# The Writer's Digest
# Writing
# Clinic

# The Writer's Digest
# Writing
# Clinic

**Expert help for improving your work**

Edited by Kelly Nickell

**WRITER'S DIGEST BOOKS**
Cincinnati, Ohio
www.writersdigest.com

Visit our Web site at www.writersdigest.com for information on more resources for writers.

To receive a free weekly e-newsletter delivering tips and updates about writing and about Writer's Digest products, register directly at our Web site at http://newsletters.fwpublications.com.

07   06   05   04   03     5   4   3   2   1

**Library of Congress Cataloging in Publication Data**

The writer's digest writing clinic: expert help for improving your work / edited by Kelly Nickell
    p.   cm.
Includes index.
ISBN 1-58297-220-6 (alk. paper)
1. Authorship   I. Title: Writing Clinic. II. Nickell, Kelly.

PN147.W685 2003                              2003041177
808'.02—dc21                                    CIP

Edited by Kelly Nickell         OCT     2003
Designed by Angela Wilcox
Cover by Chris Gliebe
Production coordinated by Michelle Ruberg

# Table of Contents

# Introduction

It's not always easy to see flaws in your own work. That's part of what makes the revision process so difficult. Where do you start—with grammar? Plot development? Or, how about your story's climax? What should you really focus on—your use of narrative voice or your slightly ambiguous subplot? Is there even anything wrong with your narrative voice, or have you simply read the material so many times that everything is starting to look a little murky?

The key to revision is learning to look at your work with an editor's eye. This skill will not only improve your own work, but it also will make you a better critique group member—or perhaps it will be the very inspiration you need to join a critique group. Learning how to edit will help you to produce great work, and that's the goal of *The Writer's Digest Writing Clinic*.

We've taken thirty-six manuscript excerpts, poems, essays, articles, query letters, synopses, and proposals submitted by real-life writers and turned them over to professional editors. The thorough critiques and exercises that appear on the following pages show you how to approach the revision process, what points to focus on, how to efficiently correct common mistakes, and how to apply these editing techniques to your own work.

A full analysis accompanies each critiqued manuscript, allowing the editor to talk you through the entire revision process and explain why each suggestion is made and how to execute it. The detailed critiques, some of which originally appeared in the pages of *Writer's Digest* magazine, include key numbered points, which are itemized in easy-to-follow numbered boxes. These coordinated points offer fuller explanations on changes and corrections made within the manuscripts. The Your Turn! exercises found in these chapters also are specifically focused to complement the material just covered. Finally, there are conclusive checklists at the close of sections two through seven that offer an overview of the material. These checklists also can double as guides for when you critique your work.

Since more than a dozen editors assisted in these critiques, you'll have the opportunity to compare a variety of different editing styles. Some editors are heavy-handed, and some are not. Some editors focus on grammar and punctuation, and some say that type of revision comes later. Just as every writer approaches the craft differently, so too do editors. You'll have to decide which method best suits your writing style and temperament. There is, however, one element these editing approaches do share. They all find a way to offer constructive and applicable advice. If an editor sees something that doesn't work, he not only identifies it, but he explains why it doesn't work and, more importantly, offers suggestions as to how the author can fix it. Learning to do this will enable you to improve your own work with far greater proficiency.

You'll also get the chance to compare editing styles between genres and forms. How does editing the first chapter of a novel differ from editing a personal essay? How do you revise a fiction query letter as opposed to a magazine query letter? When it comes to editing and revising, each type of writing has its own set of requirements, its own set of demands. Yet, the goal of all editing is the same: to improve the work. Here, you'll have the opportunity to see how such specific demands blend across genres to meet this singular objective.

We'll also discuss how to make the most out of your involvement with a writing critique group, including tips on when to take a critiquer's advice and when to politely decline it. The dynamics of a critique group can be difficult to master, especially if you've been doing the solitary writer routine for any length of time. However, a group that encourages and nourishes a free-flowing exchange of constructive suggestions and ideas can add new life to your writing—and your rewriting—process. In addition to critique group survival tips, you'll find a comprehensive grammar and punctuation primer, as well as a chart to decode standard edit marks.

The appendix section of *The Writer's Digest Writing Clinic* offers supplemental information useful to writers working alone and those participating in critique groups. Appendix A provides tips for being a strong critiquer, as well as a receptive critiquee. Submitting your work for critique is never easy. In fact, the mere act is one of bravery and hope. Opening yourself—and your writing—up to criticism takes an infinite amount of courage and confidence in your ability not only to write, but also in your ability to improve as a writer. To this end, Appendix A features three checklists to help you maximize the benefits of taking part in a group critique. The first focuses on points you, as the writer, should consider before, during, and after submitting your work for critique. The second is for members within a critique group as they independently evaluate another writer's work. The third is for the group as a whole once it's time to collectively discuss another member's work.

Appendix B focuses exclusively on what to look for in an established writing critique group, how to start your own group, and how to tell when it's time to move on to a new group. In Appendix C, you'll find a list of national writing organizations. And finally, in Appendix D, you'll find an inclusive list of respected writing books that focus on editing, technique, inspiration, and style.

The revision process doesn't have to be an arduous experience layered with dread and self-doubt. By thinking like an editor and looking at the work with objectivity and focus, you'll improve your skills as a writer and as a reviser. So, where do you start? Turn the page, and find out.

PART I

# The Value of Critiquing

# chapter 1

# Critique Basics

You've finally finished your novel. To you it reads like the finest piece of literature ever penned by human hand, but you may be biased. Your friends and family all tell you they've never read anything like it, but that seems a little ambiguous. So you join a writers' group where members critique one another's manuscripts.

And suddenly you've got feedback. The Hemingway wanna-be thinks it's too wordy. The Proust fan finds it too spare. The M.F.A. grad complains that it isn't literary enough, but the teen with the pierced tongue says it's too tame. The retired C.P.A. thinks it's too bloody, even though the screenwriter is sure you need an action scene every seventeen pages. The high school English teacher merely suggests that your thug say, "Whom the hell do you think you are?" What do you do now?

## Understand Your Critiquers

Ideally, the purpose of a critique is to help you write the story you want to write. In practice, many critique group members are more interested in helping you write the story they want to write. They'll tell you how your light, romantic farce would work better as a murder mystery. ("Just kill off a character and go from there.") Or they want your buddy comedy to turn into a thriller. They'll suggest you switch from first person to third, or change your main character's gender, or restructure your story around what is now a subplot. Essentially, they want to reduce your story to rubble and build a new one from the remains.

You're most likely to receive a take-no-prisoners critique when your critiquer is a fellow writer. Professional editors deal with a wide range of genres and styles, but many writers tend to write the kinds of books they like to read and only read the kinds of books they're trying to write. They know the techniques they themselves use and don't pay much attention to the rest. A critiquer who reads only fast-paced thrillers will be annoyed with the wealth of background detail you've built into your fantasy novel. In short, the Stephen King fan may critique you for not being Stephen King.

A few tricks will help you avoid this trap. If you're in a group where you trade critiques with other authors, pay attention to the manuscripts your fellow group members are trying to write—in case the critiquer who thinks your historical novel needs a love interest is a romance writer, for instance. If the group shares critiques publicly, note the problems your critiquers find with the other manuscripts they've worked on—they may think everybody should write a buddy comedy.

Chat with your critiquers, and find out what kinds of books they like to read. If you don't have any favorite authors in common, then be a little leery of what they have to say. If you have a choice about who critiques your story, choose someone who is widely read in your own genre, so he is familiar with the techniques you use.

## When Critiques Help

The most serious problem with heavy-handed critiquers, though, is that they're sometimes right. Sometimes your buddy comedy would work better as a thriller. Sometimes your historical novel does need a love interest. How do you tell?

Always ask for reasons for the changes your critiquers suggest—something more than, "This just doesn't work for me." When they suggest a fundamental change, it should be to bring out something even more important in your story. Perhaps by adding a romantic interest to your historical novel, you can bring out a softer, more humanizing side of an off-putting main character. By turning your romantic farce into a buddy comedy, you might jettison a forced and implausible love interest that interferes with an otherwise delightful character interaction.

If your critiquers can't produce reasons for a suggestion, then give it this test: Does it inspire you? If you have to strain to understand what your critiquers are talking about, then the suggestion probably isn't for you. The good ones hit like a revelation, leaving you itching to start your rewrites. In fact, it's not a bad rule of thumb to ignore all suggestions that don't inspire you.

People write at their best when they write from someplace deep inside, the place where inspiration lives. If you try to make changes mechanically, they will almost certainly be less than your best and may well be disastrous. There are writers who tend to revise their manuscripts as if they were trying to get a term paper past a particularly picky professor. The result is usually only the need for more editing. Genuine improvements come from the heart.

## When Critiques Hurt

Critiquers often go to the opposite extreme from reducing your story to rubble: picking on the sorts of details that should only be corrected in the final polish, if at all. They may question your verisimilitude—"Have you ever actually ridden a horse/climbed a mountain/fired a machine gun? It doesn't feel like that." Or pound you on details of word choice—"You use some form of 'to be' eighteen times on this page." Someone is always happy to shred your grammar. It's absolutely true that problems such as run-on sentences or inadvertent alliteration (like the five Ps near the end of the previous paragraph—did you notice?) can detract from your writing. Yet paying attention to these mechanical details too early in the process can interfere with your creativity.

The language you choose should flow from your characters and fit their histories and personalities. A studied attention to word choice and sentence structure can interfere with the development of your character's voice.

As to verisimilitude, well, it's not always vital. Of course, if your plot hangs on the details—if the location of the safety catch on a 30.06 rifle is the central clue to your mystery—then you'd better get the nitty-gritty right. But if the details are simply there for background or to create an atmosphere, then they're just bafflegab, a science fiction technique. Essentially, writing bafflegab means making up stuff just plausible enough to encourage your readers to suspend disbelief. For some background details, that's all you really need.

## Become a Better Critiquer

When you're faced with producing a critique for someone else, how do you avoid the mistakes we've just discussed? Of course you can critique only writers in your own genre and learn not to nitpick, but how do you help your victims—er, subjects—write the story they want to write?

You can usually spot what's most important to your fellow writers by noticing where they spend the most words. If they've written pages developing a romance or building to a plot twist, don't just tell them to ditch the romance or that you saw the plot twist coming. If possible, help them make it work. Above all, be gentle. Don't soft-pedal problems, but keep your focus on possibilities. Always remember that your job is to inspire, not to overwhelm.

Here's a critiquing caveat to keep in mind when it comes to taking outside advice: Your mileage may vary. Editorial suggestions, even those coming from a professional, should be treated as no more than suggestions—to be taken or ignored at your discretion. So listen to your critiquers. Pay attention to who they are before weighing what they say. Then follow your heart. (See Appendix A for more information on critique etiquette; see Appendix B for more information on joining or starting a critique group.)

# chapter 2

# Grammar Mechanics

Punctuation and grammar both play unique roles in your ability to critique your own work, as well as the work of others. As discussed in chapter one, worrying too early in the game about grammar and punctuation errors may hamper your creative flow. But, the mechanical side of writing shouldn't be overlooked altogether. You may find it easier to clean up such pratfalls *before* you hand over your work for critique.

Once you've mastered the mechanics, you'll be able to combine your knowledge of the fundamentals with basic editing know-how. This includes the ability to understand and execute standard proofreading notations used by professional editors. Attempting to read a harried editor's scribbles can be as easy as decoding an ancient language. By familiarizing yourself with standard editing marks, you'll simplify your revision process and make yourself an asset to any critique group. Let's start with the mechanics:

## Grammar and Punctuation

Most writers revise their work several times before allowing critiquers to read a single word. That said, it's important to remember the first step in revising is often a step back. Put your work aside for at least a day or two so you can look at it with a fresh eye before attempting any revisions. When you're ready, read the piece through as though you were seeing it for the first time.

Mark passages that seem awkward, that drag, or that lack "punch." Read dialogue passages aloud to identify any that sound stiff or unnatural. Pay attention to word choice and sentence structure. Does your writing evoke the emotions you intended? Focus on stylistic problems—lack of clarity, inappropriate pacing, disorganization, material that doesn't contribute to the theme, characters that are flat or insufficiently motivated, not enough action (or too much), etc. One of the key things to look for on this first pass is deadwood—those unnecessary words or redundancies that can clutter your prose.

On the second pass, look for grammatical and mechanical errors—check spelling, verify definitions of words, look for typographical errors within the text such as missing or duplicated words, and make sure you've punctuated everything properly.

## Pronouns

Pronouns are words that substitute for nouns. The following list will help you pinpoint the most common grammatical and mechanical errors in pronoun usage. We've included italicized examples for each:

- Things being compared must agree with each other in case. (*Judy is older than I.* Judy is the subject; I is in the subjective case.)
- Pronouns after a linking verb relate directly to the subject and, therefore, must be in the subjective case. (*It is I.*)
- Pronouns used with gerunds must be in the possessive case because gerunds are nouns. (*I cannot forgive your cheating.*)
- Reflexive and intensive pronouns (e.g., myself, yourself, ourselves) must refer to the corresponding subject present in the sentence. (Wrong: *She gave the book to myself.* Right: *She gave the book to me.*)
- Compound subjects are always plural and must take plural pronouns. (*Bob and Judy forgot their keys.*)
- Phrases and clauses interrupting the main parts of the sentence do not affect the pronouns in the basic sentence. (*Each of these boys must take his medicine.*)
- Collective nouns usually take singular pronouns, although a collective noun may take a plural pronoun when individual action within the group is indicated. (*The team won its first game. The entire class passed their tests.*)

## Verbs

Verbs are words that show action, being, or condition. The following list, with italicized examples, will help you identify the most common grammatical and mechanical errors in verb usage:

- Certain indefinite pronouns are always singular—even though plurality is implied—and always take a singular verb: e.g., another, anything, each, either, everyone, no one, nothing, someone. (*Everyone has her own opinion.*)
- Some indefinite pronouns may be singular or plural, depending on their use and take the corresponding form of the verb: any, all, none, more, most, some. (*Some of our appliances are energy efficient* [plural—more than one appliance]. *Some energy is wasted when the lights are left on* [singular—one amount of energy].)
- Collective nouns may take singular or plural forms of the verb, depending on whether the intended meaning is a collective group action (singular) or the individual actions of the members (plural). (*The team loses every week. The board cast their votes yesterday.*)
- Compound subjects always take the plural form of the verb. (*Bob and Judy live in Columbus.*)
- The form of the verb is determined by the subject, not the subjective complement. (*The problem is cockroaches. Cockroaches are the problem.*)
- Structural interruptions and additions have no influence over the verb in the basic sentence, though their subjects influence verbs within their own structure. (*Each of the men who retire this year earns a bonus.* The main sentence is "Each earns [singular] a bonus." The interruption is "of the men who retire [plural] this year.")

## Adverbs and Adjectives

Adverbs modify verbs, adjectives, or other adverbs, while adjectives modify nouns or pronouns. The following list, with italicized examples, will help you pinpoint the most common grammatical and mechanical errors in adverb and adjective usage:

- Words after intransitive verbs that modify the subject must be adjectives. (*I smell bad* refers to the subject *I* and describes the subject's state.)
- Adverbs used after intransitive verbs must modify the verb, not the subject. (*I smell badly* refers to the verb *smell* and means the subject's sense of smell functions in a below average way.)
- Adjectives cannot modify other adjectives. (Wrong: *The soup was real good.* Right: *The soup was really good.*)
- Both adjectives and adverbs have comparative and superlative forms (*sweet, sweeter, sweetest* [adjective]; *sweetly, more sweetly, most sweetly* [adverb]).
- Comparative modification involves two things only. (*Judy is older than Bob.*)
- Superlative modification involves three or more things. (*Judy is the oldest of four children.*)
- Absolute terms do not take comparative or superlative modification. (Wrong: *most unique, less square, more dead.*)

### Punctuation

Although some punctuation usage is open to the interpretation of style, most is governed by the mechanics of grammar. Here's a list of the most common mechanical forms of punctuation and their usage:

- Periods are used to end sentences and to indicate abbreviations.
- Ellipses (…) indicate the passing of time or something omitted from a direct quotation.
- Question marks end sentences that are formed as questions or direct statements that imply a question. (Question marks may be used within sentences as well as at their ends.)
- Exclamation marks are used for emphasis, especially with interjections. (They may be used within sentences as well as at their ends.)
- Semicolons join independent clauses when coordinating conjunctions are not used, series elements that have internal punctuation, and independent clauses that begin with a conjunctive adverb.
- Colons introduce something to follow.
- Commas are used with a conjunction to join independent clauses; to separate beginning clauses, phrases, and words from main clauses; and/or to connect items in a series.
- Commas also are used to join two adjectives modifying the same noun or pronoun if they modify with equal force.
- Dashes are used to create emphasis, to indicate a break in thought or to include an aside.
- Hyphens are used to divide words at the end of a line, and for adjectives made up of two or more words.
- Apostrophes indicate possession, replace omitted letters and numerals, and indicate plurals of single letters. In contractions, the apostrophe occur where the letters or numerals are omitted.
- Quotation marks are used to indicate unusual uses of words, such as slang, titles of short works, and both partial and complete direct quotations. They are not used for indirect quotations or block quotations.
- In American English usage, periods and commas always occur inside quotation marks. Semicolons and colons always occur outside quotation marks. Where

question and exclamation marks occur in direct quotations is determined by sentence meaning, and only one punctuation mark ends a quotation.

- When attribution occurs within the quotation, it is set off with a pair of commas; the quotation continues without capitalization of its first word.
- Quotations within quotations take single quotation marks.
- Parentheses enclose material helpful to the fuller meaning of the sentence and may occur within or between sentences.
- Brackets enclose explanatory material within a direct quotation.
- Italic print or underlining is used for emphasis, titles of major artistic works, bound books, and foreign expressions.
- Capital letters are used for cultural or geographic regions and regional groups, family titles not preceded by a possessive pronoun, and personal and professional titles. They also are generally used for nouns, personal pronouns, and adjectives referring to God.
- Numbers above ten that can be expressed in three or fewer words are expressed in words, not numerals; but if the writing contains many quantities, numerals should be used for all numbers.
- Numbers used for expressing time, captions, and addresses always appear as numerals, except in very formal usage. Spell out numbers that begin a sentence.

## Decode Editing Marks

The following proofreader's marks are used by most editors:

| MARK | EXPLANATION | EXAMPLE |
|---|---|---|
| ℓ | Take out character indicated. | Your manuscrippt. |
| stet | Let it stay. | stet Your manuscript. |
| # | Put in space. | Youmanuscript. |
| ⌢ | Close up completely. | Writer's Di gest School. |
| ∩ or tr | Transpose; change places | Yuot manuscript. |
| caps or ≡ | Use capital letters. | caps writer's digest school.  writer's digest school. |
| lc | Use lower case letters. | lc Your Manuscript. |
| bf or ∿∿∿ | Use bold face type. | bf Writer's Digest School.  Writer's Digest School. |
| ital or ―― | Use italic type. | ital Writer's Digest School.  Writer's Digest School. |
| ∨́ | Put in an apostrophe. | Writers Digest School. |
| ⊙ | Put in period. | Your manuscript ⊙ |
| ∨́ | Put in comma. | Your manuscript ∧ |
| ∨̇ | Put in colon. | Your manuscript ∧ |
| ∨́ | Put in semicolon. | Writer's Digest School ∧ |
| " ∨ " ∨ | Put in quotation marks. | He said,Yes. |
| (?) | Question to author. | Well known writer. |
| ‾∨ | Put in hyphen. | Well known writer. |
| !∨ | Put in exclamation. | This is great ∧ |
| ?∨ | Put in question mark. | Are you starting ∧ |
| ( ) | Put in parenthesis. | Your first rough draft. |
| ¶ or L | Start paragraph. | a writer.¶Learn to sell |
| ‖ | Even out lines. | Writer's Digest and  Writer's Digest School. |
| ⊏ | Move the line left. | Your manuscript. |
| ⊐ | Move the line right. | Your manuscript. |
| ↩ | No paragraph; run together. | a writer.  There are more needed |
| out, sc | Something missing, see copy. | out, sc Writer's School. |
| spell out | Spell it out. | spell out Your ms. |

PART II

# Fiction

**Y**ou've finally managed to get your story down on paper. Congratulations—the hard part is over! Now it's time to begin the revision process. Chapters three through fourteen take you step-by-step through this cleanup process, starting with your opening hook and ending with your closing climax.

You have an endless amount of details to consider when revising a work of fiction, and the thought of trying to address everything all at once—from subplots to dialogue and character development to denouement—can stall the process before you've even begun. Fortunately, all of these elements are interlocked—they all work together to establish a story's rhythm, its heart. As you'll see in the coming chapters, the key to successful revision is focusing on one element at a time while still keeping the story as a whole in mind.

When you revise your opening scene, for example, you'll be checking to make sure that you've established an emotional connection with your readers. This initial connection should intensify as the story progresses, so it's crucial that you ground it early. You'll also be checking to make sure that the pace and tone you've established not only work within the confines of the opening scene, but also complement your story's overarching theme. In addition, you'll want to make sure that you've created a scene that grabs a reader's interest and propels the story forward in the intended manner. You'll be checking for all of these elements—and more—as you revise your opening scene and appraise its influence on the rest of your story.

When you're critiquing another writer's fiction, ask him if there's a specific area that he'd like you to focus on. By finding out in advance what type of feedback he's looking for, you'll be able to better direct your critique. Also, try not to let any personal genre biases influence your critique. If you're a budding romance novelist critiquing a science fiction tale, ask the author to brief you on his genre before you begin your critique. You don't have to be an Anne Rice fan in order to provide a horror writer with a constructive critique—you just need to have an appreciation for the writer's work and an editor's eye.

It's also important to find a system of revision that best suits your writing style—especially when you're revising a book-length manuscript. You'll find that some writers do extensive revisions as they write. Others wait until the work is complete before they start the revision process. The choice is yours. Whichever way you do choose, though, you'll have the right set of tools.

# chapter 3

# Opening Hook

uthor Jay Heininger is off to a good start in his novel, *The Cylinder*. For one thing, he opens the action with his main character dangling over a crevasse—as an incidental background element. Alex's discovery of the mysteriously warm, smooth cylinder—one that apparently heals his knees—brings readers into a world of wonder. They're going to want to keep reading to find out what the cylinder is, what Alex does with it, and what it does with him. In short, it's a terrific hook.

But it could be sharper. You see, a hook works because it creates a strong emotional bond between the readers and the central character. In this case, readers share Alex's sense of wonder at the cylinder, and that shared emotion draws them into the world of the story. The current opening though, puts emotional distance between readers and Alex in a number of different ways.

First, the author reveals the beginning of the cylinder's message before Alex has found the cylinder itself. This message raises some intriguing questions about the cylinder—who is the author of the message and why was it left? But it also answers the

**1** Readers really should read this material along with Alex, rather than reading it before they've even met him.

**2** Note how much importance the cylinder takes on if it's capable of distracting Alex while he's hanging over a crevasse.

**3** The added material shown here in italics demonstrates how the passage could read if the author gives readers time for the discovery of the cylinder to sink in.

**4** The author can convey Alex's surprise at finding the cylinder warm by giving the discovery its own three-word paragraph.

**5** The place for the physical description of the cylinder is here, rather than in a few pages when Alex takes it out again at his apartment.

**6** Again, the author can spotlight Alex's discovery that his knees are warm by giving the discovery its own paragraph.

*The Cylinder*

*[**Note:** In order to make the editing easier to follow, some material added by the editor is printed in italics. Where the italicized material replaces the author's, the original material appears in brackets.]*

"I start my story slowly so as not to overpower you. I write from the past the distant past. So long ago that even if you looked you would find no records. ~~For I existed hundreds of millenniums before you.~~ You will not find my bones in any digs or (archeological) endeavors. ~~Me and mine and~~ the society in which I lived ~~are~~ *is* so long past that you could not find even our dust. But I know of you and that is why I left this book so that it would be found, housed in its indestructible capsule of lorfidium. This is the last that's left, all the rest consumed ~~for~~ *as* fuel ~~by~~ *for* our engines. I wonder if you will figure how to open it. I hope so. I think you will.

"In my time we had machines and cybers so advanced from yours that you could hardly imagine them. ~~Because of~~ this *is how* I know of you and your language. I place instructions on the surface of the lorfidium capsule in hopes that you will open it and ~~read~~ *learn from* my story."

Alex ~~had just read this and could not believe it. He had~~ *was hanging over the void of the crevasse when he saw the* ~~found the dull~~ cylinder. *He was on* ~~while skiing down~~ the Grand Monte in Argentierre near Chamonix, France. ~~He had been~~ on the dome, *way* above the lifts. Off piste because the area was full of crevasses which shifted and formed in the glaciers of the slope. *He skied the area often enough to know most of them, and his reflexes were still good enough that the new ones hadn't killed him yet. Although this one had come close.* ~~Alex had almost fallen in.~~ One leg ~~dangling~~ *hung* down into the [void and as he rescued himself] *darkness, his ski dangling from its bindings. Both hands were wrapped around the ice ax he'd managed to plant before he went over the edge.*

*He took a fresh grip on the ax and swiveled around to pull his knee up, and that's when* he saw the *dull glint of* odd metal.

*Slowly, gently so as to not pull the ax loose or drop his*

dangling ski, he rolled, crawled away from the edge until he
could sit up and let the adrenaline die down. When his heart
rate was back to normal, he secured his skis and poles, then
lay down and scooted carefully to the edge.

It was still there, a cylinder maybe eight inches long and
two or three across, on an ice shelf six feet or so below the
surface. And it was ... strange. From its color—a dull blue
gray—it wasn't [dull but somehow different, not] silver or alu-
minum, not some leftover water or oxygen bottle. *But what else would he find this far up the mountain?* The metal had
a force which grabbed him~~, and~~ he decided to see if he could
rescue it. ~~The crevasse was a new one that he did not know of~~
~~but these opened all the time in the glacier.~~

He drove his ice ax into the ice, attached his rope and
slowly lowered himself into the void until he could reach the
*thing. He touched it, then yanked his hand back.*
capsule. It was ~~oddly~~ warm ~~in his hand,~~ not hot but ~~room~~ tem-
perature *when* it should have been ~~the~~ bitter cold ~~of the sur-~~
~~rounding ice.~~ *But it was buried in the ice, well below where the sun could reach, even at noon. Alex touched it gingerly, then grabbed it and scrambled out* Rising out of the crevasse.

Up in the sunlight, he stared at the thing. There were no
seams, no identifying marks and ... in fact, no marks at all.
No dents, no scratches, no machining whorls. It was flawlessly
smooth, like a newly-minted coin. But it was too light to be
solid.

And warm.

He'd have to examine it in more detail. Right now it was
time to get down off the mountain. He placed the equipment and
cylinder in his pack and headed down the dome and then the
rest of the Grande Monte, *seven* ~~7~~ thousand vertical feet to the val-
ley below and the bus ~~which~~ *that* would return him to Chamonix.

It was a descent like always, ~~and~~ yet oddly different. His
knees, the product of years of skiing and ~~many operations~~ *surgery,* were
something he always needed to ignore when he skied; ~~however~~ *But today,* he
felt light on the snow and the subtle movements ~~which~~ *that* skiing
requires ~~were there as always but~~ *came without* the pain ~~was gone.~~ He flew
down the mountain side ~~as a kid not a fifty year old and~~ *with an exuberance he hadn't felt in—*
~~although his technique was~~ *He felt like he was 10 again* ~~much better then it had been at ten~~ *everything he'd developed in the 40 years since.*
~~he was a youth on the mountain. He had not felt this exuber-~~
~~ance for~~ years, racing down the mountain steeps and shallows
and contiguous roads. He ~~flew~~ *soared.* At the bottom he ~~was~~ *looked back up the slope,* not sure
what happened, but he ~~knew,~~ *noticed* his knees were warm.

most important question that occurs when Alex finds the thing—what is it? Instead of focusing on the mystery of the discovery as it happens, readers are looking ahead to where Alex finally opens the cylinder eight or ten pages later. The author should move the message to that point and let Alex and the readers discover it together.

Moving this opening message also lets the author write the initial discovery in real time rather than in a flashback. Flashbacks do have their place, but allowing readers to experience the discovery as it happens will add immediacy.

Finally, the author races through the discovery. Two paragraphs are not enough for readers to connect with Alex emotionally. For one thing, it's bad psychology. (If you had discovered something that mysterious, would you really just shove it in your pack and head for town?) For another, readers need time for the sense of wonder to take hold before they move on down the slope.

There's also the principle of proportion. If the author doesn't spend much time on the discovery, readers will feel subconsciously that it isn't important.

A few minor stylistic flourishes will further spotlight the discovery. For instance, notice the italicized paragraphs on the second page of the manuscript. These added graphs help to illustrate Alex's surprise at the cylinder's warmth. The added interior monologue, also in italics, allows readers to watch Alex's thoughts as they happen.

Finally, remember that these editorial suggestions are just that, suggestions. In this case, the added material simply demonstrates how the hook could work if the author were to stretch the cylinder discovery out a bit. Ultimately, though, this book has to be Jay Heininger's. Just remember that where most authors need to pick up their pace in the opening pages, slowing down this story a little is the best way to draw readers into it.

# Your Turn!

Add punch to your hook by applying the following tips to your work:

**1.** Ask a friend or a critique group member to read the opening pages of your novel and to place a star next to the point where he begins to feel an emotional bond with your central character. Does this point match up with what you intended? If it doesn't, rework the way the hook is presented. Are the supporting sentences too thin? Is the focus off?

**2.** Now, ask that same person to write down any questions that came to mind while he was reading. In the above story, for example, readers wanted to know what the cylinder was, who the author of the message was, etc. While these are all legitimate questions, you may find that portions of your text are unclear or confusing, resulting in reader questions that actually draw the focus away from the intended intrigue.

**3.** Now, read over your story with an eye toward pacing. Make sure you aren't rushing key elements or dragging out the wrong ones.

# chapter 4

# Point of View

This is a wonderfully tense scene. It's attention-grabbing and filled with vivid imagery—it makes a good hook for Heather Myles's novel *Haven*.

Readers understand that they're witnessing a murder, or near-murder. But what isn't clear is who the readers are supposed to be. Are they in the victim's viewpoint? The killer's? Readers must be able to orient themselves and to see the scene from a definite vantage point.

It's true that there should be some confusion. This is a dream sequence, after all, and dreams are usually confusing. But even confusion is seen through a particular consciousness. Otherwise, readers are likely to become disoriented—or worse, disinterested in the entire story.

As the story unfolds, readers initially are led to believe they're in the victim's skin, but eventually they learn that they've been watching this assault through the eyes of a third-party onlooker. That's a rather large adjustment, especially if readers have already started to identify with and fear for the victim. This sort of sudden shift can be both jarring and distracting.

1. Too much description can weaken the prose and spill over into melodrama.

2. This sentence creates quite an image, but it takes away from the action scene.

3. Excess wordage like "white," "agonizingly," and "jagged" actually detracts. For maximum impact, keep it simple and direct.

4. This is a rather long sentence. At times, the use of shorter sentences can pack more punch.

5. An active voice is stronger. The meaning would be clearer with "she stole one breath."

6. From this, it isn't immediately clear that Hannah is dreaming and not actually the victim.

Giving readers guidance won't make for a lot of rewriting; it can actually be done quite efficiently by adding a few simple phrases to the existing text.

On the other hand, if Hannah is dream-

*Haven*

Chapter 1

Shadow and Light

His thumbs overlapped, pressing like a vise against the woman's windpipe. Thick fingers surrounded her neck, ferociously tight, clenching, choking. Flashes of light illuminated her face; her eyes bulged, skin seeping with blue, tendons straining like brake cables. (These visions lashed out with such sudden clarity, as though some stagnant pond had turned impossibly glass.)

Her hair flew in wet auburn whips. Nails bitten short clawed in desperation, unable to find hold. All that was visible of him were hands and arms, pale iron posts in the dusk.

"Kggeeeeeer!" a minuscule squeal sucked past purpled lips. Then silence. She stared into his face with eyes unable to believe.

His hands were glaciers, knuckles frozen with rage. He shook her, her head juggling like a rag doll's. Everything was slow, broken frames in motion.

Finally his fingers slid loose, and in that instant before he found a surer grip, she stole one breath.

"HUUaaahhhhr!" Hannah shrieked, scared wide awake. her lungs gulped the air.

... The dream again.

Sweat cascaded down Hannah's temples, her chest blazed with fear. Not knowing where to focus in the dark, her eyes whirled in their sockets, all senses reeling. Her breath came in sharp, wheezing gasps.

"Too ... Real ... Oh, God—too real," Hannah panted. The world bucked and swayed beneath her, rippling her smack centre. The duvet started feeling like a steam press so she flung back her covers to welcome the morning's chill. Anything to chase away the dream—anything to find release.

she slowed her breathing, suckling the sweetness of the cool air. Then, cautiously, so as not to upset the seasick gut, she pivoted to dangle her feet over the edge of the bed. The room wobbled a bit, and then in slow, wide loops the blur became the dark room before her. She wiped away the perspiration with the back of her hand, trembling. A shudder escaped her lips with a moaning cry.

It was still dark, the autumn dawn not yet risen.

Gingerly, her toes felt for the chill touch of hardwood.

**10** ~~Streaks of~~ warm light stretched across the glossed floorboards, drawing her eyes to the clock. ~~Embers of~~ its LED display stated passively, 5:02 a.m.

The world dozed in its cozy blanketing of leaves, unruffled by fingers of wind. Hannah Dixon rested her feet gladly in the soothing pile of the bedroom rug spread halfway between the dresser and bed. She stood listening to the murmur of her

**11** heart, slow and even again. (In white undershirt and boxers, <u>her profile was a faint pinkish apparition</u> in the window, blinds left open to the possibility of seeing the naked sky.) Her lonely room was as still as the earth; so silent she imagined she could hear the soft snap of electronic numerals changing, slipping on towards sunrise. Too early, but there was no going back to bed.

---

ing she is actually the victim, then the scene should be presented from that point of view.

Another approach the author can use to sharpen the scene is to prune away excess modifiers. Description, as long as it's vivid and specific, will enhance almost any story, but too much can swamp it. Description such as "ferociously tight, clenching, choking," and "tendons straining like brake cables," may be a bit much in this case.

It's also important not to let description overpower the viewpoint character. Rather than tell the reader what the character is supposed to be feeling, the author needs to evoke that feeling in the reader. This is done by describing the experience rather than the emotion itself.

In the first paragraph after Hannah wakes, for instance, it would be more effective if the author tones down the account of Hannah's physical reaction and lets the reader, having seen the dream for herself, actually share the horror that affects the protagonist.

Understatement often has a more powerful impact on readers and avoids melodrama. For example:

**7** This is an awkward construction. Substituting "shrieked" for "screamed" would avoid placing two "sc" words together.

 **8** These two clauses don't work together. Make them separate sentences.

**9** This hints at a comic book image. Maybe something like, "Her eyes darted wildly."

**10** For stronger prose, take out some of the modifiers.

**11** If this is in Hannah's viewpoint, she can't see herself from the outside.

Hannah woke damp with sweat, her heart pounding. Her eyes stared through darkness, searching for something familiar to tell her where she was, and that she was safe. Her breath came in sharp, wheezing gasps.

"Too real … Oh God, too real," she panted, whispering. The duvet felt like a steam press. She flung back her covers to welcome the morning's chill.

The trick is to get inside your character's head and try to feel her honest emotions. Accomplishing this keeps the author on course with her viewpoint character and allows the readers to share in the character's experiences.

# Your Turn!

Clarify your point of view by applying the following tips to your work:

**1.** Ask two fellow writers or critique group members to read the first chapter of your novel. Next, ask them to identify your point of view (POV) character. Did they each pick the same character? If not, or if the character they did pick isn't the one you intended, it's time to do some rewriting.

**2.** Once you've clearly established your POV character, ask your two loyal readers to take another look at your first chapter. This time, ask them to write down three or four lines describing the POV character. Is she coming across as selfish? Too self-deprecating? A little too good to be true? You may find out that the character you meant to be seen as cautious and smart is coming across as a fearful know-it-all.

**3.** Now it's your turn to analyze chapter one. Read through the chapter, and underline all the sentences that tell readers what the viewpoint character is feeling. Use a different colored pen to underline the sentences that show readers what that character is feeling. Are you telling more than showing? If so, try reworking some of the telling sentences you underlined. Remember, as in the story above, an easy way to show instead of tell is by describing the experience instead of the emotion.

# chapter 5

# Narrative Voice

**W**riting in your point of view character's voice, as Tony Colatruglio does in this scene from his novel *The Thunder, the Ballet, and Her Perfect World,* lets your readers see the world as your character sees it, sharing his or her experiences. But what do you do when your point of view character has an experience that's beyond words, either because it's too rich for everyday language or because your character, through youth or lack of education, doesn't have the words at hand? Whose words do you use? Let's find out.

Take Sally's moments of transcendent joy. If she were asked to describe how she felt riding across the meadows, she might be able to come up with the description the author gives here. But since she's not a professional poet, she would probably have to work at it. And she certainly wouldn't be thinking in these terms while she's riding. So the author does the only thing he can do—describe her experience using his own words, letting his narrative voice pull away from his character's voice.

There are dangers in this technique. One is that you become so caught up in your

**1** At the beginning of the scene, the author's in Sally's voice ("I want to ride horses forever," is something she might say). The author shouldn't mention Sally's thrill. Rather, he should describe the animal clearing the creek, and let readers feel the thrill for themselves.

**2** Here, Sally's still thinking consciously, naming the horses in turn, dreaming about riding, but the experience of the moment—the burnt-orange evergreens, the blue sky, and the voice that describes them—is starting to sneak in.

**3** And here the author's really slipped into the moment.

own voice that you lose track of the character's state of mind, eulogizing on rapture in general rather than describing the specific joy one specific character is experiencing at one specific moment. This problem is the source of most purple prose gracing slush piles.

Another danger is that you stumble as you move back and forth between your ele-

"Stride, girl," ~~she~~ said to Foxy as they ~~cleared~~ neared the creek. ~~"Now let me feel the thunder."~~

**1** The ~~thrill of the~~ massive animal ~~unhesitatingly~~ leapt over the water ~~then~~ landed gently and evenly to gallop off for more adventure and ~~made~~ Sally Dumont wanted to ride horses forever, especially at twilight. She could spend hours on horseback, with ~~talking to the horses,~~ then all around again in turn. Talking to them, **2** admiring the contradiction of the evergreens burning orange in the sun's afterglow ~~and~~ while the otherwise blue sky was ~~cast~~ cast in pink streaks and swirls in the western horizon overhead. Mostly, though, she loved the ~~feel of the~~ thunder under her galloping across the lush expanse. Strength with grace, only horses could be both simultaneously, and she lived to be part of it.

~~The~~ thunder and ~~the~~ ballet on four, frail legs, ~~and she could ride them forever over every acre of her perfect world. First~~ Foxy, then Queenie, then Regal, then Princess ~~and all the others.~~ Even when she was ~~sleeping~~ cuddled with Peter under the warm blankets, she was still riding her horses, dreaming of sunsets and ~~of~~ saddles and of the freest winds whipping through her hair, as they were **3** just at that moment, when the trees and the sky belied their true colors, and when Foxy was perfectly the thunder and the ballet over a world that was as contented and innocent as Sally and the sky ~~and the other horses back at the stables.~~

Dusk had thrown its shadows over Lil' Hallow, ~~as Peter and Sally Dumont more casually called their paradise, a fifty-acre horse farm perfectly isolated in northern North Dakota. An army of evergreens lined the perimeter of the meadows. In~~ the fading light, the trunks and fuller boughs of the evergreens at the edge of the meadow into ~~appeared as~~ had turned shapeless, shadowy shrouds. From these a graceful illusion of nature slowly ~~projected itself~~ took form as magically as ~~that of~~ a deer's shape ~~frame~~ **4** finally coming to eye as it stands cloaked among the brush.

Into that illusion ~~Twenty four years old and newlywed,~~ Sally rode ~~a white and dray thoroughbred,~~ Foxy ~~her most beloved horse. She was wearing western-cut blue jeans, tan cowboy boots, and a white sweater. She disdained the formal apparel of shows and competitions: glossy spurs, top boots, white breeches, derbies and top hats, and the many other garments. She couldn't ride in a clown suit like that. It would shield the wind from her hair and~~

~~soul. She wouldn't be able to move freely with the horses. They~~
~~would sense it and nervously hold back. So Sally kept the~~
~~atmosphere lose and casual, the horses rewarded her and they~~
~~rode like the freest wind.~~

Her
~~Sally's~~ long straight hair and ~~the horse's~~ long black tail
flew in the wind and the horse's momentum stirred. ~~This was~~
~~freedom. Each stride brought rhythmic clopping of the hooves~~
~~against the grass. "Thata girl." The reins jingled. The straps~~
~~of the leather saddle slapped slightly. "Let yourself ride."~~

Then,
~~But~~ just as the rim for the sun finally faded into the
horizon, Sally slowed and turned the horse so that they faced
(Foxy)
the afterglow. ~~"Our favorite spot."~~ The ~~horse~~ neighed softly
her
and threw ~~its~~ head side-to-side ~~as if it agreed.~~
Sally    ed
"You're really happy tonight," ~~she said,~~ patting the
Foxy's
~~horse's~~ neck. "I know, I know, I love it just as much as you
do. I could just die out here—but only if heaven has land like
this so we can ride forever. ~~Wouldn't want to give this up—or~~
~~you,~~ And the sunset, too. And all the other horses. ~~Nothing.~~
~~I'm not giving up a single thing.~~ Think it does girl? Think
(Foxy)
heaven has a place for horses and riding?" ~~The horse~~ neighed
again, more loudly, ears twitching. ("I think so too, but that's
—¶ well,
a long time away.

⑤    ~~They were~~ standing in a spotlight ~~upon~~ on a stage ~~because over~~
beam                        as
~~them was~~ a bright ~~glow that had~~ descended from some balcony
high in the sky ~~and the spot where the sun might have just~~
~~set.~~ Behind and around them were the shadows where the audience
Foxy
should have been clapping. ~~The horse~~ neighed and proudly held
her                    her                              she
~~its~~ head high, ~~its~~ ears turning and twitching as though ~~it~~ were
listening for that applause. The chirruping of crickets could
have been that applause and the sea of fire-flies, the camera
flashes. Each second, the light before them receded further, as
though a stagehand were turning away the spotlight and saving
it for another performance on another perfect evening, which
would no doubt be tomorrow, and the next day, and the next
day—every day as far as Sally was concerned.

⑥    "Can't stay out forever. Giddyup."

**4** Once the author's reached this point, he shouldn't drop back out to work in facts. All of that can come later. For now, he should stick with her experiences.

**5** This metaphor of the meadow at sunset as a stage is just a bit too self-conscious—Sally would be aware she's seeing the meadow in these terms. It's a good way to make the transition back to Sally's everyday voice.

**6** And, of course, by the time Sally's talking to the horse, she's fully back in her own voice.

vated voice and the character's everyday voice. After all, you can't stick with the elevated voice throughout the scene without keeping the character, in this case Sally, in a state of constant epiphany. The key to smooth transitions is to stay right with Sally's state of mind. When she starts to let herself go, the author must let his language go too. When she comes down, the author must tone his language back down too. It also helps to make the transitions gradual, if only so readers can keep up.

Remember, an elevated voice is used to get readers in the same mood as the character. If you jump back and forth too quickly between the character's everyday voice to your elevated voice, you don't sustain that mood.

Also, unless you're really a master of this technique, use it sparingly. In moderation, it can give your characters a rich internal life, an added dimension that many authors don't even attempt. At great length it can be exhausting, even emotionally coercive, as if you expect your readers to be in a state of heightened awareness for pages at a time.

Finally, because this is an advanced literary technique, the "rules" are a lot looser than with more basic techniques. In this case, the author may, for instance, feel it's important to have Sally keep easing in and out of that joy as she rides, rather than having it happen all at once. But you must remain aware of the technique and how you're using it—this is the best way to use it effectively.

# Your Turn!

Ground your narrative voice by applying the following tips to your work:

**1.** Write a paragraph describing a warm and sunny day—only write it from your main character's perspective. Use words and phrases she would use. Does she ramble? Or, use lots of adjectives? This will give you a quick reference paragraph to help you zero in on your character's voice.

**2.** Now, compare the paragraph's tone and style to your novel's first chapter. Is the character's voice similar in both pieces? Underline lines that sound more like you than your character.

**3.** Look at the points where your voice betrays your character's. Rework these passages to reflect your character.

# chapter 6

# Dialogue

I n this excerpt from his novel, *Ride of the Valkyrie*, David M. Ryan sets up some interesting settings and scenes. But he also makes some rather egregious errors that would damage his chances at publication.

The most important rule of writing successful, interesting, and dramatic fiction is this: Show, don't tell. Most rules of writing can be broken—or at least bent—without doing too much damage to a novel. But showing rather than telling is the essence of fiction. Telling a story through narration and exposition is almost guaranteed to drive readers away. If you tell the story, you block the reader from becoming a part of the adventure—and you prevent the empathy that should exist between character and reader.

Readers must be able to experience a story through the senses and perceptions of the protagonist. That character's pain, joy, wrath, and fear must be shown to the reader for a bond to form. If you simply tell the reader what's happening, you insert yourself between reader and character, making a good idea as tedious as paging through an

**1** "It's" is a contraction of the term it is. As written, the sentence would read, ". . . pulled a German Luger from it is holster . . ."

**2** This should be a single sentence. Instead, it's a quote followed by a sentence fragment.

**3** Standard, completely articulated sentences work much better than sound bites.

**4** The most effective and compelling dialogue is that which stands alone.

auto parts catalog. For example, toward the end of this excerpt, the author writes, "Bakaric gave the German a lascivious wink." Structurally and grammatically the sentence is fine, and it conveys a bit of information to the reader. But that's all it does. The author should take this opportunity to indicate more strongly the sort of man Bakaric is. Grab the reader with something like:

*Ride of the Valkyrie*

by

David M. Ryan

Prologue

*Austria-Croatia border, March 1945*

The young man screamed as he was taken from the train. Two big soldiers with the red and white checkered shoulder patch of the Ustasa dragged him through the car, leaving toe marks from his boots in the dirt and mud of the coach's wood plank flooring. *[handwritten: Which spelling?]*

Through the wisps of steam from the locomotive, Albert Koenig could see the terrified face of the boy-soldier. The would-be spy was on his knees in front of the militia commander, begging for his life. The Ustatsa officer pulled a German Luger from it's holster, placed the ugly black muzzle against the boy's head and slowly pulled the trigger. The parabellum round blew a red wind from the boy's forehead where it exited. *[handwritten: This is a bit confusing.]*

Koenig turned away from the grimy window and the dead boy on the tracks. When he looked up the militia leader was asking him for his papers. He wondered if he would be soon joining the boy. The loyalties of the Yugoslav fighters seemed to change with the wind. Today they were ethnic Germans, fighting for Hitler and the glorious Fatherland. Tomorrow, fighting each other for who knows what? As the Croat major studied his travel orders, Koenig decided he really didn't care. *[handwritten: This works well.]*

*[handwritten: Use a comma here, not a period.]*

"Oberst Koenig, you are to come with me," The Ustasa major said in clipped German.

"Who are you?" Koenig asked respectfully, studying the chiseled features of the man. An ugly scar ran from his left eye to his jaw.

"I am Major Josep Bakaric. I was sent by Oberst lieutenant Petzer to see to your safe delivery."

Koenig breathed a silent sigh of relief. "How did you know I would be on this train?"

"As of two days ago, there is only one train in and out of Croatia. Units along the border were also watching for you.

With the war lost, your comrade felt it would be safer to travel under escort to our base."

Koenig noticed the fascist major's eyes. They were dark and cold—totally without feeling or sympathy. He allowed himself to be ushered to a waiting Opel Kapitan, driver already at the wheel. The major seated himself in front and ordered two of the militia to sit on either side of Koenig in the back. As far as Koenig could tell they headed east, the engine of the old car smoking badly. The rest of the militia unit was left at the train station to settle old scores. A custom as ancient as the Balkans.

**③**

"Where are we going?" Koenig asked trying to sound unconcerned. Major Bakaric's certainty that Germany had already lost the war made Koenig decidedly uneasy.

"We are bivouacked north of Zagreb. There is an abandoned copper mine there."

"I thought the area around Zagreb was held by that peasant Tito and his partisans?" Koenig commented.

**④**

"And units of General Konev's Fifteenth Mechanized Infantry," Bakaric added.

*use a comma here, not a period.*

As if to punctuate the last statement, Russian artillery began a barrage somewhere in the distance, reflecting in the clouds like lightning. "We will have to find another route out. This road will be theirs by morning."

"Are the partisans and Russians aware of your cargo?"

"I don't think so. They don't know our position yet. If we can not flank them and go northwest towards Austria with the convoy, all will be lost."

Koenig pulled a silver cigarette case from his tunic and began to light one of the American Camel cigarettes he so loved.

"No! No, Oberst!" One of the men in the back seat covered the lighter with his hand. "I will show you."

The soldier took the cigarette lighter and bent down behind the front seat, cupping the flame in his hands to minimize the light. He then handed Koenig the cigarette in cupped hands and showed him how to smoke without becoming a target.

Major Bakaric saw what had transpired, leaned over the seat and said one word.

*This paragraph establishes the danger/drama quite effectively.*

"Snipers."

They drove through the Slovenian countryside in silence. It was hard to see anything.

*fragment*

(A study in indigo.) Only the occasional thatched roof of a farm-house or barn could be seen ∧*when* illuminated by a shell burst.

*fragment*

(Mostly empty darkness.) It fit Koenig's mood.

The old Opel was open and provided little in the way of protection from attackers and even less from the cold. Koenig pulled his coat tighter against his body and dug his chin into his collar.

*refer to #4 and the critique*

"Why did you shoot the boy?" He asked the major without looking up.

"He was a spy." Major Bakaric said coldly, staring straight ahead.

After some time the militia major seemed to relax. "You may smoke openly now, Colonel."

"What has changed?" Koenig asked as he passed cigarettes around.

"We are now in territory held by the Ustasa!" The major said with a sweeping motion of his arm.

Koenig did not see any sentries or checkpoints, but he knew they had passed some unseen boundary, some secret gate into sanctuary that only the major and his men understood. The men also visibly relaxed as the Opel turned into a deeply rutted side road lined by small oak trees and juniper bushes. The ter-rain began to rise slightly and then dipped suddenly into coun-tryside made up of rugged hills.

*Who said this? The Major?*

"We have made this area our temporary base. Until a safe route can be established, it would be unsafe to move the cargo from here."

Something about the sarcastic way Bakaric made this last statement left Koenig feeling wary. He wondered if this sly Croat knew the real contents of the trucks.

"I must tell you it is imperative that these weapons move back to the German lines as soon as possible," Koenig ordered in his most Prussian manner. *use a comma*

"If you wish the Communists to have them we will move imme-diately." Bakaric sneered.

Did the German High Command really think this clever Ustasa

major would swallow the ruse that they were transporting captured Russian biological weapons to be used in a last stand against the Allied forces?

**5** The carefully crated Rumanian treasury of gold bars the Germans had taken on their retreat from Russia had been marked with the skull and crossbones. "Poison! Danger!" was stamped all over it, but (it) didn't fool the Croats for a minute.

Koenig remembered, all too well, the scene in the bunker with the madmen. The Fuhrer at the map table, moving divisions that didn't exist. Frau Goebbles serving sandwiches and swaying to "Sentimental Journey" on the phonograph.

The Generals planned on using the stolen gold and art treasures from a dozen countries to finance the "Fourth Reich" *What happened to the Third Reich? It was supposed to last a thousand years!* Isn't this a thought? (What fools they were!) He would do his best to follow their orders and get this particular shipment to the Swiss border, but once there, instead of a numbered Nazi account, it would go into the personal account of Albert Koenig ⎯use a period.

The Ustatsa major became more arrogant with each kilometer. Koenig knew he was in the lion's den. He could feel the hot breath of the beast on his neck. He also knew the power of gold. There was enough for everyone. use a period. If he could just convince Bakaric of his plan, they could forget this lost cause and live in luxury the rest of their lives.

As the ancient Opel rattled on, the land about them changed into a cratered moonscape. It looked as though the fields had been a target of a massive Allied bombing raid. In fact, ~~they~~ the gaping holes were the result of a huge open-pit copper mine.

The moonlight cast an eerie green glow on the water-filled holes. Here and there were ~~also~~ the shafts that led into the sides of the hills. These were the deep mines that held the more pure veins of ore.

Perched on the hillsides were the small houses of the miners. Warm yellow light spilled through the windows of one of the shacks. In front of this one the car came to a lurching halt. Koenig and Bakaric got out and began climbing the steps carved from the earth into the hillside. The Ustasa major turned and instructed the driver to put the car out of sight in the large entrance to one of the mines.

"Soon you will meet my wife," Bakaric said proudly.

*to use a comma*

"She stays with you here?" Koenig was always amazed at the lack of discipline among the militia groups.

"Where else? Our home is now occupied by Soviet forces."

Koenig grunted his understanding.

"There is another woman here as well. They take care of our uniforms, cook the food, clean and many other things." <u>Bakaric gave the German a lascivious wink.</u> *Explain this. Provide details to show readers what kind of man Bakaric is.*

When the door to the miner's shack opened, Colonel Koenig understood why Bakaric would bring his wife. She was beautiful. She was also pregnant.

Koenig found many Eastern women unattractive. By the time they reached thirty, they had given birth to several children and had the short, wide bodies of the peasant. He also found their Slavic features harsh and unappealing. Bakaric's wife had none of these faults. She was tall and had the aquiline features of an aristocrat. *Too vague.*

**6** Koenig bowed slightly at the waist while gently taking her hand. As he rose he sensed an unspoken truth had passed between Bakaric and his wife. For only a second he saw them looking at each other. It was almost as if a farmer was sizing him up. *Ja! This one will be good in the pot!*

**5** The "it" in this sentence refers to the gold bars, and that's not the author's intent. The crates are marked with warning signs, not the gold bars.

**6** This is vague. What precipitated Koenig's sense that an unspoken truth had passed between Bakaric and his wife? The author needs to show something that generated Koenig's thoughts.

Bakaric's pocked face seemed to somehow broaden as his grin revealed yellowed teeth and his right eyelid dropped slowly over his eye, held there for a long moment, and then jerked upward. A quick wave of disgust swept over Koenig. *This mindless pig is bragging about his prowess with these poor women, he thought. I'll enjoy pulling the trigger on him.*

The author also is having some difficulties in properly structuring and punctuating dialogue and narrative throughout this excerpt. Take a look at point three, for example. The author writes:

> "Oberst Koenig, you are to come with me." The Ustasa Major said in clipped German.

He ends the dialogue with a period and then tacks a sentence fragment to it. If he'd used the comma the situation calls for, the line would work fine. Correctly punctuated, it would read:

> "Oberst Koenig, you are to come with me," the Ustasa Major said in clipped German.

The days of copyeditors spending days correcting punctuation and grammar are long gone—if they ever existed. Editors expect—even demand—error-free manuscripts. Review the use and placement of the comma. This little symbol is important to coherence in writing.

This author has a keen eye for detail, and that's a major part of what makes his writing strong and compelling. He presents the bleakness of Bakaric's domain very well.

It is, however, important to note that the fragment fad has died in current fiction, much to the delight of English teachers and linguists—and most readers. Fragments are now seen by editors as exactly what they are: aberrations in structure—sound bites that are fine for TV advertising but have little place in serious writing. The author should consider deleting all the fragments and offering complete sentences instead.

As for his dialogue, the author handles it well except for the punctuation. The aura of mystery and impending violence of Koenig seeps through his terse and realistic phrasing. Bakaric speaks precisely in character. The author does add what are, in essence, stage directions to otherwise tight and often chilling dialogue. The best dialogue stands alone. For example, "Bakaric sneered," "Koenig commented," and other such phrases slow the pace and damage the immediacy of the scene. The author does a fine job of establishing the emotions present, and readers will hear the tones he wants them to hear. His dialogue is his strongest suit, and it doesn't need to be buttressed.

When the author cleans up the things mentioned here, he'll find that his writing is more dramatic, more logical, easier to read—and infinitely more salable.

# Your Turn!

Perfect your dialogue by applying the following tips to your work:

**1.** Do a quick punctuation check of your dialogue. Remember: Periods and commas always go inside quotation marks. Dashes, semicolons, question marks, and exclamation points go inside quotation marks only when they apply to the material within quotations.

**2.** Next, read through your dialogue, and underline dangling fragments. Also underline anything that sounds like a stage direction. If you did a lot of underlining, try cutting such extraneous lines when you revise. Let your dialogue stand on its own merit.

# chapter 7

# Exposition

The opening scene of George Onstot's *Rash Acts* is strong, but it's also drowning in exposition. Using some exposition is understandable, since the background of this story—high society in British Columbia—is probably unfamiliar to many readers. The author needs to fill them in on local details like the gentrification of Gastown and the existence of the Ministry of Cultural Pride. At the same time, he needs to fill them in on his characters' personal backgrounds—Ryan's divorce and career, Rash's problems with the Barrister's Board over the leaky condos. Readers need to know these things before they get into the story.

But they don't need to know as much as the author gives them, and they certainly don't need to have it all delivered through straight exposition. The author has packed this dinner meeting with so much explained information that the dialogue never picks up momentum. In fact, he has often substituted exposition for dialogue, telling readers what Rash and Ryan said rather than showing the characters saying it. This means that readers never get a feel for the most important thing—the friend-

**1** Readers need to know that Rash picked an inconvenient restaurant in order to please Ryan because that sets up Rash's state of mind going into the scene. They don't need to know why the restaurant was inconvenient.

**2** Readers don't need to know Rash wasn't suited for the Cultural Pride Ministry, either. And if they do for some reason that hasn't been revealed yet, the author should find a way to work it into the small talk.

**3** Note how much of this material repeats the material in the first paragraph. The author really only needs to say it once.

ship between Rash and Ryan. Their friendship comes out best through their voices, their reactions, the way they play off of one another as they talk. The author needs to let readers hear it in action.

So what do you do with too much exposition? Some of it can be converted into dialogue. In fact, a good rule of thumb is that

[**Note:** *Rash Patel, the Minister of Cultural Pride, asks his old friend Ryan Patterson, a popular financial commentator, to meet to help him escape a scandal.*]

**(1)** Rash was eager to please me, which was why he'd suggested Ricci's. It was out of his way, in Gastown. ~~When not in Tsawwassen, he was, of course, in Victoria, the provincial capital. Gastown, considered Vancouver's "historical" district (Strathcona, not far away, is much more historical, if somewhat seedier), today is filled with souvenir shops that I find depressing, even considering my livelihood. But you couldn't beat the food at Ricci's.~~ I went in and ~~waited for~~ Rash *arrived a few minutes later.* ~~He walked in, his movements brisk.~~ After a curt greeting and handshake, he settled in across the table. *He didn't look well; he had lost weight and his* *boyishly long, black* hair was threaded with conspicuous strands of gray. Still, ~~his boyishly long hair was mostly bright black,~~ his large dark eyes *were* amazing. He dressed elegantly, as always: camel's-hair sportscoat, olive slacks, beautiful paisley tie, lavender dress shirt. ~~We had succeeded because of~~ **(2)** ~~our looks. He'd become a media fashion plate, the guy whose clothes were as newsworthy as his ideas. He didn't mind the interest in his appearance and attire so much; what irked him was his current work. Rash couldn't relate to the Cultural Pride portfolio. It was just too esoteric; it required sensitivity. He could relate to money, employment, immediate gratification. Getting paid and getting laid (as he would say). He'd have been better suited to Education or Finance.~~

*and* ~~He~~ ordered a vodka and tonic. I had a glass of white wine. ~~The waiter seemed not to recognize either of us.~~ Gastown, once **(3)** excitingly dangerous while I was at UBC, had been tamed. PR firms and ad agencies had moved in, condos were built. Ricci's had grown in popularity with the tourists. The management had cut back on the portions and raised the prices slightly. ~~This I resented.~~ Still, nowhere else could you find such a fine plate of tortellini. "You've been following the leaky condo crisis?" Rash asked.

~~This was at the heart of his problems. I had followed it well, since it was~~ *"Sure, it's* my job to follow Vancouverites' financial affairs *quite a mess."* ~~and as outrages went, this one was a whopper. For a~~

**❹** "Why is the Barrister's Board coming after me? All I did was put up the money. How was I to know the construction workers would cut the windows down to fit too small, so the guys then stick lengths of wood underneath them to make them fit. It's not my fault."

"I agree," I said. "In fact, if it were me, I honestly wouldn't be worried."

"Well, it isn't you, is it? It's me."

**❺** He finished his drink and ordered another one. The alcohol soothed him. "So, do you have a girlfriend yet?"

Celeste and I had divorced several years earlier. More accurately, she'd left me, accusing me in our divorce decree of being a 24-karat obsessive-compulsive workaholic. My beautiful auburn-haired girl didn't know she was marrying the kind of all media, a man of galloping ambition. She held off on getting pregnant until things quieted down a bit for us. They never did. We parted, our settlement modest (she could have done better). "I have offers." friends try to fix me up with sisters, cousins and even a few daughters and nieces. "And you're not interested?" hardly! I just don't have the time.

**❻** "Well," he said, "at least you've got fame and money. And on your own terms. Admirable."

That's the messenger as much as the message. "If I looked more like...oh, say, Rush Limbaugh, I wouldn't be nearly as popular."

"No, you've got it wrong. It's that prematurely graying New York voice of yours." I chuckled. "That's me." Canada's Toughlove financial guru.

~~cient. On the air I scolded economically pinched young callers~~ ℓ
~~confessing to making epic long-distance phone calls to sweet~~ ℓ
~~hearts. To baffled retirees I gave explanations, in what bor-~~ ℓ
~~dered on caretaker speech, of tax forms and RRSP brochures. And~~ ℓ
~~if I had been a bit adventurous in my own investments (and~~ ℓ
~~absurdly lucky), I guided my followers down a considerably~~ ℓ

**(7)** ~~safer path. I preached to them,~~ "Work hard, save religiously,
buy generic."

---

**4** Much of this can come out, and the author can still fully convey what happened.

**5** As a rule, if dialogue wouldn't take up any more space than exposition, use dialogue.

**6** A character trait like Ryan's ego comes across much more effectively if readers see it in action.

**7** Ryan's one-sentence summary of his financial advice is all readers need to know about what he does.

if dialogue doesn't take any more space than exposition, use dialogue. In this case, there's no reason Rash can't cover the basic facts of the leaky condo controversy as he complains to Ryan about his treatment by the Barrister's Board, or that Ryan can't give a witty summary of his career as part of his small talk. The author will have to be careful to keep his characters from telling each other things they already know, since exposition by any other name …

You also can recast some exposition as interior monologue. In this case, when Ryan meets Rash, for instance, it wouldn't be out of place for Ryan to notice how haggard Rash looks and how carefully he's dressed. Ryan knows Rash is going through a tough time and might check for physical signs as to just how tough. It's also appropriate to include a quick explanation of Gastown's gentrification, since Ryan knows the district and would be aware of how the changes have affected Ricci's restaurant.

Finally, as is evident from the edited pages of this excerpt, you can usually cut a lot of exposition. The key to knowing what to cut is to ask, "What do readers need to know in order to understand this scene?" Rash and Ryan are meeting over Rash's problems with the leaky condos, and the scene is building to where Rash asks Ryan to write a letter of clemency. Here, readers need to know about the condos and Rash's role in the problems (though not in as much detail as is given here), and they need to get a feel for the friendship.

Readers don't, however, need a lengthy history of Ryan's divorce. Also, Ryan's appraisal of Rash when he walks into the restaurant probably wouldn't include a commentary on Rash's relationship to the

Ministry of Cultural Pride. He's interested in Rash's condition, not his career problems. And readers only need to know that Ricci's place was out of the way for Rash—not why.

If readers do need to know this material, the way to bring it out is to create a scene where Rash's relationship to the Ministry or Ryan's relationship to his ex-wife is important. The author could even have Rash run into a board member at Ricci's or have Ryan run into Celeste. A little bit of dialogue can tell readers as much about those relationships as half a page of exposition.

# Your Turn!

Keep your use of exposition in check by applying the following tips to your work:

**1.** Take a look at your first major scene involving more than one character. Draw a star next to each new line of dialogue. Select a different colored pen, and draw a box around each new chunk of extended exposition. Does your exposition overwhelm your dialogue? If so, try to balance the two out a bit. Remember the rule from the story above: If dialogue doesn't take up any more space than exposition, use dialogue.

**2.** Next, turn some of your blocked-off exposition into interior monologue. Start by underlining any text that states or describes a fact. For example, in the story above, there's a description of Rash in the first paragraph. This could easily be turned into a bit of interior monologue on the part of Ryan. Could any of these any of the passages you underlined work the same way?

**3.** Now, take one more pass over the scene you've been working on, and ask yourself the following question: What do readers need to know in order to understand this scene? Select a colored pen, and circle each bit of essential information. The key here isn't what you circle, but what you don't circle. How much extraneous information do you have? Can you find a more appropriate place for the information? Can you cut the information altogether?

# chapter 8

# Tone

I n this short story excerpt from *Murder on a Sunday Afternoon,* author Adrian M. Tocklin presents a darkly humorous account of a woman stuck in a netherworld of nasty old people haunting grocery store aisles, a world readers will be happy to avoid. That is the strength—and ultimately the burden—of this story.

On the strong side, the author has material aplenty for such a tale. The narrator coming into contact with creatures she can't stand is the stuff at the heart of fiction—conflict. But the story, to be successful, must maintain a consistent tone throughout, especially because of the central event: a churchgoing, married woman committing a horrible crime in a horrible way.

Think of tone as a set of expectations for readers. The beginning of any story (or novel or screenplay) creates a tonal foundation upon which readers rest their anticipation. If you frustrate readers by changing tone in the middle of the story, or near the end, the fictional edifice you're trying to create will crumble.

With dark humor, there is the added task of modulating two normally opposite

**1** A good opening line can stand alone as the opening paragraph.

**2** This isn't specific enough. The author needs to give readers a picture of the lead character quickly. Slip in some background.

**3** What's the connection? This needs to be developed more. What happens at her church? What might have happened that very morning to help explain her actions?

**4** Here is where more dialogue would help.

**5** Instead of the narrator's philosophy, expand the scene started earlier. Create tension.

**6** Seek fresher, more humorous images.

tones. Killing and death are usually treated in documentary style in literary or genre fiction. Humor has its own conventions. Combining them requires a deftness of touch that is worth striving for, but rarely

*Murder on a Sunday Afternoon*

**1**   Today after Ȼhurch I decided to murder a nasty old lady.⌗
Don't get me wrong. I'm a good person, and I never killed any-
body before. But these old people can really get on your
nerves.

It started at Publix, where as everybody knows you can't go
if you're in a hurry. For you and me, a trip to Publix means
we need a carton of milk. But retirees consider a visit to
Publix an important social event. They like to savor their time
*Expand on this.*
**2**   there, and if they can aggravate <u>someone younger</u> while they're
at it, so much the better. Last week I was heading for the "8
or less items" checkout line when this old woman scooted past
me carrying a grocery basket in each hand. She flew by in such
a whoosh that I was sure the sunglasses perched atop her little
head would fly off. But they didn't. The old gal took her
sweet time removing ⑩ frozen dinners and ③ packages of cook-
ies, and then without looking plopped the empty baskets behind
her, right on top of my bread. She ignored the checkout girl's
repeated "Paper or Plastic?" request. I swear the hearing turns
conveniently on and off once they move to Florida, just like
they forget how to count. Next the request for ② cartons of
Chesterfield Kings, which the bag boy had to get from the back.
*Don't need this "tell" phrase.*
~~And so on. Such is the grocery shopping experience in Florida.~~ ℓ

The only thing worse is waiting at Eckerd's for my husband's insulin prescription. There, you have to stand behind
old guys with tubes from portable oxygen tanks stuck up their
nose. Most of them reek of tobacco. Like they don't understand
the connection. Right.                    *What happened at church to make her snap?*
**3**   But I digress. There I was this afternoon <u>still dressed up
from church</u>, clean panty hose and all. I was standing behind my
grocery cart examining the decaffeinated coffee selections.
Don't you hate that the coffee companies have stopped putting
coffee in cans? Those cans were great for sugar and flour and
leftover nails. Now they just give you those stupid vacuum bags
and once you open them the coffee falls out and makes a mess
on the kitchen floor. Maybe it's a conspiracy with the
Tupperware people to get you to buy Tupperware ~~to hold the cof-~~ ℓ

fee. ~~I bet if we looked it up on the Internet, we would find~~ ℓ
~~that Tupperware is owned by Folgers or some Columbian coffee~~ ℓ
~~producer.~~ ℓ *One line too many on a topic that's a throwaway.*

Anyway, there I stood minding my own business when this
shriveled old crone barrels around the corner and rams into the
front of my cart. I expected a quick apology and would have
gone on my way. If she had just apologized, none of this would
have happened. Instead she glared up at me through thick black-
rimmed glasses and barked, ↩

└ "You're going the wrong way!"

"I beg your pardon?"

"You're going the wrong way! This is my side of the aisle.
Move over!"

~~I looked at her.~~ She had the face of someone who had spent
decades disapproving of everyone she met. Deep lines of con-
tempt etched her mouth. I imagined her playing Bridge every day
with women she loathed. Her hair was dyed an awful shade of
chestnut, flared out in stiff peaks. Brown spots competed for
space on her hands and wrists with wrinkles and too much gold
**4** jewelry. You would not have wanted her as a mother.

~~In hindsight~~, it's hard to know exactly what it was that
made me snap. Maybe it wasn't just her, although she was a
particularly nasty specimen. Maybe it was just years of shopping at Publix in Florida. Maybe it was years of trying to get
around groups of old women blocking the aisles while they discussed their grandchildren. Years of not being able to pass the
old men who could not decide whether to get on the Toledo
scale by the exit doors. Years of waiting while they used
checks in the "Cash Only" line. And they know exactly what
they're doing. It has nothing to do with being old or infirm.
No, this is the only power they have left, and they take it
out on the rest of us.

Maybe it was because she was so sure of herself when she
slammed into my cart. So sure, and so wrong. Grocery aisles are
not like streets. There are no preset right- and left-hand
lanes. You also never park your cart and stand next to it
**5** while shopping, although that is what these old people all do.
Then the rest of us have to keep saying, "Excuse me, to get

around them, and all we get are dirty looks. No, you stand

**5** behind or in front of your cart. Then there is plenty of room
for two shoppers to go down the same aisle at the same time.
It is very simple. *use better imagery.*

**6** I could have said all this to the <u>leathery witch</u> who held
her ground and smirked up at me through pinched red lips. I
could have pushed back on the grocery cart and knocked her
down. (After all,) she was half my size. But right then I decid-
*cut echos*
ed on a better solution. She would pay the price for them all.
So all I said was, "I'm so sorry ma'am. Forgive me for getting
in your way." Then I backed up the cart, gave her a big smile,
and walked on. (After all,) I did not want her telling her
friends and family about the wicked person she met at Publix.
If she said anything, it would only be how nice it was that
young people were finally learning their manners.

A rack of stuffing packages straddled two aisles at the
end. I pushed the cart in front of it and turned to watch her.
From the back, she looked like a dozen other antique ladies in
Publix that afternoon. Except for the red hair, and maybe the
way she held herself. As if everyone else in Publix were her
servants. The usual nylon jogging suit, the white sneakers, and
of course the shopping list. If they must carry a list, why do
they insist on leaving it in the grocery cart when they are
finished? The rest of us inherit carts littered with illegibly
scrawled remnants of some old person's life. Yuck. And what's
with the jogging suits? The only exercise these people get is
squeezing the handle at the self-service gas pump, or bending
into a booth for the $2.99 breakfast at Denny's.

She strolled down the aisle, and I waited. I just knew that
she was going to stop her cart next to the bread, walk over to
the paper towels, and block the aisle for that nice couple with
the baby coming towards me. Sure enough, that is what she did.
Every time they tried to pass, she would back up. I wanted to
grab a bag of charcoal briquettes and hit her on the head. But
I had guests coming for dinner and did not have time for the
police. So I waited and watched. The couple eventually got by,
and she muttered something behind their backs as they passed. I

**7** reached for a bottle of bleach. <u>This was going to be fun.</u>

I only needed about ⟨20⟩ seconds alone with her. But I couldn't do it in Publix because they have surveillance cameras everywhere. Besides, I had to get something out of the car first. If I stayed much longer at the end of the aisle someone might notice me watching her, or the cameras might pick it up later. At the opposite end, she turned right and started coming down the next aisle towards me. Good. She was actually shopping, not just coming in for one or two things. I had time to get what I needed for the dinner party while still keeping an eye on her. ~~After all, why should I have to make another trip to Publix?~~

I grabbed some stuffing and headed for the chicken breasts. The witch was now skipping an aisle and going to vegetables and seafood. <u>How wonderful it would have been to stuff her in the lobster tank.</u> All those little lobster claws snapping at her nose and eyes. But this was not to be. As she interrogated the produce clerk about the source of their oranges, I tossed broccoli in my cart.

"Young man, I hope these oranges are not from Chile," she said.

"I don't know ma'am," the clerk replied.

"Well go find out. I don't want to eat anything from Chile."

*not clear enough*

<u>I hoped that the produce manager was out on a cigarette break,</u> and headed for checkout. I had to get to my car before she left. Luckily, there were no delays today in the Express lane. I glanced over my shoulder at the tabloid rack on the way out, and still did not see her. So far so good.

The great thing about Publix is that the layout is almost the same in every store. You enter through automatic double doors on either the right or the left, with the front of the store either a wall or plate glass windows. There is about 75 feet between each side, so I would be able to watch both exits from the car.

I had never paid attention to outside surveillance cameras before. Were there any? I thought back to a news story about a purse-snatcher in this parking lot about a month before. Had there been photos? I don't think so. They interviewed the old ladies whose bags had been grabbed, but they never showed pho-

tos like they do after convenience store robberies. Maybe
Publix had added cameras since then. Damn. I would have to act
as if there were cameras everywhere. That meant putting the
grocery bags in the front seat so no one would see me taking
out the bleach. What if they had zoom lenses? Well, I'd worry
**8** about that when I got in the car.

achieved. *Catch-22* is a classic example of the form, as is the film *Dr. Strangelove.*

Consider the story in musical terms. If it begins as pop, it can't end with hip-hop. If it starts out like the Louis Armstrong Orchestra, it can't finish like Nirvana. You can go off on riffs, but these must have some connection to the style you established at the outset. There are, however, several simple techniques for achieving tonal balance within a novel or short story.

First, in order for this story to work, the author has to do a lot more work to convince readers that his narrator is capable of such an act. It isn't enough that the character tells readers she's annoyed by all the shopping geezers. At point four, for example, the narrator tells readers she doesn't know what made her snap. Readers feel the same way. Later, the narrator gives a list of annoyances, but once again this is the narrator *telling*—not *showing*. Instead, readers need to feel the character's annoyance by experiencing it.

E.M. Forster said the test for a good character is whether she can surprise readers in a convincing way. Many times, new writers—itching for a shock—will have the lead character do something far out, yet completely unjustified by any setup. That leads to the reading equivalent of a sugar rush. There's a quick high, but a massive letdown afterward.

The solution is to give some glimpse of the narrator's life *before* the events. You can do this either in an opening scene (What is the character's home life like? Why is the character ready to snap?) or in some internal monologue flashbacks. In this case, the cold premeditation of this woman's act makes this background work essential.

Here, the author needs to bring to the actual murder more of the tone he establishes in the beginning. One way to do that is to make the crime less premeditated, and more comically spontaneous. That would preserve the story's dark humor, which is not present in the murder scene as written.

Irony often plays a large part in a darkly humorous piece. The author should think about expanding that element of his story. While he has set up the irony of a church

**7** There's not enough background for readers to believe these statements.

**8** Conflict being the heart of fiction, why not add some obstacles, like a security guard or chatty shopper?

soloist committing murder, he never really tells readers what the significance is. Irony without explanation becomes mere puffery; it wants to say something about the world but hasn't thought it through quite enough.

Another way you can maintain tone is through dialogue. There is one funny exchange here where the lady says that she doesn't want to eat "anything from Chile." That's the sort of quirky, irrational, and annoying element the story needs more of.

The author should write several such scenes, and write them for all they are worth. This is an exercise you can do with your own work as well. Let yourself go.

Create dialogue exchanges and illustrative actions. Write more scenes than you will ever use, then choose the best one or two, the ones that capture the tone you're going for, and incorporate them into the story.

You also can use the subtext of dialogue to give readers a glimpse inside the narrator's head. The words a character uses should not only communicate, but characterize. Work with the tone of voice and verbal ticks the narrator would display.

Dark humor is very difficult to write. This author has a good start here: an off-kilter view of a social annoyance that lends itself to humor and irony.

# Your Turn!

Ground your narrative voice by applying the following tips to your work:

**1.** Have a friend or critique group member read over the first chapter of your novel or your entire short story. Ask him to draw a star next to each point where he senses a jarring change in tone. This will give you a better understanding as to how a reader is perceiving your work.

**2.** Once he's finished, take a look at what he's marked. Were you aware of these tonal changes—were they intentional or unintentional?

**3.** If the tonal changes are intentional, and your reader still finds them jar-

ring, try adding in a few transitional sentences to bridge the gap.

**4.** If they are unintentional, reread each starred paragraph or section. Then, try using dialogue to maintain your story's tone. For example, as is suggested in the above critique, pick one of your starred sections and rewrite it several times using different exchanges of dialogue to influence your tone. When you're finished, choose the version that best captures the tone you want to achieve, and use it in the place of the starred section.

# chapter 9

# Details

This is a tense scene from Ruth M. McCarty's *Preston Point.* Even before readers learn what the novel's main character, Dotty, is afraid of, the author conveys the fear in the way Dotty's overwhelmed by her son Eddie's accident and panicked about dinner. The author then sustains the fear when she makes it clear that, even after Dotty's gotten Eddie and dinner under control, Wayne, her husband, is still a threat. Unfortunately, in trying to keep the scene as tense as possible, the author leaves out too many crucial details.

The author's instincts are good. One way you can create a sense of time rushing forward is to trim the descriptive details to an absolute minimum. In the case of this story, this approach is even more effective if readers know from the beginning what Dotty's in for if the dinner isn't perfect. They can dread Wayne's return even as they watch it rush toward them.

But even when the details are kept to a minimum, you still have to give readers enough to follow the action clearly. In this excerpt, for example, when Dotty makes the sudden transition from wiping Eddie's

**1** The author needs to explain why Dotty doesn't move for a moment. Also, she shouldn't tell readers that Dotty hears Eddie crying; she should show Dotty hearing him crying.

**2** There's a major detail missing. If the author has Dotty look in Eddie's mouth, she should tell readers what Dotty sees.

**3** This is where the author really needs to track things mentioned in the scene more closely—the dishrag, the glass of water, Eddie himself.

pants to handing him a glass of water, without any sign of where the water came from, readers are apt to feel left behind.

How do you decide how much detail is enough? There are no rules. Here, the author could have conveyed Dotty's fear just as effectively by showing the character drowning in detail. For example, she could have Dotty focus on the state of the meatballs while she's washing Eddie. Or, the author could spend half a paragraph with

*Preston Point*

by Ruth M. McCarty

[**Note:** *Dotty is having a difficult time preparing dinner—the spaghetti sauce boiled over earlier. Eddie is four.*]

**①** Eddie screamed. Startled, Dotty dropped one of the eggs on the vinyl floor. ∧ *Then, for a second she merely stood there, while he began to cry and the crying turned to words.* ~~She could hear him crying.~~

"I burned my mouth ⊙," *this.* ~~he said.~~

~~Shit, I can't do it.~~ (ital.)

Dotty ran to the living room. "I told you to be careful!
**②** Let me see." She looked into her son's mouth, ∧ *A little redness, no blistering, thank God.* ~~tears running down his face.~~ "Come into the kitchen, I'll give you a glass of water," she said. "It ∧ will make you feel better."

Eddie followed her. She walked to the sink, reaching for a glass and turning on the tap. "Watch out for the ~~egg~~-"

It was too late. Eddie was wiping his eyes and didn't see it. His foot *slid out from under him,* ~~slipped~~ and he landed on the ~~yolk.~~ *egg.* He began crying again.

Dotty wanted to ~~cry.~~ *join him. Instead,* she ~~grabbed Eddie~~ *took him* by the arm, ~~pulling~~ *and dragged*
**③** him to his feet. ~~Reaching for~~ *Then she grabbed* the dishrag, *and* ~~she~~ tried to wipe his pants, *without much luck. She slung the rag in the sink and handed him his water.* ∧"Stop crying ~~," she said, handing him a glass of water,~~ *and* "Drink this, then go change your pants." *She shooed him out then* ~~Dotty~~ started to wipe the floor *with* (She knew she sounded crazy) ~~as she laughed.~~ Eddie's pants had soaked up most of the egg, but a slimy mess still needed cleaning. ~~She ran~~ the now dirty dishrag over the floor. *Then, suddenly, she began to laugh.* but she couldn't help it. *When the floor was more or less clean, she tossed the rag in the trash—it was old anyway—then* ~~She~~ raced to roll the meatballs, *She put* ~~putting~~ them in a glass
**④** dish. ~~I'll have to~~ *so she could* nuke them before *(ital.)* ~~I put~~ *she added* them into the sauce *then* ~~She~~ filled a pot with hot water, *and* turned the burner to high. *She glanced at the clock. Wayne would be home any minute. Yanking* ~~Now to set the table. Pulling~~ open cabinets and drawers, she *then stood back and stared at it.* *had she forgotten* set the table, ∧*Salt, pepper, sugar, butter, bread, milk* ~~did I forget~~ anything? ←(ital.)

~~Dotty threw the dishrag into the trash. It was old anyways.~~ The meatballs were ready to go into the sauce, the table set, and the water boiling. It was going to be all right. She broke the thin spaghetti in half, dropp~~ing~~ *ed* it into the water and began ~~the task of~~ cleaning the now-dried spaghetti sauce from the stove and the wall.

Dotty was just finishing when ~~she heard~~ Wayne's truck ~~in~~ *pulled into* the driveway. She ~~pulled~~ *lifted* the curtain ~~out from the frame, only~~ *and* a fraction, not wanting him to see her, ~~She~~ *him* watched ~~as he~~ opened the door, *He* stumbl~~ing~~*ed*, turning his ankle *as he did. Oh no. She watched as he* slammed the door and kicked it.

Oh, God, please let him like the supper. She checked the table again. *Napkins.* ~~I forgot~~ *She'd forgotten* to put out napkins. Sweating now she raced to the counter, ~~pulling~~ *jerking* three napkins out of the holder, fold~~ing~~*ed* them in half and ~~putting~~ *stuck* them under the forks. Dotty took one last look. Everything was okay. ~~She had managed to get the kitchen clean, the table set, and the food cooked.~~ Maybe tonight ~~will~~ *would* be different. She ran a comb through her hair and pulled her lipstick from her apron pocket. *Maybe if ~~I~~ she look~~ed~~ good tonight he'~~ll~~*d* be happy.*

Wayne limped into the kitchen, slamming the door shut. He crossed the room to the refrigerator ~~and~~ pulled out a can of beer~~, chug-a-lugging it. He~~ *and chugged it down, then* crushed the can and ~~then~~ turned to Dotty. "Where the hell ~~is~~*'s* my supper?"

"Hello Wayne." She smiled. "I just have to drain the spaghetti. How was your day?"
He ~~sat at the table, ignoring her.~~ *dropped into his chair without a word.*

Dotty dithering about what to do with the dirty washrag. But there are a couple of rules of thumb that you can follow when trying to determine just how much detail is enough.

On one hand, readers need to do some of the imaginative work. You, as the author, have to give them a chance to fill in some of the details—in this case, the design of the vinyl on Dotty's kitchen floor, or the degree of rust (or presence of a gun rack) on Wayne's pickup truck—based on their memories of similar people in similar situations. When readers are given room to fill in these details, they custom-tailor characters and situations to their own experience, making them much more real. Besides,

waking up readers' imaginations is a good way to draw them into the story.

On the other hand, you also have to give readers' imaginations a framework to fill in—enough detail to define the characters in broad terms and establish the character traits the story needs. For example, readers would imagine Dotty and Wayne as slightly different people if, instead of vinyl, their flooring was terra-cotta tile, say, or unfinished plywood, or if they were having an arugula salad with a balsamic vinaigrette rather than spaghetti and meatballs.

Finally, you have to remember to track your action and props, filling in enough details so your characters move smoothly from one moment to the next. Granted,

**4** A quick note about italics and interior monologue: When you're writing from your character's point of view, you can keep most routine interior monologue. For example, Dotty's review of what she needed to place on the table, is in the third person, past tense. You can, however, use italics for internal voices, such as the author did with the "I can't do it" comment or the brief prayer about the supper.

**5** The author doesn't have to keep saying that Dotty heard or watched aspects of Wayne's arrival. The readers know. The only time the author might want to use this construction is when she wants to emphasize Dotty's attention, as when Dotty first gets a hint of the mood Wayne's in by the way he climbs out of his truck.

there are certain common actions that can be abbreviated. For instance, you can go straight from the sound of the telephone ringing to the first "hello" without mentioning that the character has picked up the receiver. But when Dotty suddenly switches from holding a dishrag to holding a glass of water, or when she has interior monologue about her laughter before readers have seen her laugh, then the author is leaving gaps that readers will find jarring. The goal here is continuity, not a strobe effect.

The details you choose depend on what you need to convey about your characters for the sake of the story. The author of this story may disagree with some of the added details—or she may want to add more. Just remember that, in general, you need to include enough detail to create the characters you want and no more.

# Your Turn!

Use details to enrich your story by applying the following tips to your work:

**1.** Ask a friend or critique group member to read over your first scene with an eye on detail.

**2.** Next, ask your reader to describe his impressions of your main character and setting based on the framework of details you provided in the text. Did you provide enough detail for your reader to envision your character and setting in the manner that you intended? Or, did you provide too many details, leaving nothing to your reader's imagination?

**3.** Now it's your turn to analyze that first scene. Reread your work, and focus only on the details surrounding your character's actions and the props in the scene with which your character interacts. As in the above critique, it can be distracting for readers when a character suddenly goes from holding a dishrag to holding a glass of water. Highlight sections of the text that lack such crucial transitional details. Then, rework them sections by adding in more details.

# chapter 10

# Scenes

This well-crafted scene from Angela Fox's novel, *Fowl Play*, will keep readers laughing throughout, while simultaneously creating suspense. The author also does a great job at building every scene on the one before it and the one after it, which reminds me of something Dorothy Wall and Thaisa Frank say in their book, *Finding Your Writer's Voice*: "You understand instinctively that a good plot functions like a series of billiard balls hitting against each other."

For those balls to keep moving and hitting each other, however, your cue stick has to connect with the balls in the first place. This is accomplished by making sure your character has an "intention" in each scene that will take him through the scene to its ultimate "collision." In Jack Bickham's book *Scene & Structure*, he identifies the three major scene elements as goal, conflict, and disaster. Let's modify these to intention, journey, and collision. These new labels leave more room for scene development that is not necessarily as serious as "conflict" and "disaster" seem to indicate.

For example, in this scene the emphasis is on getting through the next scheduled

**1** The scene should start with "I didn't do it!" It's more of a grabber, and it's the key statement of Meg's intention for this scene.

**2** How about making Meg responsible for Sherman's topple from the log? She's already said she doesn't want him up there. When he falls, everyone can look at her accusingly, and she can blurt out, "I didn't do it." It's another opportunity for her to state her intention, albeit unconsciously.

**3** Insert a few lines of narrative into this dialogue to reveal how relieved Meg will be when the heat is off of her and everyone clearly can see that Sherman is the killer.

**4** There who was? Who is "she"? Pammy's replacement?

rehearsal of the children's TV show without the show's star, Pammy Peacock, who recently was murdered. As mentioned in a scene not included in this excerpt, the killer most likely is someone on the set of this show. No one in this story is free from sus-

[**Note:** *In this excerpt from Fowl Play, the main character,
Meg, is a writer for a children's TV show. She's also suspected
of murdering one of the show's lead character's, Pammy
Peacock.*]

That afternoon at rehearsal, it felt like all eyes were on
me as I blocked out a scene between Sherman and Edith. Today
was the day to set up the scenes and run the characters
through their lines. They ~~got~~ *would get* a feel for the set and ~~tried~~ *try* to
work without scripts as much as possible. The dance coordinator
could also eyeball which moves were working and which needed
some adjustment. David and I ~~kept~~ *would keep* a lookout for which lines
didn't ring quite right or which jokes fell flat. We'd huddle
with Jon to make tweaks here and there for the actors to pencil into their script books. It was all quite informal, and
usually quite long.

*I forced*
~~Forcing~~ myself to concentrate on the job at hand, *and* ~~I~~ pretended everything was normal. After all, I owed it to the show
to give it my best, to analyze how every line was said, where
each actor stood. Still, it was hard. Every five seconds or so,
I felt like screaming, "I didn't do it!" I imagined my words
echoing throughout the Happy Forest, all the way back to the
painted mountains in the distance. David slid up next to me.
"Whatever you're thinking, stop it."

"Easy for you to say."

"Let's just concentrate on getting done with this, then
catching Sherman in the act tonight." He wandered away to talk
to the lighting guys.

I felt my eyes narrow every time I looked at the overgrown
bunny. We hadn't spoken since our confrontation that morning in
Pammy's dressing room. There he stood, perched upon a log,
(delivering lines) about respect for nature and wildlife. He
looked like a circus bear on a ball, except he wasn't as talented. One wrong move and he was ~~going~~ *sure* to lose it.

I could feel myself leaning to the left, then the right,
tottering with him. I realized I really should rescue him from
the scene. It had looked good on paper, but it was ~~really~~ too
obscene with Sherman up there, ready to crush anyone lingering
beneath.

*Move to later in the opening.*

*Let's hear the lines—use dialogue,
bring Sherman to life.*

*wonderful description—good use of details.*

Sweat stains soaked the underarms of his royal purple silk shirt. His ballooning sleeves were like wings, as he continuously strained his fingers upward and outward in a feeble attempt to balance the mass of his body. When he finished his lines, he unconsciously began to puff out his already ample cheeks and blow in short, hard breaths, as if that would somehow keep him upright.

"Jon," I leaned towards him as he chewed on his pencil, "We have to get Bouncy Bunny off the log. It doesn't look right with Sherman up there."

"Let him figure it out. He does his job. You do yours," said Jon a bit too arrogantly for my taste.

"Well, he's doing what's in the script," I said to the back of Jon's head, "but I'm just realizing now I shouldn't have written it with him up there. It's not flowing."

**②** Jon turned and sighed, *Can't sigh a sentence—use a period.* "I don't see him complaining, Meg. Only you."

*Make Meg responsible somehow.*

Stung, I returned to the scene in front of us. <u>Sherman had fallen off the log</u> and was getting back on, looking around to see if anyone had noticed. Edith rolled her script and tapped her pink pump nervously for a cigarette. Bunko Bob was arguing with the choreographer. It was not a happy forest.

David ambled back over from across the set, hands in the pockets of his classic blue jeans, his white shirt contrasting sharply with his deep tan.

"Look at him, like a big old grape," David said in a low tone, nodding back at Sherman, who had sat down on the log and was wiping his forehead with a handkerchief that matched his silk shirt.

"So how do you want to do this?" I bit at my lip nervously.

"Well, we have to catch him in the act," David said, as he turned and propped himself against the wall where I was leaning, "so I'm thinking we watch his dressing room and then when he leaves, we follow him."

I put my hands in my pockets and thought for a second about his plan. "There's really not much around Sherman's room, besides the other actor's rooms. What do you say we hang out with Bunko for a bit?"

"Next door, huh? Good."

I didn't like to misuse a friendship like that, but ~~his~~ was [*Bunko's room*]
the perfect vantage point. Besides, when we caught Sherman in
the act, we'd be doing everybody a favor.

I smiled devilishly, [*Can't smile a sentence—use a period.*] "I can't wait to see Sherman in the

Tinseltown Times." [*Italics*]

"You have the perfect photo too."

"The one where we put him in pink toe shoes?"

**3** "Oh yeah," David grinned. "The night he had too much
whiskey and passed out."

"Which night was that again?"

"Nah," he leaned in closer, "I was thinking about the time
you snapped that shot of him making change in that homeless
guy's cup."

"After he chaired that fundraiser for the poor?"

"Exactly."

"Ah, the choices." It would be nice to have them again.
Lately, things had felt a little tight.

Jon called for quiet on the set. Pammy's replacement would
be giving her debut performance in the next scene. I just hoped
she'd be able to jump right in. Once this rehearsal was finished, David and I could get down to the real business at
hand.

"So," Edith Elephant began, "You sure look different today,
Pammy."

**4** And there (she) was, peering from the Happy Forest [*who?*]
tree house. "Really?" Thin and stoop-shouldered, she looked
more like a fruit bat than a peacock. "Well, I feel the same. [*Excellent line.*]
After all, friends like us for who we are on the inside, not
for what we look like on the outside." [*Great line, so corny.*]
——— The script was bad, the replacement was bad and no one
seemed to notice, least of all Edith.

**5** "You're right. Let's play. Here, come along and rhyme with
me!," ~~laughed~~ the plump, aging actress, prancing [*ed*] about the
room, script dangling from the hand above her head.

"Please stay. Don't leave me in this tree," read the woman,
squinting at her script.

"Can't! I'm busy as a bee!" Edith began spinning slowly.

[*Let Meg blame David for this—she's under stress.*]

"I get it, Edith! You're rhyming with me."

Jon interrupted the growing melee with a sharp "Okay!"

The frightened (actress) looked up and fiddled nervously with
her reading glasses. Edith kept spinning.

*[handwritten: replacement or Edith?]*

Thus, we spent the better part of an hour turning a pale
version of Pammy into something we could all be proud of. We
walked with her, talked with her, strutted with her. The only
truly noteworthy moment was when Edith—momentarily disoriented
from all the spinning—launched her generous body straight at
the timid looking new bird *with* disastrous results. Both went down
in a heap as a rainbow of tiny beads from her broken necklace
raced across the floor. I've never heard anyone hit such a high
pitch as she screamed in surprise. Ten minutes and one crushed
pair of bifocals later, both were composed enough to continue
with the reading. Not that it mattered. Like Edith, the
replacement had flopped.

Jon approached the exhausted applicant. "Ms. Whatever-your-
name-was, you're fired. Meg, you're reading Pammy's lines."

"Why me?"

"You wrote them."

"David did."

"Close enough."

Edith tittered as I clutched my script between my teeth and
climbed up to the tree house to begin the scene.

"You're such a trooper, dear!"

I ignored her. If this would help us get through this
afternoon, then so much the better. However, as we began to
read, I felt myself warming to the character of Pammy Peacock
and to my presence on stage. It was fun, especially the scene
where I got to throw spongy, oversized fruit down at Sherman's
Bouncy Bunny character. He winced as I tossed it a bit more
forcefully than was altogether necessary. This was great thera-
py.

At last, the final scene was read to everyone's satisfaction. All the costuming decisions had been made.

"You were great," David nudged me as the sets were rolled
from their places for reworking.

"Well, you know, some devote their lives to intellectual
discovery. Others to pious works. For me, it's giant elephants

*[handwritten in left margin: Don't resolve her paranoia yet by having her warm too much.]*

and bunnies."

"Ah yes, the Mother Theresa of daytime programming." Something else caught his attention. "Here comes Jon."

"Meg! Great! That was a really natural read—especially when you tripped Sherman with that tree branch."

"Yeah, well I ad‚libbed that part."

"Perfect! Now how'd you like to replace Pammy in this week's episode?"

In truth, I did not like, but decided to give him a break before delivering my final verdict. I was learning to be composed. "For real?"

"For real!"

"No."        *More internalizing of Meg here* . . .

"Think harder."

❽ "No." Pammy's costume consisted of a white leotard, shiny yellow tights and tufts of feathers that did nothing to enhance or hide a body that wasn't stick thin.

"You're not thinking."

"No." There was no way they were getting me into that fluffy feathered skull cap, and I didn't even want to know how they attached that yellow beak onto one's nose.

"I'm going to let you think about this tonight, but I don't really see where I have a choice." With that, he stalked away. I turned to David, but was blindsided by the harsh flash of a camera. How had the press gotten in?

*Italics*
"Jack Terrill, <u>Tinseltown Tribune</u>. So you found Ms. Porchot's body, now you're taking her role on the show. What would you say to people who wonder if you in fact murdered her?"

I stared at him, blinking back purple spots.

"I liked her."

"Yeah, but you liked her job even more, now didn't you dear?"  *Make this dialogue stronger.*

"No comment," I fumbled.

❾ "Was the brutal slaying planned or did you do it in a fit of passion?"  *Let Meg lose it here at the end.*

~~I couldn't think of anything else to say as his camera~~ ¶
~~flashed again.~~ ¶

~~"Good one, dear. But next time, lose the gum."~~ ¶

picion, but the main finger of guilt seems to be pointing at the central character, Meg, the show's writer.

Every scene, then, should emphasize not an external goal like getting through the show, but Meg's personal intention—either external or internal, but preferably both. The reason for this emphasis is because the character's intention is what propels each scene forward and engages readers. The character has to want something, and the more desperately she wants it, the more your reader will be on the edge of her chair.

Meg's intention in the scene shown here could be any number of things. It could be as simple as moving the suspicion away from herself. Or it could be as complicated as trying to shift the suspicion onto another character so that someone else is in the spotlight—someone like Sherman a.k.a. Bouncy Bunny. Meg's, and everyone else's, overall intention—i.e., the plot—is to identify and expose the murderer. And so Meg goes through various antics to help the police find the killer.

But underlying this—and an even more important motivation for Meg—is that Meg must find the killer so that she is not arrested for the murder. Things don't look good for Meg, especially since she was the only one at the scene of the crime immediately after it was said to have occurred. Meg's intention in every scene should somehow further the idea of her innocence.

The viewpoint character's intention needs to be clear at the beginning of the scene. The author might even want to open this scene with the line "I didn't do it!" on the tip of Meg's tongue. Or maybe Meg actually blurts it out, but means to say something else. For example, Edith or Sherman could be looking for their lost

**(5)** Meg—the show's writer—is admitting to herself that the script is bad. How about letting her say something out loud to again deny responsibility? Maybe blame the bad lines on David? That way Meg's again denying that she killed Pammy Peacock—she's a bit obsessed with pointing this out.

**(6)** Here, Edith could blame Meg for writing the kinds of lines that would cause her to fall on her face, shattering her necklace. Meg is becoming full of guilt.

**(7)** Show Meg's despair before transforming it to glee.

**(8)** This snatch of dialogue needs a purpose; could Meg be paranoid that Jon is trying to punish her because he believes she's guilty of Pammy's murder?

**(9)** Show more of Meg's frustration—maybe even rage—as the reporter shows up. This is a collision that will end this scene. It needs to be dramatic.

scripts, and Meg could suddenly scream she didn't do it—clearly overreacting.

At this point, Meg's journey takes her through a series of events that will distract everyone and get the attention off of Meg. The way the author has it now is funny, but it lacks focus and the furtherance of Meg's intention. The author misses a real opportunity here to propel the story forward.

The author also misses a chance to add more humor, because when people are trying to get the attention away from themselves, they'll go to lengths that can sometimes get a little crazy. For example, maybe some evidence has turned up that shows the murderer was definitely a bungling idiot. When Sherman almost falls off the log, Meg can find ways to connect this to things the murderer did and therefore implicate Sherman. Or maybe Edith Elephant does or says something that Meg jumps on to implicate her as the murderer. This could, of course, be a ridiculous stretch and even her co-writer, David, is rolling his eyes. But Meg is on a mission. She's desperate. The author needs to make Meg more desperate—make every step of her journey though this scene full of her desperation to prove that someone, anyone, other than her committed the murder.

As mentioned earlier, each scene needs to end with a collision—the outcome of a character's intention, something horrible. You never want to resolve a situation at the end of a scene, because you want readers to stay up all night reading your novel.

In this case, the *Tinseltown Tribune*

showing up is actually a great collision as it reveals that no matter Meg's intention to get the attention off of her, here is this newspaper reporter flashing cameras all around her, and everyone is there watching—what a mess. Perfect. This is especially funny given the dialogue that takes place earlier in the scene between David and Meg where she's gleefully imagining the photo of a guilty Sherman in his pink toe shoes in the same newspaper.

Intention. Journey. Collision. When planning your novel, think about these three words for each scene, and you can't go wrong. Intention: Your cue stick is connecting with your billiard balls. Journey: Your balls are rolling forward. Collision: The balls collide with the wall of the table, crazily bounce off the table or drop into the intended pocket.

All of this will ensure that your reader will keep turning pages long past the midnight hour.

# Your Turn!

Keep you scenes connected by applying the following tips to your work:

**1.** Take a look at your first three scenes. Write "PI" next to the points were your main character's personal intentions become clear. Do the intentions propel the scenes forward and add insight into your character? Are they consistent with your intended storyline?

**2.** Now, it's time to chart your character's journey. Within the same scenes, write "J" next to thoughts and actions that are inspired by your character's personal intentions. Is your character's journey apparent in each scene? Do the marked points move the scenes forward?

**3.** It's collision time! This time, write "C" next to point where the outcome of your character's intention finally occurs. Remember, unlike intention, collision should be revealed late in each scene. Compare your collisions with your intentions—do they complement each other? Are your character's thoughts and actions consistent with each scene's climactic moment?

# chapter 11

# Scene Endings

good scene ending, like good dialogue, has to simulate real life without actually imitating it. Reality rarely provides you with good exit lines, so when you end every scene with a sharp, crisp ending, your work starts to feel artificial. On the other hand, you can't simply let your characters drift on to other things, as Charles Scott does in this scene from his novel, *Fever Spike*. While it's more true to life, it ultimately feels flabby and accidental.

How do you give your scenes sharp yet authentic-seeming endings? Well, you are allowed an occasional cliff-hanger, where you end your scene with your main character in imminent danger. Sometimes you can also get away with ending a scene on a surprise revelation or on a moment of ominous foreboding. As a rule of thumb, though, the greater the danger, surprise, or foreboding, the less often you can use it in an ending. You don't want readers to burn out before they get to the end of your novel.

One way to end more mundane scenes is to use an image or an exchange of dialogue that summarizes or typifies the main emotion of the scene. For instance, scenes where

**1** The dialogue needs to be trimmed back. The author's letting his legislative sensibility get too involved in his writing. Normal dialogue contains a lot more ambiguity. Cut phrases that specify precisely what the characters are talking about.

**2** There should be a bit more give-and-take between the characters—they tend a bit toward speeches. This might be in character for politicians, but not in private dialogue.

**3** Try moving some of this dialogue to the end of this scene where it will give the ending an emotional twist (see point eight).

the conflict between two characters escalates can end with one of them storming out. A scene where a scheming character begins his machinations can end with a particularly egregious lie. Ending at a summarizing moment leaves the main emotion of the scene sharp and fresh in readers' minds and launches them into the remainder of

## Fever Spike

[**Note:** *The United States is threatened with a deadly new virus. The president, while moving forward with a vaccination campaign, wants to reassure people and avoid panic. In direct defiance of the president's orders, the surgeon general has just given a clear warning of the danger. The president is discussing his response with his chief of staff.*]

**❶** "Well," Bob said, "~~it won't be too hard to get~~ *"we'd start with"* a campaign of leaks saying you're not satisfied with her [the surgeon general's] performance. Too slow to identify the problem ~~and bring it to your attention~~, too slow to get the vaccine campaign going, that sort of thing. Then in a week or two we can identify some specific snafu in the vaccination campaign ~~in~~ some—*one*—thing that big you know there will be ~~something the press will make a big deal of~~ and you can ~~explicitly~~ hold her responsible for it and fire her. That'll make you look decisive without making you responsible for what happens next."

**❷** The president paused and tapped his pad with his pen. "~~As a minor theme, add~~ *How about* a careful leak that we feel she ~~first~~ underestimated the situation, then compensated by overestimating it, and we're losing confidence in her judgment. That ~~kind of a leak~~ will help mollify the retail folks. *"You mean"* ~~She made the mistake of using exaggerated numbers on what's going to happen next.~~ That's the old |trick| ~~we always see out of the~~ bureaucracy ~~and the interest groups~~. Claim something really bad is going to happen to scare people, then claim credit for saving the situation when ~~things don't~~ *it doesn't?* turn out that badly. ... You do think they're exaggerating this, don't you?"  *Move this graph to point 8.*

**❸** "Yes, Mr. President, I do. I hate to be cynical, but ~~you outlined the strategy we always see. Those~~ *her* claims are based on bureaucratic politics. This is the 21st century, for God's sake. ~~We can deal with epidemics.~~ We have a vaccine and you've done the right thing to get us moving on using it. In a couple of months most people will be vaccinated and that will be that. ~~Still we have to be careful. If the bureaucracy is even 20% right, and that or something a bit worse is likely, by spring~~

~~time when the crisis is over the Congress will be in full cry~~
~~on a witch hunt for those responsible. We need to make sure~~
~~that their target is the former Surgeon General, not you."~~

**4** ~~"Agreed. I think our leak strategy is the way to go."~~ The
timing of the actual firing could be important. I don't want to
fire anyone the week before Christmas, that always looks bad.
Beyond that … "

"No problem.

"I need at least a week for the leaks to be effective,
maybe more. ~~Let me get started and then we can reevaluate the~~
timing next week. By then we'll know more about how far off
her predictions on the number of cases are, and we'll have more
time for the inevitable vaccine campaign snafu. That may influence our timing. A good snafu will give us the kind of opportunity we can't pass up and that may be more important than
timing." *That's right. In fact,*

~~"Yeah. Of course,~~ if she's far enough off on her estimates
of how bad the problem is, I could fire her for that too. This
business of everybody *turning* ~~exaggerating~~ problems into ~~major~~ crises
is *getting out of hand.* ~~much too common.~~ It's usually environmentalists, but the
public health people and the consumer advocates can be just as
bad. *We could use* ~~I'm looking for a chance to make~~ an example ~~out of someone to try to rein it in.~~

*agree about needing an example, but I don't think she should be it.*

"Mr. President, I ~~really don't think that would be a good
idea in this case.~~ This one's already bad enough that people
aren't going to get too excited about someone exaggerating it,
and we know it's going to get worse before ~~we get everyone~~ *it gets better.*
~~vaccinated. We can put out a leak or two that we think she's~~
~~exaggerating the problem, but the public reason for firing her~~
~~should be something else, like being slow to deal with it.~~ Save
your example for some case where the TV can't find real victims

**6** to interview ~~you need~~ the modern equivalent of ~~an~~ asbestos
~~problem, where the solution advocated is either a waste of~~
~~money or even does some harm. Even if it's exaggerated, this~~
~~problem is too real for that."~~

**7** "Okay, I guess you're right. Do your leaks, but we'll base
the firing on bad management. *Also* ~~when we get the snafu in the vaccine campaign.~~ *"Good. And* Keep in the back of your mind that sometime in
the next six months I want to make an example out of someone

*Move this graph to point 7.*

*Insert graph from point 4.*

for exaggerating a problem with inflated numbers. ②~~The practice~~⑨
*The President picked up a file. "Now, if you'll excuse me."*
~~is getting out of hand because there've been no consequences~~ ₹
~~for doing it. It's making it hard for me to figure out which~~ ₹
~~problems really are important and which aren't. I shouldn't~~ ₹
~~entirely rely on the public opinion polls for that … Now, on~~ ₹
~~this problem with the farm bill, did you talk to … "~~ ₹

[**Note:** This would be a good place to the put the dialogue cut at point three. Also, note the italicized dialogue that has been added to the original manuscript.]

**8** *"Very good, sir."* Bob Got up and made for the door.
*"Um … Bob?"*
*He turned. "Yes, sir?"*
*"You do think they're exaggerating, don't you?"*
*"Yes, Mr. President, I do. I hate to be cynical, but her claims are based on bureaucratic politics. This is the 21st century, for God's sake. We have a vaccine, and you've done the right thing to get us moving on using it. In a couple of months most people will be vaccinated and that will be that."*
*"I thought so. Good night, Bob."*

---

**4** This section of dialogue would work better later in the scene (see point seven).

**5** Again, it may be in character for politicians to talk in this kind of detail, but readers don't need to read all of this.

**6** There's no need to define why asbestos is a problem.

**7** This would be a good place to put the dialogue cut from point four.

**8** Note the dialogue added at the end. This also would be a good place to put the dialogue cut from point three.

the story. The summarizing moment doesn't seem contrived because it involves an emotion that has been present in the scene from the beginning—an emotion that's part of the landscape.

For example, later in this excerpt, there's a scene where a railroad engineer, Fred, finds a train stalled on the track ahead of him because its engineer, an old friend of his, has succumbed to the epidemic—thought to be caused by asbestos. Fred places his friend's body in a nearby outbuilding, then runs his friend's train into the next switchyard to clear the track. Rather than follow Fred all the way to the switchyard as the author does, end the scene where Fred starts his friend's train moving and blows a crossing signal on the air horn that is also a final salute. That moment, which captures the sadness of the discovery, is the right spot to end the scene.

Another way to conclude is with a moment that plays against the rest of the scene in some way, giving the main emotion an unexpected twist to propel readers forward. If the dominant emotion is cruelty, let a little tenderness shine through at the end, or vice versa. An emotional twist at the end of a scene is a bit more artificial than a simple emotional summary, so you can't use this sort of ending too often. But humans are prone to doubt in the midst of confidence and hope in the midst of dread, so they experience emotional twists more often than they do cliff-hangers. Since the emotional reversal still builds on the dominant mood of the scene, it's not difficult to make it feel authentic.

In this story, for example, during most of the president's conference, he and his chief of staff don't take the epidemic as seriously as readers know they should. The only exception is that humanizing moment of doubt the president experiences midway through. If the author were to move that moment of doubt to the end, especially if he makes it an afterthought, it would give the ending a slight twist that flips readers forward into the story.

Note that in both the examples given here, the scene ending the author was looking for was already there. It usually will be, since a good ending builds on what has been happening in the scene. So if you hit a scene that seems to peter out, look back a little bit. It may be that the scene actually ended a few paragraphs earlier, and all you need is a cut to make the ending clear.

# Your Turn!

End your scenes on a high note by applying the following tips to your work:

**1.** Select five scenes from your novel. Classify the ending used in each scene based on the various endings described in the above critique. Did you end with a cliff-hanger? A surprise revelation or moment of foreboding? With a dialogue exchange meant to summarize a scene's main emotion? With a moment that plays against the rest of the scene?

**2.** Once you've defined your endings, take a look at what you have. Do all of your scenes end in a cliff-hanger or in surprise revelations?

**3.** Now that you've analyzed your endings, select a scene that seems to end on an awkward or flat note. Try spicing it up by changing your approach. If you ended the scene with a surprise revelation, try rewriting it using an exchange of dialogue. Then, rewrite your rewrite using a moment or an emotion that plays against the tone established in earlier portions of the scene. Keep trying different methods until the scene ends on a note that's sure to propel readers forward.

# chapter 12

# Raising the Stakes

ain, sadness, and teardrop earrings are intuitively linked in this strong excerpt from *Texas Teardrops*, by June F. Forte. Strong sentences and a clearly realized world characterize the story, which easily leaps many of the most difficult hurdles that all stories face. Among the writer's tricks the author pulls off especially well is the knack for keeping the action going, moving the characters through space and time, and making the scenes clear without writing too much.

When you examine a story—whether it's written by you or someone else—it helps to ask questions that address the work on two different levels:

**1.** Does the story work on a micro level? Are the sentence patterns varied, well paced, and interesting? Are the word choices concise, correct, and pleasing?

**2.** Does the story work on a macro level? Do readers feel what's at stake? Does the story create and maintain tension? Why should readers care?

In this case, the author is skilled at varying her sentences, changing their patterns and rhythms. For the most part, her words create a vivid picture in the reader's mind

**1** Ideally, the first paragraph should establish what's at stake in the story or at least alert readers to the story's central conflict(s).

**2** The sentence literally says that as Gail relaxes her grip, she taps the horn, an obvious impossibility. It's easily fixed (e.g., "After relaxing her grip …").

**3** The phrase "on tip toes," placed where it is in the sentence, refers to the doorman; the author means to describe Nora.

**4** Beware of overused phrases, such as "black as night."

**5** Put a comma before the name at the end of a sentence if it's the name of the person to whom the sentence is addressed.

(e.g., the "Texas rain that sheeted across the windshield"). However, she does let her story become unnecessarily wordy at times (as with "reflected dimly off the high-gloss finish of the black Corvette").

Writing should always move smoothly

*Texas Teardrops*

*rain—sadness—teardrop*

Gail Morgan was late. The unusual darkness of the day made
it seem even later. She knitted her brow [cliché] and craned her neck
to see the pavement in front of her car.) [why?] The seesaw sweep of
the wiper blades weren't [wasn't] erasing the torrent of Texas rain that
**(1)** sheeted across the windshield. Store lights reflected dimly off [weak]
the high-gloss finish of the black Corvette as it hugged the
wet asphalt of downtown San Antonio. Gail turned the car into
Alamo Plaza. Gearing down and pumping the brake pedal, she
reined the powerful car to a stop in front of the Menger
Hotel.

**(2)** Relaxing her grip on the wheel, she tapped two short blasts
of the horn. [action a little useless] She watched the familiar Simon step back from his
post at the door and offered her mother his gold-braided arm. [POV dips into Nora or Simon]
As they emerged from the warmth of the lobby, the doorman
**(3)** snapped an oversized umbrella open over Nora's head and, on tip
toes, [as written, this phrase refers to the doorman] steered her to the waiting car. Amused, Gail smiled as
she leaned over the leather seat and pushed open the passenger
**(4)** door. Her collar-length, black-as-night [weak word choice] hair swung back from
her face exposing a diamond-studded earlobe.

**(5)** "I thought you had forgotten me, Gail." Nora Breen snatched
the belt of her raincoat out of the closing car door and settled back in the seat. "I hate this car. It's a kiddy car. I
**(6)** feel like I'm sitting on the floor." [This is a good place to add tension by having Nora express concern about driving in the storm.]
Gail steered into a U-turn and headed out of the city.
"Sorry, Mother. Anne Marie and I were shopping. The time just
got away from us."

"Where is your sister? No, let me guess—shopping still. You
and Anne Marie are always shopping, Gail. I wish you'd both take
more of an interest in the Breen Foundation and a little less
in *haute couture*." Nora removed the kidskin glove from her
right hand and loosened the yellow silk scarf (from) [around?] her neck.
"The foundation will be your responsibility one day and …"

As they drove through the heavy rain, Nora chatted off and
on about the foundation and the Board luncheon she had just
left. Gail, preoccupied with the road, managed to nod and comment at the appropriate pauses. Twenty minutes out of the city,

[right margin, rotated:] Remember to establish what's at stake early in the story.

63

they left the highway and turned onto the deserted two-lane access road. Easing her grip on the wheel, Gail turned to look at her mother. The large tear-shaped opal dangling from Nora's left ear caught her eye.

*Raise the stakes here by reiterating Nora's trepidations and Gail's disinterest in taking over the foundation.*

"Mother," she <u>drawled in exaggeration</u>, "I bought the most fabulous evening suit for the Schaeffer's party this weekend—pink brocade." Gail switched her attention to the rear/view mirror and began flicking a clump of (non/existent) mascara from her lashes. "You'll just die when you see it. Souzie Shaeffer will be absolutely green. You simply must let me borrow your Texas Teardrop earrings."

*unclear*

*Is it "Schaeffer" or "Shaeffer"?*

**7**

*Leans toward exposition in dialogue—a no-no*

"Honestly, Gail, you haven't heard a word I've said. You can thank the business Daddy worked so hard to build for your lavish lifestyle. The foundation was his dream, a payback to the state he loved so much. And to think neither of his daughters care a hoot about it." Sighing, Nora shook her head and looked out the side window. (She could see the earrings in the glass.) "I remember the night your father gave me these," she said, touching the gold Texas-shaped supports that anchored them to her ears. Nora turned and faced her elder daughter. Her voice softened, "We had struggled for years, just getting by, then suddenly everything started going right. John made a windfall profit, and it just kept getting better. 'You've earned them, Nora,' he'd say. 'For all the years and all the tears you never let me see.' Apart from you girls, these earrings—not the ranch nor the vacations, not fancy cars nor the furs—mean the most to me."

*gerund problem, as per #2*

*POV shift*

**8**

**9**

*POV Nora*

*the sudden POV shift here from Gail to Nora is jarring.*

*this sounds odd as speech. Try reading it aloud.*

*You're shifting POV here. In this type of story, it's usually best to confine your third-person narrative to a single person.*

"And you will let me borrow them, won't you mother?" Gail offered Nora her most winning smile.

*Gail*

Nora laughed at Gail's childlike ploy. "I regret that you and Olin have no children. They may have taken some of the selfishness out of you and given him someone else to dote on."

*Nora*

"Anne Marie has children."

"Anne Marie has a nanny and a housekeeper who, thank God, pay some small attention to those children." Nora waved her hand to the right. "Here we are. I hope the road is safe."

Without signaling, Gail turned the car onto the unmarked dirt road that wound its way for nearly five miles through scrub oak and range to the brick gateway of the Breen compound.

The Rockin' B was a 2,000-acre spread, a gentleman's estate. Expertly run by hired hands, it was home to a small herd of champion Longhorn breeding stock.

After John Breen's death, Olin Morgan, wealthy in his own right, had developed his father-in-law's hobby into a lucrative side business.

The ring of the cell phone startled Nora from her thoughts. "Watch the road, Gail. You're going to stall ~~the car~~ out in the low spots. They're covered with water."

Gail reached for the phone. "Hello?"

"Hi, Sugar, where are you?"

*Again, continue to raise the stakes here.*

"We're almost home, Olin. Where are you?"

"I'm stuck in Austin for the night. Thought I'd call so you wouldn't worry. My meetin' ran over. It's rainin' up a storm here."

*Careful with pseudo-dialect, don't overuse.*

"Here too. I can hardly see the hood of the car."

"So I hear. I just talked to Jake. He and the boys are riding out now to round up the cattle, get 'em to high ground for the night. My guess is we lost a few already. The creek should be bustin' its banks. You be careful, darlin', you hear? I'll be home early tomorrow."

"I promise. Bye, Olin." Gail returned the phone to its cradle and peered out at the road. She unconsciously bit her lip. The rain was still coming hard, and the wind seemed to be picking up. As they rounded the curve, she could see water streaming over the wooden bridge—just how high it was, she could only guess.

*the bridge? Watch pronoun referents.*

"You're not going to try to get through that are you?" Nora twisted the ends of her scarf. "I wish ~~you had~~ you'd brought the truck."

"It'll be just fine, Mother. If you're afraid, close your eyes." Gail shifted to first gear and inched onto the bridge. She could feel the planks sink under the weight of the car. The rain was battering the windshield, and she couldn't see at all past the hood. The side window wasn't any better. She opened it and felt a blast of wet wind hit her face. Looking down, she could barely see the edge of the open bridge as it rose and fell with the force of the water surging beneath it.

On the other side of the car, Nora sat tensed and

Trim dialogue wherever possible—try saying it out loud.

frightened. Gripping the knotted scarf like a rosary, she prayed out loud. "Dear God, get us home safely …"

The car sputtered and died. Gail turned the key ⊘ *illogical* ∧ <u>frantically pressing</u> her foot on the gas. Nothing. It wouldn't crank. She pumped the pedal and tried again. "We have to get out of here," Nora screamed ⊘ ∧ pulling her seat belt free. The sound of the bridge breaking muffled her next words.

A rush of water lifted the car like a rubber raft and dumped it <u>upright into the creek</u>. *word choice* The impact <u>jerked</u> Gail against the steering wheel. She watched in horror as her mother was thrown up, then forward. Nora's head shattered the windshield, and she fell slumped against the dashboard.

Gail pulled her mother back against the leather seat. Releasing her own seat belt, Gail reached over the unconscious Nora and rolled the passenger window down. She boosted herself out,through the driver's side window and clung to the outside of the door. Submerged to her neck in the frigid water, Gail edged her way around the bobbing car to the passenger's side. The strength of the water flattened her against the car. She fought to reach the door. With all the strength she could muster, Gail lunged for the open window and missed. "Mother," she cried. The word broke apart as a wave of water filled her mouth. Choking and coughing, she fought to regain her breath.

Battered by the raging current, Gail struggled to keep sight of the Corvette in the distance. It whipped through the cresting water like a tilt-a-wheel run amok. She watched as one end of the yellow scarf fluttered out the open window. It hung momentarily in the wind, then fell wet and limp against the door panel just as the car disappeared around the bend.

**⓬** Panic rose in her chest. She grabbed at a dark <u>unseemly</u> *Choose your words carefully.* shape passing to her left. It was a dead steer. Gail dug her fingers into its hide, then moved her grip to its foreleg, leaving pieces of acrylic nails behind. The lifeless buoy dragged her behind as they catapulted down the swollen creek. At the bend where the car had disappeared, the steer crashed into the bank with such force it ricocheted into a strand of half-submerged trees and lodged between two trunks.

from the page to the reader's brain, and for that reason, it is important that you trim the inevitable excesses that appear in early drafts. Read manuscripts at least twice with an eye for unwarranted wordiness.

In *Texas Teardrops*, it is the second level—the macro level—of questions that reveals the most apparent weaknesses. Readers have to know what is at stake long before the end of the story. This information is essential in order for the vivid scene of the bridge collapsing to be emotionally effective and for the story's ultimate ending to be emotionally satisfying.

To be fulfilling, a story must raise expectations and then fully meet them. In this case, the author brings the story to a conclusion, but she doesn't satisfy expectations because she hasn't sufficiently raised them.

One way to determine if you have established what's at stake is to boil your story down to a few sentences. For instance, *Texas Teardrops* could be described this way:

Gail picks up her wealthy mother, Nora, and drives her home in a downpour. On the way, they talk about how Nora hopes Gail or her sister will take over the family's Breen Foundation when Nora passes away. When they are nearly home, the car crosses a small, wooden bridge over which a stream rages. The bridge gives way, and although Gail manages to escape, her mother does not. Gail decides to take over her mother's duties at the foundation.

Obviously, there is much more to the story than that—the family's wealth, the background about Nora's aspirations for her daughters and "Daddy's" hopes for the foundation he created, the fact that Gail and her sister only seem to be interested in shopping, the centrality of the teardrop

earrings—but the primary events, as with all stories, shake out to a few sentences.

Once you have the events of your story laid out in a few sentences, you can begin to see what needs to be improved. In this case, readers need to know sooner what is at stake. Perhaps Nora is concerned from the outset about the final bridge they will have to cross, but Gail pooh-poohs her concerns. For instance, in the first paragraph, the author can let readers know that Gail is cer-

**6** This is a good place to introduce Nora's aversion to riding in this particular rainstorm.

**7** Raise the stakes—and reader expectations—by making it clear that Gail has no intention of taking over the foundation.

**8** The point of view shifts briefly here from Gail to Nora. This can be jarring for readers.

**9** In a few paragraphs, the author moves from Nora's POV to Gail's and back to Nora's again. It's usually best to confine third-person narrative to a single character.

**10** The trick to raising the stakes is to do it early so that the story conjures tension in readers, a tension that grows until it reaches its culmination in the bridge collapse.

**11** This is another example of being unclear about referents, a pronoun referent in this case. The "it" here refers to the bridge, whereas the author means the water.

**12** This is a weak word choice. What is an "unseemly" shape?

tain Nora is going to be afraid to ride home in this storm. Perhaps Nora even tries to talk Gail into waiting until the rain lets up. Or, at point four in the manuscript, maybe Nora expresses her concern by saying something like, "I thought you had more sense than to drive in this type of weather."

The author's description of the weather is vivid enough that readers know that it's a severe rainstorm, but they don't know it's a dangerous rainstorm, and they don't feel the danger as the story unfolds. By raising the stakes early on, readers will be on alert.

Readers also don't have any sense that Gail would be giving something up if she were to take over the foundation. Maybe Gail—as we could learn as soon as Nora brings up the foundation—decided long ago that she is not smart enough or capable enough to take over the foundation. Gail plans to enjoy her life—shopping, seeing, and being seen. Her husband's work on the ranch is enough for her to feel like she's contributing to the world.

Just remember that you need to make sure that something is at stake, and it needs to be clear very early in the narrative. The stakes should be raised on at least two levels: the physical danger and the psychological stresses.

Conveying a sense that a complete world exists beyond the boundaries of a story, and implying that there is more to tell even though it is unsaid is difficult for writers to do. The author's success here indicates that she vividly imagined the characters, the family, and their place in the world. She can draw on that to make the readers understand what's at stake, feel the tension, cry when Nora dies, and feel satisfied when Gail decides to take over her mother's duties at the foundation.

# Your Turn!

Sustain the tension in your story by applying the following tips to your work:

**1.** Determine if your story is working on the macro level by first summarizing the story in a few short sentences. As in the above critique, this exercise helps clarify a story's primary events.

**2.** Once you have summarized your story and you're clear on the central events, take a look at your short story or the first chapter of you novel, and place a star next to the occurrence of each primary event you come across.

**3.** Now that you know exactly what your primary events are and precisely where they occur within your text, it's time to check for tension. Reread the text preceding your each primary event. Do readers know what's at stake? Do you increase tension by including dialogue that hints at looming events? Do you provide details that allow readers to share in the emotions and sensations of the characters?

# Climax

Let's take a look at the last few pages of "Mona on Darkening Ground," a short story by Katherine Harvey. The writing here is detailed and well paced. Where the author needs help is in the last stages of the plot: climax and denouement.

In a basic classical plot outline, a story starts with high drama (delivered through a strong character, lavish settings, a major conflict, or stunning writing—and combinations thereof). Then, the story inevitably dips and loses steam, but obviously heats up quickly and boils toward the big climax— and the plot explodes. That's followed by descending action, the denouement or cooling-off period, and then this section rises at the end for a last pop. The end.

When structuring sentences, paragraphs, or chapters, each cuts off at the climax. The governing rule is this: Sentences are written like jokes; the punch line is at the end. And the principle obviously extends from the basic units of writing into the longer units—paragraphs and chapters. Hence this submission appears, at first reading at least, to be a chapter rather than a short story.

 Too many conjunctions (when, when, while). Delete some and shorten the sentences.

 Here "myself" is clumsy and abstract.

 Follow Hemingway's advice: Be brief. Use short sentences.

 The paragraph climaxes with "never let go." The scene shifts, so start a new paragraph.

 The "gaze" and "faze" rhyme is too close. Make a change.

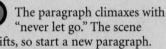 Without a comma, this can be misread as "clouds passing over the moon and shadows."

7 "Every inch of her ... body" is a cliché, and "body" repeats in the next sentence.

The trick with a climax is that it must deliver fireworks. There must be a dazzling payoff for readers, who've invested time into the story. This short story succeeds in following the classical plot outline until the

"Mona on Darkening Ground"

When Mona finally came home the shaking stopped. ~~When~~ our
front door creaked open to reveal her silhouette, and waves of pure
clean water crashed over me ~~and~~ while the last ripples settled,
**(1)** I could feel that vibration again. ~~After taking~~ I took a long satisfying breath to replace the thousands of ragged gasps I'd been
forcing to stay alive. I looked into her eyes and the deal was
done. The ordeal ~~was~~ over. She was my savior now, and I knew
that my existence depended on hers more than she had ever
depended on mine. "Hello, Dada," she said. "What are you doing
on the floor?"

I struggled to get up, but the mess I had made caused me
to slip around like a fish. Mona leaned over and extended her
hands to me. I took them and stood, her face wrinkled as she
took in the smell my sickness created in her absence. "My poor
Dada, you just can't get along without me, can you? Let me
help you to the shower and I'll get this all cleaned up.
Before you know it, you'll be right as rain. I can't tell you
about all that has happened to me in California until we're all
settled again."

**(2)** After the house and ~~myself~~ my equally filthy body had been purified, Mona took me
outside to the spot where I found her, and She sat down. Instead of
snow, this time there was fresh dewy grass to soften her place.
She began to tell me about her adventures. "I have been reborn
as a woman of the world," she sighed, ~~and continued,~~ "I'm going
to move to Los Angeles as soon as my new agent sends over the
contracts for me to sign. I will be a film star the likes of
which this little town, and the world for that matter, has
never seen. I always knew that there was something special
inside of me, a gift that must be shared not just with the
little people of this place, but with all of the little people
in every corner of the earth. I will reach them all; none have
the power to resist me. You must know this more than anyone,
Dada. You just experienced what I can do.

"As I was walking from the train station to the edge of
Tunachee, I saw people rising up like Lazarus. You see, you
weren't the only one who suffered while I was gone. Every last
citizen in our little settlement went through the same ordeal

to varying degrees. It actually pleases me that you had double the pain that they seemed to have endured because that means that I had complete power over you. People that didn't know me so personally got through these last two weeks with only mild stomach pain and headache; they spent this whole time tending to those, like you, who were fully incapacitated. This thing inside of me, it has grown stronger and more insistent with each passing year. Now is the time for me to break out of this cocoon of a little town. I can resist the pulses no longer."

I remained quiet. I had no words to express the betrayal, confusion, and loss that I felt. She, my darling angel, this woman I considered my daughter, was joyfully leaving me to die without her to chase the shakes away.

"Dada, I did love you, but that was before I realized just how important I am. I can't waste my time here anymore, these pulses are pulling me in a direction away from you, and I must go, I have a higher purpose that I don't really understand yet, but I know that my decision to leave is the right one. In two days, I leave. I came back only to get my things and say good-bye. I can only hope for you that what you've just experienced doesn't repeat itself. If it does, console yourself in the fact that I will go on to conquer this world and that I could never have aspired to such lofty heights if you had not saved me long ago."

The very idea sickened me. I began to move even before she finished speaking. I went next door first and gathered Coretta, her husband, and their four girls. Next to the Beckersons' for Samuel and Haverton, their boys, and Jake who lived over their garage. I kept walking through Tuna until I had everyone behind me and then I turned back for home. All of my people were still in various stages of recovery. If we allowed Mona to leave, we would all surely die eventually without whatever it was about her that kept us alive and healthy. The plan was to band together and demand that she stay. If Mona refused, we would take her by force, and by God, we would never let go. With about three hundred of us assembled around my little house, she confidently strode out the door.

Instead of the warm and pleasant faces she was used to

**5** meeting here, this time she received only grimaces and dark menacing ~~gazes~~ *stares*. Unfazed, she began to say her good-byes and best wishes. She was prevented from going on when a rock hit her square in the mouth. I don't know who threw it or from what direction, but that first explosion of blood made everyone hungry for more. It was reckless to abuse our only hope for life, but I think that Tunachee's brothers and sisters were not going to be put down again by her elixir or her absence.

The rocks, tree branches, pine cones—anything we could get our hands on—rained down like wildfire on Mona. Her wailing began and I was taken back to the night when I found her. There was a fat moon draping its pale light on the darkness, light that reflected on the surface of the snow, lending the atmosphere a silvery supernatural sheen. When I first began to hear the child's screams I ran outside and tried to see, but

**6** there were long clouds passing over the moon, and shadows crept over the woods where there was light only moments before. Now, in ~~the~~ *this* moment, in the same place many years later, the noonday sky began to darken with rain clouds that were nowhere to be seen an hour before. Mona was howling in pain and anger, bleeding from cuts that criss/crossed over every inch of her former-

**7** ly sublime ~~body~~ *flesh*. I began to weep for her, not out of pity or for love, but for her power that was finally crawling out of her body in the form of thousands of insects.

Her shape was withering, crumpling upon itself, ~~as~~ wasps shot out of her hair, ~~and~~ beetles squeezed ~~out of~~ *from* her eyes. There were centipedes dripping from the exposed ropes of muscles in her arms and legs, swarms of ants swirling over her breasts and abdomen. The crowd jumped back, astonished by the sight. Mona's fingers broke off into stick bugs; her palms

**8** ripped opened and dirty brown praying mantises popped out. This pulsing mass of bugs was no longer Mona at all. *(Add climactic image)* ~~The light from the sun was nearly blotted out when~~ the clouds split open to

**9** release torrents of rain. *(Add drama)* We all stood there, drenched by the water, unshakable, and watched as the *column of* creatures washed away to leave behind, in that famous spot, a perfect little baby girl.

**8** These images need to build to a stronger climax.

**9** Add a new paragraph for the denouement.

climax and denouement. In the beginning, Mona is a baby left in front of our narrator's house. A single man, he raises her alone. Mona is stunning and smart, the darling of her little town of "Tuna." At eighteen, she goes to Hollywood. When she's gone for two weeks instead of two days, the towns-people, especially her "dada," fall very ill. They recover when she returns, and that's where this critique begins.

Everything's fine until the end. The author delivers a wonderfully imaginative scene, with the insects breaking out of Mona's body, and the details piling up. But what's missing is the crescendo, the ultimate moment when hundreds of rockets burst in a huge, sky-wide spectacle.

The author needs to add a few more lines after the "mass of bugs was no longer Mona at all." For instance:

It bristled upward into an amorphous column of pincers, antennae, thorny legs and gleaming exoskeletons. And at that moment a thunderbolt roared above, lighting the insects in a flash of silver.

Then there needs to be a new paragraph to signal the denouement and the shift from the bugs to the people. (Notice there's an additional sentence to heighten the drama.)

The clouds split open to release torrents of rain. We had never, in all our years in Tuna, seen it pour like this. The crowd stood there, drenched …

The only problem left is the oddness of the last image, the "perfect little baby girl." Where did she come from? Is it Mona again? The author can easily answer these questions as she continues the story.

---

# Your Turn!

Give your climax a boost by applying the following tips to your work:

**1.** Identify your story's key stages, and then place a "C" next to the start of your story's crescendo, "the ultimate moment when hundreds of rockets burst in a huge, sky-wide spectacle." If you have a difficult time deciding where to put the "C," your climax may still need some work. After all, this is what your story has been building toward all along.

**2.** This time, place a "D" next to the start of your story's denouement, the point where the final outcome is fully realized by characters and readers alike. If you have a difficult time discerning your climax from your denouement, keep in mind that the denouement wraps up loose ends created by the story's conflicts.

# Fiction Checklist

Keep these questions in mind as you revise or critique your novel or short story:

✓ Does the opening scene make an emotional connection with you as a reader? Does the scene hint at future conflict?

✓ Does the pacing of the opening scene set the proper tone for the book's theme and story line?

✓ Is the POV consistent throughout the story? Would the story work better if told from a different POV? Is the POV character fully developed and believable?

✓ As the author, does your voice ever overshadow that of your story's narrator?

✓ Does your dialogue realistic and natural? Do you make proper use of tag lines?

✓ Is the story drowning in exposition? Are there sections of exposition that would work better as dialogue?

✓ Do you maintain a consistent tone throughout the story?

✓ Do you use details to increase the story's believability? Do readers have a clear picture of the main characters and the setting?

✓ Does each individual scene connect to advance the story's plot line and theme? Do any scenes seem awkward or out of place?

✓ Does each scene end on an intriguing note that keeps readers interested, or do some scenes just seem to fall flat?

✓ Is there a discernable element of tension throughout the story? Do you adequately raise the stakes as the plot advances? Does the pacing of each scene complement the story's tension level? Does the tension level complement the story's overarching theme?

✓ Are the story's climax and denouement believable—and worth the read? Can readers spot the story's ultimate crescendo, or is it all a little ambiguous? Are there any loose ends that you forgot to address?

PART III

# Nonfiction

**R**evising and critiquing nonfiction requires attentiveness to structure as well as to content. Chapters fourteen through seventeen demonstrate the different skill sets needed to properly critique memoirs, personal essays, and magazine articles. While all of the forms share the nonfiction label, each places unique demands on both writers and revisers.

A memoir, for example, offers a window into the writer's personal history. It's the story of the writer's memories and feelings toward certain events. The factuality of the book's events is slanted by the author's perceptions; her reality becomes the book's reality. When you're critiquing a memoir, whether it's your own or that of a fellow writer, it's important to make sure that the reality presented in the book is interesting enough to hook a reader's interest. Just as with fiction, the characters and settings in a memoir must be fully developed. The story itself must be broad enough to attract an array of readers, while still maintaining that crucial element of originality.

Personal essays showcase an author's personal story or her individual perceptions on a given subject. These pieces can average anywhere from five hundred to three thousand words in length. Some points to look out for when critiquing or revising this type of work include: clichéd themes (e.g., the death of a grandparent, vacations, high school or college graduation), vague descriptions, and over sentimentalizing and/or moralizing an event.

With a magazine or newspaper article, where the usual objective is to inform readers on a specific subject or event in a relatively small amount of space, the revision process tends to be fairly concentrated. Certain facts must be included, so the focus is tight by nature. Creativity is delivered via word choice and structure.

When you critique an article, pay special attention to the opening paragraph. Does it immediately arouse your interest and draw you into the story? Is it leaden with one too many facts? If it's an anecdotal lead, does it complement the rest of the story? Does the author revisit the anecdote—or elements of it—later in the article? Does the article itself raise any unintended questions? Are the facts explained in a coherent and accurate manner? Are all of the quotes properly attributed?

The next four chapters will take a look at all of the forms just described. So, whichever form you may be writing, rewriting, or critiquing, you'll be able to identify weak spots and make concise improvements.

# chapter 14

# Theme in Memoirs

uthor Pamela Moore has done an marvelous job of writing through her pain in order to pull together the first few chapters of her memoir, *The Pieces of My Heart*. She has a lot of information she wants to include in the story; now all she needs to do is focus and structure this information.

Let's start by clearly defining this book's theme. Theme is a story's major external and internal conflict and the resolution to that conflict. When you're writing a memoir, it's important to ask yourself what your life has been about. Answer this in one sentence. It may seem simplistic to try to sum up your life like this, but this process focuses the story and keeps it on track.

A few movie themes come to mind: *American Beauty* (everyone finds beauty in a different way, and one person cannot tell another person what beauty is—beauty is truly in the eye of the beholder); *American History X* (you can transform your own life, but you can't transform anyone else's, everyone has to learn his own lesson).

Every good story has one overriding theme. If your theme isn't completely clear before you start writing, keep thinking

**1** The integration of the birthday party and the news about the husband's affair is a powerful scene with which to open a memoir.

**2** This is probably an important flashback, but save it for the next chapter, after the story action gets rolling.

**3** This sounds like such a telling moment in the breakdown of the marriage, but the author's moved into a flashback within a flashback. Save it for later.

**4** Readers don't care about Steve's drive or his need for cash. Stay close to the present action.

about it. Sometimes it reveals itself as you go along.

The best way to tell a story is through a series of scenes that, once connected, communicate your theme to readers. In this case, the author starts out beautifully in the first chapter with the phone call from Debbie. The dialogue in this scene is snappy and alive. She sets the scene—the birth-

*The Pieces of My Heart*

Chapter One

~~When the phone rang, I wasn't expecting the news I was~~ ~~about to hear from a casual friend.~~ The timing couldn't have been worse, what with the lively group of eight- to ten-year-old boys in our home for a Saturday afternoon birthday party. It was ~~January 13, 1979,~~ the day after Jeremy's tenth birthday. *I had been* ~~We were in the basement, where Kevin, Jeremy, Brian, 7, and I had lived since the fall of 1976.~~ ~~I~~ watch~~ed~~ *ing* *as they* the boys, ~~including Brian,~~ played in the downstairs recreation room.

"Oh, Pam, I'm so sorry to be the one telling you this but I can't stand it any longer," Debbie said, her voice quivering. "Kevin has a girlfriend and it's time you knew about it," ~~she said.~~ "He's playing you for a fool and you're the only one in ton who doesn't know. I'm sorry ..."

I stood in frozen silence, *now* slumped against the wall around the corner from where the boys were playing, not wanting to believe what this woman I hardly knew was telling me. I could feel my cheeks burning and my heart pounding inside my chest. The rest of my body went numb.

"How do you know?" I asked. "Are you sure?"

"Yes, I'm sure," she said, "It's been going on for a long time. You've got to know, Pam."

"Yesterday was Jeremy's birthday. We're having a party," I said, my hands trembling ~~now~~ as I shifted the phone to my other ear. "I can't talk." I hung up the receiver, wishing I could be somewhere else, anywhere but here. *How could he do this to me? How could this be happening?* But then I remembered six months earlier when my best friend, Carol, made a similar attempt to tell me something I didn't want to hear.

While driving home from a luncheon, I *had* told Carol, matter-of-factly, if she ever heard anything about Kevin, even though it would be difficult for her to tell me, I wanted to know. I must have suspected the possibility that Kevin could be unfaithful.

Without speaking, Carol pulled the car to the side of the road and turned off the ignition. She placed her hand on mine

and looked straight into my eyes. I sat, motionless, afraid
even to breathe.

"Kevin has a girlfriend," she said. "I don't know who she
is, but I know he's seeing someone."

Later that day, when I confronted Kevin with what Carol
told me, he surprised me by lashing out at Carol. Flatly denying her story, he called her a "vicious gossip," and told me
to drop her as a friend

If, back then I had been honest with myself, I would have
admitted that our marriage was a disappointment to both of us.
After thirteen years as husband and wife, we were growing farther and farther apart in our interests, values, and attitudes
about so many things. With two beautiful young sons to raise
and no savings, we were not in a position to even consider
divorce.

Nearly a year before, on ~~February 26, 1978,~~ our 12th wedding anniversary, Kevin gave me a card that hurt me deeply. On
the front was a little yellow duck floating on blue water
underneath the words, "*There it goes ...*" Inside the little
duck is laying on its side next to a drain, with the words,
"*Another year down the drain.*"

When I opened it, I didn't know whether to laugh or cry,
but, of course, I laughed, or at least pretended not to mind.
Later that day, I ripped the card in half and threw it away. I
didn't want to think about what it meant for Kevin to give me
such a card.

Until the phone call on Jeremy's tenth birthday, I had
managed to avoid looking honestly at the condition of my marriage—and my life.

In my heart, I wanted to believe I had a good marriage, a
happy home, and a promising future. God knew I tried as hard
as anyone to make my husband happy and to be a good mother. I
honored my marriage vows, yet the harder I tried, the worse it
seemed our marriage became.

"Mom, when are we going to have birthday cake?" Jeremy's
voice broke the silence of my tormented thoughts, as I
anguished over who was telling the truth—my friends or my husband.

By now, it was 1:30 in the afternoon. The boys and I had just returned from a sledding excursion. ~~It was~~ a typical January day, with icy winds blowing snow sideways across the white and open fairways. We had planned to go sledding for several hours but the wind-chill factor forced us to shorten our stay. ~~Brian was so cold I had to carry him most of the way to the car.~~

Steve, the 25-year-old son of ~~my~~ a friend, ~~drove~~ had driven over from Weston to help me with the party since Kevin chose not to be there. ~~Steve was a school teacher who needed extra cash. Whatever I paid him wasn't much, but he seemed to think it was worth it. I think he felt sorry for me because I had no help with the party. Whatever the reason,~~ I was thankful Steve was there so I could take a few minutes away from the boys and their activities to gather my thoughts. ~~Besides, it was comforting to have a "man" around the house, a comfort I missed since Kevin was rarely at home.~~

Now I knew where ~~he~~ Kevin had been all these months, literally years, since he later told me his "other" relationship began in 1976.

Somehow, I got through the next several hours. We opened presents and had cake and ice cream while Steve entertained the boys with magic tricks. Just as the last two birthday party guests were leaving, Kevin came home and walked straight through the living room into the kitchen.

My heart began pounding so hard I thought it would leap out of my chest. I knew the moment of truth had arrived and I was determined to hear and accept it this time, no matter what. I walked into the kitchen and told Kevin I wanted to speak with him privately, in the bedroom. He could tell by my voice and the look in my eye that I meant what I was saying.

As we turned to go toward the bedroom, I told Jeremy and Brian to play in the living room while their Dad and I talked. I followed as Kevin walked into the bedroom and laid down on the bed with his hands folded behind his head, looking up at the ceiling. I locked the door and stood by the dresser. ~~What a pathetic sight this was, I thought to myself, this husband of~~

~~mine who betrayed me, a liar and a womanizer, a man who wasn't~~ ℓ
~~man enough to tell me the truth.~~ ℓ

"Do you have a girlfriend?" I asked point blank.

Kevin ~~said nothing and~~ *or* continued to stare at the ceiling.

"Look me in the eye and answer my question," I demanded.
"Do you have a girlfriend?"

"Yes," he murmured, his face flushed and pale at the same
time.

Reacting with a gesture that surprised even myself, I
ripped off my wedding rings and threw them across the room.

**(5)** Tears streamed down my cheeks as angry words spilled out of

**(6)** my mouth. The horror of that moment, as I absorbed the truth
of my husband's infidelity, left me weak and trembling.

---

**(5)** The author shouldn't tell readers angry words spilled from her mouth. She should show this to readers. Let them hear the words.

**(6)** This is where the author can end the chapter. Adding anything else to this will only weaken this incredible "moment of truth."

day party, a happy event. Then the author learns about her husband's affair, and the contrast is powerful.

In the first chapter of a memoir, you need to accomplish five essentials: 1) introduce the main characters, 2) establish the story's emotion, 3) show readers the setting, 4) create suspense, and 5) move readers into the main conflict, both internal and external. Nothing else.

Here, readers don't need to know about Kevin's birthday card, Steve needing extra cash, or the author's conversation with Carol that took place months earlier—no

flashbacks are needed in the first chapter. The author can tell readers these things when they need to know them—later in the book. It's also possible that readers may never need to learn some this information.

The author also needs to play out the party scene—to *show* herself going through the motions of celebrating while she's dying inside. She needs to *show* readers the innocence of her children who have no idea that their world is about to fall apart. She must have struggled with whether or not to confront Kevin about the affair. She should play up this struggle while doing the party thing with her son, moving in and out of these two dimensions until Kevin makes his entrance. Finally, the author needs to show readers how she feels as he comes through the door.

When you're writing a memoir, you can use dialogue, action, and emotion to convey your story. Show confrontations, but don't end the chapter with narrative. The narrative preceding this excerpt doesn't lend itself well to the pacing of the story. You want your first chapter to move quickly.

Expository writing slows down the pace. In this case, the author has just been told her husband is having an affair. At this point, readers do not care about where and how she was born. All readers care about at this point is the present scene of action.

The author should end this chapter with everything up in the air for the two of them—she might throw her wedding ring or yell something like, "How could you lie to me?" Maybe she even wants to end it with the question, leaving Kevin's "yes" for the next chapter.

The goal at the end of each chapter is always the same—to pull readers into the next. If you construct your story in a series of scenes that communicate a theme to readers, that is exactly what will happen. Readers will keep reading and reading and reading until the end.

# Your Turn!

Find your memoir's theme by applying the following tips to your work:

**1.** As demonstrated in the above critique, "every good story has one overriding theme." What's your story's theme? In single sentences, complete each of the following statements:

- My life has been about …
- My memoir is a story about …
- My memoir's overarching and universal theme is …

**2.** Once you have identified your theme, look at the first chapter of your memoir, and make sure that you've covered the five "essential" points discussed in the above critique. Start by listing the main characters you introduce in the first chapter. Remember, there's no need to introduce your entire cast all at once. If your character list is too long, try cutting it down by saving a few introductions for later chapters.

**3.** Next, write down the emotion that the chapter establishes, and compare it with your theme. Do your dialogue and exposition convey the intended emotion?

**4.** Now describe the setting. What's going on? Does the setting complement the emotional tone you're trying to establish?

**5.** Check the chapter's suspense level: Is the tension mounting? Is your pacing appropriate for the level of suspense you want? If not, try altering your exposition to speed up or slow down the scene.

**6.** Lastly, it's time to make sure that you introduce readers into the main conflict—without giving too much away. Keep your theme in mind here so that you're conscious of what you're working toward.

# chapter 15

# Personal Essays

**M**indy Halleck's personal experience essay, "Mr. Ed," has the potential to connect with readers because they've all been in a blissful place in their lives, and then—suddenly—everything is out of whack.

When you write about a personal experience, ask yourself: What is this story about? Whether you include the story in your memoir or market it to a magazine, it's your job to show readers how the experience has informed your life, and answering this question will help you to do that.

The key to this story's theme is found in the last paragraph where the author says she is "not writing about death, but learning about life." This needs to be set up from the start as a conflict—either internal, external, or both—and then woven through the horse incident in the same way that various colors of thread are woven into a tapestry.

One reason readers miss the introduction of this story's theme is because it's buried in the opening. The first paragraph is a description of the weather, and then the author mentions the heavy hooves. Instead, she should start with something like, "I came to Ireland to write about death." Then

 This description is necessary, but not as the opening. Weave it in once the story action is rolling.

 Start the story here with dialogue and action.

 The author should develop the story's universal theme here.

**4** This is a beautifully-crafted paragraph integrating the internal theme into the external description of the setting.

**5** This can be cut—it doesn't further the story line.

**6** The laughter breaks the seriousness of the situation. Save it for the second phone call.

move to the paragraph that introduces Josef, the proprietor, so that readers immediately are thrust into action and dialogue.

She should wait to mention the horse's hooves until after she sets her laptop on the table. Readers need a bit of background to help them understand why the author's

"Mr. Ed"

by M.S. Halleck

My second morning in Ireland I awoke to wind, rain and a stormy black-gray sky that overwhelmed the cheery countryside, it's heaviness falling into my room through the rose pink and yellow cotton curtains. I opened the window a bit, to let the wind blow through me and chase the dampness of the steam heat from the room while I finished unpacking. Below my window I heard the sounds of heavy hooves, a horse or a cow. I didn't know . I wouldn't know. I looked below, saw nothing and went back to settling in.

The bookshelves stood tall and solid, packed with Irish literature, and the collections of an eclectic mind. I could tell the room had been still and undisturbed for some time. Dust lightly covered the books and the steam heat took awhile to warm things up. But the room was a perfect writers nest for me. I embraced it as the womb that would birth the writer in me, After all it was why I came to Ireland, to write it all out.

While my laptop geared up for use and I finished unpacking my belongings into the wardrobe closet and small vanity area, I took in the smelled fresh coffee from down stairs in the kitchen. Josef, the proprietor, called up the stairs to me, "Hello there. Are ya doin' alright now?" He was asked in a friendly tone. "Yes, I replied, "Everything's perfect. I stood close to the private hallway at the top of the stairs so I could hear him better, then, glanced back into the room. This I saw what would be my writing place for the next month.

I felt warm, independent and eager to get started. I knew that in this room Here I would write about all the deaths in my family and how frightened I felt. But I also knew that Then once I'd written it all down, I'd find my way through it and back to life again. I knew the seriousness of it all, my task at hand. I welcomed it and dreaded it. But I was ready.

"There's hot coffee and some biscuits if you like. We're off to the store for the mornin' paper. Be back in bit, Love. He. called up to me. "You make yourself comfy. His Josef's voice was so friendly, with a hint of Irish accent. Thank you. See you

~~in a bit, "I responded.~~ ⟍

I set my laptop on the table next to the window and fussed about a bit with the plug-in converters. I knew this would be a long day of writing and I didn't want ~~its~~ *the* battery to wear out. The cool outside air and the warm steam heat blended together to create just the right feel of warmth and fresh air. I pulled the handle on the large oak framed window closer to the lock and left it ajar just a tiny bit.

Just then, as I heard them pull the front door shut behind them, a rainbow filled the countryside and embraced the rolling green hills of County Clare. The golden hue filled my room with a whisper of color and a promise that I would find my way. Much the same as the darkness of the stormy sky had given birth to the soft colors of the rainbow, I knew I had to go into my darkness, my pernicious depression, to find my own rainbow.

As they pulled out of the drive and onto the gravel roads that wind through the hills and disappear into an abyss of green and gray mist, the coffee enticed me out of my writer's nest.

I heard the ~~hoofs~~ *hooves* again, hitting stone and at an even faster pace. I leaned out of the window and looked down. *This time* I saw the top of a gray white horse running along the side of the house, from the back to the front. Then I realized he'd gone onto the front porch. I stood straight up, trying to wrap my city girl mind around ~~the fact that there's~~ *it. There was a horse on the front porch.*

I scurried down the spiral staircase and ~~spilled~~ into the living room. I saw nothing out the window. The house was quiet and filled with the smell of fresh coffee, still tugging at my sleepy senses. In the kitchen I ~~stumbled over the rough slate floor and~~ riffled through the cupboards until I found a clean cup.

I poured the coffee and wrapped my hands around the cup as I pulled it to my face. The warmth filled my hands and tingled through my arms. The smell filled my jet-lagged senses with a familiar creature comfort. ~~They knew I was from Seattle and that I love my coffee. Gracious hosts that they are, they~~

*Every word needs to move the story forward.*

85

~~bought a delicious French roast. I was in coffee heaven.~~

~~I stood looking out the kitchen window, about a half a mile~~
~~away, a field with a ruin of what looked like a medieval cas-~~
~~tle in the middle of it. Black and white cows surrounded the~~
~~toppled stone and appeared to be getting their feed from inside~~
~~it. "Hmm, recycling real estate." I thought to myself.~~

About then I heard a noise from the living room and went [Describe the noise.]
to check it out. ~~The front door was half glass and half wood.~~
~~I could see clearly who or what was at the door. I stood not~~
~~two feet from the door, in amazement. So startled, that I~~ [I started and]
spilled my coffee all over my fleece pajamas. At the front
door, wiggling the door handle with his mouth, was the horse.

In my [entire] life I'd only seen a full-grown horse up close, maybe
once or twice. He looked ~~up~~ at me; ~~standing~~ [through the glass part of the door. I] paralyzed, mouth [stared]
open and coffee stained, then [he] put his head down again, workin'
on that door handle. He wanted in. I didn't know what to do.
Who to call. If I should be frightened or not. So I called my
husband in Seattle. ~~I knew~~ even with the time difference he'd
still be awake. "There's a horse on the front porch and he's
tryin' to get in the house." "What do I do? You grew up in the
country, what do I do?" I screeched into the phone in a shrill
whisper. So as not to disturb the horse, I guess.

"Huh? What are you doing? Where are you?" His groggy voice
came across the line. ~~Then it all struck me as funny, not~~ [Not yet, too soon for laughter— reduces tension.]
~~scary. I felt the tension lapse from my shoulders and back~~
~~as the humor of it all welled up inside me.~~ "You aren't going
6. to believe this," ~~I explained to him with a laugh.~~ "There's a
horse that looks like Mr. Ed trying to break into this house.
Nobody's home except me and I had to tell somebody. There's a
horse on the porch who wants in. A horse!" ~~I kept repeating as~~
~~my husband laughed.~~

I watched as the horse worked the handle. I sat on the
floor in front of the doorway, drank my coffee and talked ~~and~~
~~laughed~~ with my husband. Finally Mr. Ed shook his head in frustration and marched [away] across the front yard, leaving the break-in
for another day.

~~I thought.~~

~~We said our good-byes, I love you's and miss you's.~~ [Relieved,] I hung up the phone, got a fresh cup of coffee and headed up the spiral staircase to the writer's nest that would be my haven, to write. To purge all the darkness, swollen and aching inside of me. To heal.

Still somewhat jet-lagged and sleepy, I sat at my laptop looking out the window, ~~looking~~ searching for the words to pull what was inside of me out into the light. I waited for just the right phrase or word to cross my thoughts and ignite this writing of mine. I sat. Nothing came.

Instead, suddenly I heard ~~there was~~ a loud noise from downstairs, ~~that pulled on me.~~ I crept down the stairs and snuck around the corner to the kitchen, ~~where the noise had come from.~~ "Oh my God!" I shouted, and then covered my mouth so I wouldn't scream and upset him. I didn't know what a horse would do if upset or agitated. There he stood ~~Mr. Ed was standing in the kitchen~~ on that rough black slate floor, ~~He'd gotten in. Smack~~ in the middle of the kitchen ~~place~~ next to the wood stove. Mr. Ed had ~~He'd~~ somehow maneuvered the sliding patio door open and come on in. There he stood, big as day. What did I do now? ~~I didn't know what to do.~~

~~Then again it struck me as funny, and pulled me from the drama of my melancholy mood.~~ This horse wantin' in the house so bad. The front door not giving in to his persuasive powers, him having another idea of how to break in. This was no regular horse, I could see that.

Not yet —later

I leaned next to the wall for a moment to catch my breath and decide again not to be afraid of this huge animal, so foreign to me, a city girl all my life. Some feeling of camaraderie came over me and I wondered if ~~decided~~ he possibly ~~probably~~ just wanted some heat and good conversation.

I carefully inched my way to the coffee pot, wondering if horses bite. I poured another cup and stood there in my pajamas, leaning against the counter, talkin' to Mr. Ed. He would nod in agreement every so often and even made eye contact once or twice. But then I noticed Mr. Ed had an accompanying fly in his nose, and in that instant I realized he was a large beast, not a friendly neighbor come for coffee.

I realized too in that very same startling instant, that he might leave something behind, here in the kitchen, on the

floor. I knew it wouldn't be a small offering and I knew for
sure that I didn't want to clean it up. ~~Not knowing~~ *I didn't know* how long
my host would be gone, ~~I~~ *and* I figured I should try to do something.
So, I called my husband. Again. ~~Him,~~ now in a deep sleep in
Seattle "Hi honey, he's in the house. What do I do?"

~~Another groggy~~ "What?"

"The horse, he's in the kitchen and I don't know how to
get him out"

"You gotta be kiddin' me!" I ~~heard~~ *imagined* him rustle *ing* the covers
and turn *ing* on the lamp next to our familiar bed. ~~I could picture~~
~~him, light on, him holding the phone in one hand and his~~
~~sleepy head with the other. Eyes closed, black curly hair in~~
~~every direction.~~ "Just lead him out of the house. He won't
bite, but don't stand behind him, he might kick" *Here's where you can insert the laughter and your humorous perspective of the situation*
⑦ *I heard a* ~~About that time, the~~ car ~~pulled back~~ into the drive "Thank
God. They're home." I told my husband to go back to sleep and
hung up the phone as they came in the front door.

**[Note: Josef and his mother return and lead the horse out;
they discuss how Carter (a.k.a. Mr. Ed) likes to visit them
when he's lonely or while his owner is away.]**

*I* curled up on the sofa in the kitchen next to the wood
stove that Carter liked so much, had coffee and chatted with
Caitlin while she fried Irish potatoes and 'breakfast meats,'
as they called them. ~~She, I discovered was the eclectic, well~~
~~read and curious mind that collected the books in my room.~~

⑧ I didn't blame Mr. Ed. This ~~is~~ *was* a nice place to just be.
Still and warm. I knew the best thing I could do, was surren-
der to his oh, subtle suggestion. Funny, I thought, the messen-
gers and guidance God sometimes sends me. A horse named after a
great man ~~leading~~ *led* me to the spot where I should spend my second day in Ireland. Not writing about death, but learning about
life.

traveled all the way to Ireland to write. She can take some of the opening description and weave it in here now that she's interacting with the setting. This is more effective than just telling readers about the setting.

The author also can up the external conflict with the horse as well as the internal conflict—to heal and write about death. Readers need to understand her mission, but this should occur gradually.

**7** This is the crisis/climax, when the external situation will be resolved. The author needs to reveal an internal understanding about the situation. As the situation resolves itself, she can include her laughter.

**8** This is the resolution paragraph, where the author tells readers what she's learned about herself.

In addition, some of the description can be cut to create a faster pace—readers probably don't need the entire coffee paragraph. Remember, when you're writing this type of piece, every sentence, every paragraph of your story should be focused on the point.

The description of the horse entering the house is excellent, as is the author's initial reaction. This would be a perfect place to add in some dialogue—what does she say to the horse? The author also should continue to weave the internal theme into this scene as she calls her husband again and when Josef and his mother return.

The external and internal crisis of the story should collide here, after which should come an epiphany about both—what the horse is about and what the author's writing is about. But the author will have to be careful not to drag this out, and this is where the story needs a bit of work. Readers need to understand what happened for the author in those moments with the horse. What did she learn? Stillness and warmth in the kitchen isn't enough. The horse came to bring the author a message, and she needs to communicate that to readers. The message is universal—not just for the author, but for readers.

The external structure is here—some things just need to be moved around. The internal theme is also here; the author just has to access a deeper layer and express it.

# Your Turn!

Personalize your story by applying the following tips to your work:

**1.** Sometimes, you're simply too close to a story to see what's missing. Ask a friend or critique member to read your essay. Then, ask him to tell you what he thinks the story is about—really about. For example, on the surface "Mr. Ed" seems to be about a woman visiting Ireland and her encounter with a horse. But "Mr. Ed" is really about how one woman's experience of writing about death teaches her about life.

**2.** When you're writing a personal experience piece, you must be prepared to reveal your inner thoughts. If you don't, your story will seem flat and underdeveloped. Keep in mind, however, there's a fine line between sharing your inner thoughts and offering of an overdrawn lesson to beleaguered readers. If you find your story lacking its most valuable asset—you—try rewriting it and inserting all of your thoughts. This will make it easier to cut away the ones that don't complement your theme. Plus, by overwriting, you may uncover inner thoughts you never knew you had.

# chapter 16

# Humor in Essays

Author Kathy Walker has selected a wonderful subject here—belly dancing—that lends itself well to a humor piece. The most difficult part of writing humor is sustaining it from beginning to end. But before you can focus on humor in your essay, you have to identify the theme or major conflict.

Every article or story needs a conflict, and it's best if there are connected external and internal conflicts to communicate a universal message. The external conflict in this excerpt from "The Belly Dances" is obvious—the author wants to excel at her new hobby of belly dancing. In this personal essay's first paragraph, which is not shown here, the author identifies one internal conflict—which is developed through the external conflict or events: How can a once sexually repressed woman find the joy of erotic liberation in her middle-aged singlehood?

The problem here is that the author concludes with a resolution not to this conflict, but to one she doesn't even bring up—how a woman can express herself for herself, and not for any man who happens to be in her life. Which is it? Since the story flows along

**1** Readers are interested in the author's progression—both internal and external. She needs to tell readers about it.

**2** This scene with Jules needs to do something. The author should use it to develop the internal conflict by talking to Jules about her struggle to let go. What is her fear of letting go about? What "jewels" of wisdom does Jules have to offer?

**3** There is an opportunity here to introduce more humor.

the line of the first conflict, let's assume that's the one the author wants to explore and at the end resolve.

The ongoing banter that the dance instructor, Yolinda, keeps up is pretty funny; readers can see all of these middle-aged women, their bellies swiveling and their breasts "held proudly aloft." (Great line.) Now, if the author wants to sustain the humor and develop the internal conflict, she needs to show herself resisting Yolinda's efforts to make her "let go," while

[**Note:** *We begin "The Belly Dances" on the second page.]*

... "Now ladies!" Yolinda continues, "Just move your bellies, nothing else. Pull-up-and-to-the-side, now down, and-to-the-other-side," she sing-songs. "Smoothly now, around in a circle!"

Do you know how it feels when you are not used to thinking about your belly at all (in fact, you are usually trying to ignore it), and here you are being told to push it strenuously around in a circle? It makes your spine tingle. It makes a lot of things tingle. *Good line...*

Yolinda is cooing, "Just let everything loose girls! Let it all go, wiggle it out! Oh yes, we are letting it go! Now, isolate your upper body and only move above your waist. Push those shoulders forward, one after the other. Shake, shake!!"

Very quickly, this motion turns into a breast shaking exercise, there is no way around it. My dilemma is, do I let go and just shake, or do I hold back? Just then, someone from across the room calls out, "It's not my shoulders that are shaking!" We all titter. The sound mingles with the tinkling noises from the jewelry we have wrapped around our bodies. I let go and begin to shake.

*The use of present tense works well for this piece.*

The next afternoon, I'm telling my best friend all about it. "I mean, honestly, Jules! It's so blatantly erotic!"

Jules is actually a nickname, and it's pronounced "Jewels," which is a perfect name for her because she is always coming up with them. We are flopped across my bed in my cozy bedroom like a couple of 17-year-olds chatting about "boys" and life and, now, belly dancing.

My ranting continues. "It's so cool! Here're all these average women who work in offices and they come to this yoga studio and spend their lunch hours belly dancing! And there is every body type in there you can imagine, from stick-shapes to pear-shapes. But it doesn't matter. For that one hour we're all beautiful."

*Too many exclamation points actually weaken the writing.*

"That's wonderful," Jules says softly. She is lying on her back gazing up at my star-studded ceiling. "It seems like women might really need this, to be able to let loose and let go, especially in our society where we're almost taught to be sexually inhibited."

"Right!" I said. "And the class keeps getting bigger and bigger. Women need this. It connects us with our sexuality. I think it gets us to notice our bodies, or stay in tune with them. I mean, you can't ignore your body when you are jiggling parts of it all around the room!"

Jules nods, warming up to the subject. "It's like a rejuvenation, almost like a transformation for these women to be able to let loose and move their bodies in ways we're taught not to move."

"Yess!" I shout, jumping up and dancing around my bedroom. It is hard for me to keep still when I talk. "Women need to connect to themselves and this gives us a chance to be sexy and sexual. And not only that, but IT'S OK. It gives us permission to love our bodies."

"I bet it feels really liberating to be able to do that. I know I couldn't do it." Then, she looks straight at me and says, "I think you really need this."

"Oh, Jules, I really do," I say dreamily. I suddenly stop moving and just stand there. "It's so good for me. I love feeling the freedom of it. I love moving and flowing and feeling erotic. ~~And I think it works because there're no men there to watch. Lets us be uninhibited.~~"

~~"Uninhibited," she echoes, lost in her own reverie.~~

A few classes later, we are all a little better, a little looser. We are getting into it. I have loosened up to the point of baring my midriff—the audacity of it! The part of a woman's body that rarely sees the light of day is on display. I wrap a sarong around my hips, then add a gorgeous belly dancing scarf encrusted with silver beads and tiny metal coinlike bangles. At the slightest motion of your hips, it creates a soft, irresistible, shivery jingle. It calls to you, "Just let go and let me sing, ting, ping!"

But this dance is not just about letting go. It's very hard work to isolate just one part of your body and let it move deeply and freely while keeping the rest still. It requires a degree of strength, flexibility, and coordination that I never thought I could master. But something about it touches me

*Make this scene accomplish something.*

deeply and keeps bringing me back to learn more. It looks so

**③** flowing and effortless when it's done right. *And when it is done wrong? This is an opportunity for more humor.*

If you have ever seen a belly dancer, you know what I mean. There is something incredibly mesmerizing about seeing a woman's nude midriff undulate and watching her hips and belly move back and forth so quickly yet so smoothly. When a belly dancer performs, ~~no one can~~ *you can't* take ~~their~~ *your* eyes off of her. You are ~~hypnotized.~~ *mesmerized.*

In class, Yolinda is beckoning to us. "Now move your knees up and down in tiny little movements, very fast, and shimmy! Let it all wiggle and jiggle!"

As we start our shimmy, someone's jingly hip scarf suddenly falls clean off her hips to the floor. She ~~had~~ *has* jiggled it right off.

Yolinda says, "AH, I see it's working!*y*" We all laugh.

When the music stops, we all stand there for a second, looking at one another sheepishly and then the whole room bursts simultaneously into a shy giggle, that we had been so bold, so audacious, and it was OK. Not just OK, but great, good, wonderful!*oo*

"NICE, ladies! Good form." Yolinda is complimenting us on our shimmies. We all shimmer and gleam in the afterglow.

"I see you are all doing well," she congratulates us. "Coming along nicely! It is starting to happen. You are all getting something out of this. I see it in your smiles, and in your movements."

The highlight of the class is putting ~~it~~ *y* all ∧*of the movements* together at the end. We play our own music with finger cymbals, very fast, CHink-ching-CHINK! CHink-ching-CHINK! All the while, step-touching around the room, pushing up our hips, then dropping them strongly downward, right-left, right-left, one after the other, not forgetting to hold our heads high, drop our shoulders, smile, breathe deeply (because it's all about the breath, anyway), and coordinate our hands and arms in sensuous, flowing motions to balance with our feet. It's one of the hardest things I have ever done. *Harder than what? This is another opportunity for humor.*

At the end of class, I have a feeling of oneness with the group, and I sense the energy flow of our combined feminine

spirits. As I begin to disrobe from my precious hip scarf, I
blurt out to some nearby classmates, "You know, this class
feels like we're in a harem!"

"Yeah, it does!" someone replies. "And I like it!"

**(4)** ~~The pretty blonde woman next to me says, "Yeah, but no men!~~ 𝒈
~~This wouldn't be happening if there were men around!"~~ 𝒈
~~"That's for sure!" we chorus.~~ 𝒈

**(5)** So what am I learning? How to perform the mechanics of
these movements, which is hard enough. But maybe I am here to
learn something more. How to LET GO enough to really dance this
dance. How to give myself permission to be beautiful, sensual,
*Because that is exactly what I am.*
**(6)** and feminine. ~~And how to express myself in this way, not for~~ 𝒈
~~any man who happens to be in my life, but just for me.~~ 𝒈
*This needs to end on a funny line.*

**(4)** Readers need something more
here. What has all of this
gyrating been about for the author?
She needs to tell readers what the
turning point was—at what moment
did she give herself permission to be
sensual and feminine? The author
also needs to explore what letting go
means and how belly dancing
defused her fears.

**(5)** But isn't the goal to be able to
let go no matter who's
around—to be free no matter what?

**(6)** This story should end on a
humorous note.

at the same time wanting to be good at this
belly dancing thing.

This is what creates humor. It's that tension between wanting to please her teacher
and do well, and not being able to because
her body refuses to perform. What is her
resistance to letting go all about? Without
going too deep, because after all this a

humor piece, the author needs to answer
this question. Is she embarrassed by the way
her body looks? Has she never moved her
body in this way before? Does she feel silly?
Does she think Yolinda is full of it—sure,
easy for her to teach this class with a body
like Barbie's?

When she gets to the scene with Jules,
the author should be fed up, maybe blaming Yolinda, maybe blaming herself, but not
getting the letting go thing so that this all
becomes natural. Isn't this about the author
learning to love her body just the way it is?
This scene works well because her enthusi-
asm accelerates the more she explains the
class to her friend. But this scene needs to
pull its weight and do something to further
the story's theme. Perhaps Jules says something—in a funny way to sustain the
humor—that helps the author to let go.
Maybe Jules lives up to her name and offers
a jewel of advice that propels the author
into the next class and the final conclusion
of this piece.

The author also should shorten the last scene as this is the one that will reveal her transformation. It shouldn't be a repeat of the first scene. What made her finally get it? What happened inside of her that made belly dancing finally "flowing and effortless." What happened that made Yolinda say, "It is starting to happen"? Finally, the author should delete the last conversation about how none of this would be happening if there were men around—that is beyond the scope of this particular article.

The key to this type of piece is to pump up the humor so that the "message" doesn't dilute the story and make it serious. The goal here is to instruct, to offer another's perspective of a situation, while making the reader laugh at herself because she's been in the same position and is quite familiar with the emotions involved.

# Your Turn!

Add humor to your personal essay by applying the following tips to your work:

**1.** State the goal of your piece. Is it to instruct? To inform? Is it a testimonial to an item or a way of thinking?

**2.** As shown in the above essay, tension often works to create humor. Find the source of your tension by reading your story and identifying your central conflict—both internal and external.

**3.** Now that you've identified these key points, it's time to look for the laughs. The goal here is to use humor to sustain and propel your central conflicts forward throughout the piece. Take advantage of dialogue exchanges. Use them to explore your internal conflict in a humorous manner.

**4.** Descriptions also offer an excellent source of humor. As with any story remember to show, not tell. If you provide richly descriptive scenes, readers will have an easier time sharing in the laughs. Play up your story's familiar and universal experiences

**5.** Finally, take a look at your ending. Does your closing "message" overpower the humor that runs throughout the rest of your story? If so, try cutting back on your exposition and reemphasizing the universality of the story's message. For example, in "The Belly Dances," the author's closing paragraph takes a serious turn as she explores all of the lessons she's learned. However, something as simple as a short reference to an earlier laugh may be all you need to give readers one last smile.

# chapter 17

# Anecdotes in Articles

James Elmore has written a good article with some valuable information. Since it's intended for his local paper, his wanting to give it a more conversational—or "popular"—style is completely appropriate.

Let's start with the title. This can be restated in a catchier way, and with the elements introduced in the order of their appearance. For example: "Schizophrenia: Faulty Parenting or Faulty Neurology?"

The author is off to a fine start by focusing on one person. He can make his opening even more anecdotal by leaving out the first two sentences and beginning with:

> "Vulcan is angry at you! Get out of here!"
>
>   After that outburst, Cheri falls silent. *(At this point, the author might briefly describe what Cheri does when she's silent. What physical activity accompanies her outburst and its aftermath?)* A victim of schizophrenia for eighteen years, Cheri is still haunted by her delusional demons.

 To make the opening paragraph even stronger, the author should start with Cheri speaking.

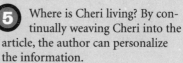 Making a person the star of the story, as the author does here, will best interest readers and illustrate the issues involved.

 Shorter sentences make the piece sound less academic.

**4** This is a good place for the author to mention some of the risks.

**5** Where is Cheri living? By continually weaving Cheri into the article, the author can personalize the information.

**6** This is a wonderful analogy.

**7** The author does a nice job here of bringing the article full circle by relating it back Cheri.

# FAULTY NEUROLOGY, NOT FAULTY PARENTING, CAUSES SCHIZOPHRENIA

## By James Elmore

I don't question whether our work in the Community Mental Health Center is important when I see a patient like Cheri. After 18 years of schizophrenia her delusional demons still haunt her. "Vulcan is angry at you! Get out of here!" Following her frightening outburst, silence.

Twenty-five years ago Cheri's problem was a mystery; ~~then,~~ *In those days, many people believed schizophrenia was caused by flawed parenting.* ~~flawed parenting was a popular theory as to the cause.~~ Based on brain research by the National Institutes of Mental Health we now know the problem lies in the developing tissues of the brain.

*Cheri is treated with* Today clozapine, ~~one of~~ a new ~~group of~~ more effective psychiatric medications for serious mental illness, *it was first* marketed in 1990. *Because it* ~~is prescribed for Cheri. It~~ has risks *clozapine* ~~and~~ is reserved for the most severe and unresponsive cases, but *it* keeps Cheri out of a long-term hospital.

By far, the majority of people with schizophrenia live in the community ~~and~~ with medications, mental health case management and family support, *they can* enjoy the pleasures of daily living. *Research at the NIMH* ~~National Institutes of Mental Health research~~ indicates that prenatal oxygen insufficiency, exposure to viruses or toxins, delivery complications, and low birth weight along with a genetic abnormality of the frontal brain may be the causes of schizophrenia. ~~But,~~ symptoms usually don't occur until early adulthood, when the brain's final maturation is taking place. *What are these genetic abnormalities?* Scientists have noted an increase in the size of the spaces of the brain containing cerebrospinal fluid and decreased size of the cortical surface areas; this means a loss of tissue where essential thinking processes take place. Important nerve connections from frontal lobes to lateral lobes and deep nerve centers are *thereby* lost.

The results are the symptoms we see in those with schizophrenia: apathy and withdrawal *caused by* ~~from~~ frontal lobe changes, auditory hallucinations, delusions and unusual behaviors from changes in the temporal or lateral lobes.

**6** To understand this process, imagine a computer with very few, very slow programs and a virus. Its output will have many errors, bewildering the user. It's No wonder that people with untreated or severe schizophrenia often appear confused, paranoid and speak and behave in strange ways. Keep in mind, though, that most people whose schizophrenia is controlled by medication can relate to others ~~nor~~ in a normal manner. ~~mally.~~

Schizophrenia affects 1.8 million people in the U.S. and 1% of the world's population. Breakthroughs in brain research and psychopharmacology signal a future in which new medicines and therapies will address specific brain changes and their underlying causes. This will mean ~~For~~ a better quality of life for millions, perhaps **7** within Cheri's lifetime.

---

Most readers like to get a picture of what they're reading. In a word or two, the author needs to tell them something about Cheri. Even mentioning her age will give readers a reference point.

Next, put paragraph five right after three, which seems to follow naturally. Also, shorter sentences will make the tone more conversational:

> According to researchers at the NIMH *(which you spelled out in full earlier)*, a number of factors can contribute to schizophrenia. Among them are an insufficient oxygen supply before birth, exposure to viruses or toxins, delivery complications, and low birth weight. Any of these, along with a genetic abnormality of the frontal brain, may cause the disease. Though these factors are present from birth, symptoms usually don't occur until early adulthood, when the brain is reaching its final maturity.
>
> What are these genetic abnormalities? Scientists have noted ...

And on with paragraphs six, seven, eight, and nine. End with paragraph four, tying it in with the clozapine mentioned earlier. To emphasize the point—since apparently Cheri still suffers with her delusional demons even with clozapine—the author should try to describe how the medication helped her. What was she like before she started taking it? How does she live now? Is she out of the hospital? With her family? In a group home? While the author may want to keep the article short, a little more information will help to personalize Cheri, thus adding more depth and power to the entire article.

# Your Turn!

Weave an anecdote into your article by applying the following tips to your work:

**1.** Reread your opening paragraph. Did you use the standard inverted pyramid, supplying readers with the basic who, what, when, where, and why? Or, did you personalize the material by starting off with an anecdotal lead? If you introduce an anecdote midway through your opening paragraph, consider cutting the first few lines, and leading with your anecdote.

**2.** If you took the inverted pyramid route, it's time to think about your topic: Who is most affected by the topic of your story? Who is involved? Who gains or loses the most? In researching your subject matter, it's likely that you've spoken with someone who has been involved with or impacted by your topic. It's this person's unique perspective that you can use to hook readers into your article. But remember, this person isn't what the story's about—she is only a part of the story. Be sure you don't lose sight of your story's focus.

**3.** Do be careful not to let your focal point cause confusion within the article. In the above critique, for example, Cheri's story brought up as many questions as it answered. To be sure you've covered all the bases, ask a friend or critique group member to read over your article. Have him place a star next to each point where he wants to know more information. This will help clarify any potential gaps in your work.

**4.** Now take a look at your ending. Does it relate back to your opening—tying everything up for readers? If not, try rewriting your closing paragraph so that it refers back to your opening. You may even want to consider including a closing quote from the person.

# Nonfiction Checklist

Keep these questions in mind as you revise or critique your memoir, essay, or article:

## Memoirs

✓ Can you identify the memoir's theme? Is it well developed and maintained throughout the manuscript?

✓ Are the main characters introduced naturally throughout the story, or does each make an appearance by page 5?

✓ Does the dialogue and exposition support both the story line and the book's overarching theme?

✓ Does each chapter maintain an adequate level of tension?

✓ Do you establish a realistic sense of place and time?

✓ Is the main conflict present throughout the memoir, or does it seem to disappear at certain points?

## Personal Essays

✓ Does the essay have a clear focus and theme? Or, does it read more like a simple play-by-play record of events?

✓ Do you present your thoughts and feelings in a natural and believable manner? Can readers feel the emotions you're describing?

✓ Do you provide descriptions of key events? Can readers relate to these events.

✓ Can you easily identify major turning points in the essay, or do these points seem to blend into the story's background?

## Articles

✓ Does the article have a strong opening hook? Do you get a sense of the article's focus from the opening? Will readers be intrigued?

✓ Would an anecdote or quote enhance the opening hook?

✓ Does the article have a human focal point? If not, does it need one?

✓ Is the information presented in a natural order that readers will be able to follow and comprehend?

✓ Does the article address questions appropriate to the topic? Does the article inadvertently raise more questions than it answers?

✓ Does the ending satisfy you as a reader? Does it relate back to the article's opening? Does it answer any questions raised within the article.

PART IV

# Poetry

evising poetry mandates precision of craft, a respect for duality, and an intimate understanding of the ebb and flow of language. Chapters eighteen through twenty-one explore the various principles and skills needed to properly undertake such a revision process. Each chapter carefully deconstructs a submitted poem, and then offers a revised version of the poem. This allows you to see how each editing technique described by the critiquer builds on the existing poem's structure and theme without altering the poet's intended vision.

In chapter eighteen, for example, the primary focus is on shortening the poem's length while also increasing its tension level. This critique, while focusing specifically on the submitted lyric poem, explores one of the biggest challenges associated with editing poetry of any type: How do you identify, modify, or cut clichéd images and underdeveloped lines without corrupting the poem's innate sense of beauty and self-expression?

By cutting overly general phrases and reworking line breaks, the critiquer reduces the original poem presented in chapter eighteen from twenty-two lines to nine. Since the changes were made with clear objectives in mind—to increase tension and solidify the poem's concrete imagery—the integrity of the work is actually enhanced

by the cuts. This approach to the editing process allows for both an appreciation of the existing poem and an appreciation for the poem's potential for improvement.

As Kim Addonizio and Dorianne Laux state in *The Poet's Companion*, "True revision is just that: a re-visioning of the poem's potential and the strategies it has used so far." So, before you begin to edit a poem, look first for its heart. What is the author really writing about? What is she really trying to say? Once you have a strong understanding of a poem's focus, you'll find it easier to spot those incidents or phrases that act like clutter more than complement. Making slight adjustments to line breaks also can open a poem to new levels of meaning and possibility.

Poetry, as a form, presents unique opportunities for writers to expand their editing abilities. It's not necessary to be a published poet in order to cultivate a respect for the artistic endeavors of poets. Nor is it necessary to have two or three poetry chapbooks to your name in order to offer constructive guidance to a poet. It is crucial, however, that you nourish your love of language and develop your editing skills as they relate specifically to poetry. Once you're armed with the tools demonstrated in the next four chapters, you'll be able to polish your own poetry, as well as that of other writers.

**chapter 18**

# Basic Flaws

**W**endy DeWachter's rhymed free verse lyric poem on writer's block—aptly titled "No Poem"—presents an opportunity to learn vital lessons about verse, chief among them that poetry can be mastered with some attention to craft.

To correct flaws, you have to be able to identify them, beginning with the first line. That's where craft comes in.

The opening line here is weak, followed by lines containing the antiquated "Tis" contraction and clichéd phrases. Also, the author is padding lines simply to execute the rhyme, an affliction that recurs throughout the lyric. In fairness, "No Poem" was the weakest of those submitted by the author for critique. But in a sense, it held the most promise because a sterling poem lies within the draft.

The fifth line, "Remembering only one line," is intriguing. What line is she referring to here? Because the author never explores that, her poem lacks tension. Tension generates irony, and irony generates truth.

In this poem, everything happens predictably. A more powerful lyric would

 **1** Gerunds can become repetitive and sound unpleasant. Use the root form of the verb.

**2** Break the stanza here to enhance motion.

**3** Inserting line breaks will suspend meaning and add to the tension.

 **4** Deploy sensory images in the ending.

 **5** Try another stanza break for more tension.

**6** Notice how this new closing line generates irony.

involve a line or an image that distracts the poet, like "birds that do not sing."

As far as basics go, this poem contains another overlooked consideration of craft: length. If you want to publish poetry, think like an editor who routinely considers whether the topic of a poem is worth the number of lines.

"No Poem"

I do not ~~know what to say~~
~~'Tis hard to write everyday~~
~~Same old thing~~ repeating
~~Great thoughts receding~~
**❶** Remember~~ing only~~ one line
Entertaining an idea ~~of mine~~
**❷** ~~Attempting to~~ capture a ~~moment~~
Track~~ing~~ where it went
~~Today is rather slow~~
~~Organizing things I know~~
~~Shaping it into a poem~~
Extravagant images roam
~~Enticing my eyes with words~~
~~Yearning thoughts fly~~ like birds
~~Obscure visions remain~~ in sight
~~Unable,~~ still, ~~to write~~
~~Again I try, again nothing~~
~~There is nothing over which to~~ sing.
~~Gathering things I secure the lock~~
~~Anxious over the writers block~~
~~I guess I have nothing to say~~
~~No poem will be written today.~~

In this case, the poem should be short, especially since it contains only two concrete images, one of birds and another of the poet securing a lock. The latter seems to appear because it rhymes with block. It isn't needed.

The author does have some crisp active verbs, "track" and "capture," for instance, that provide motion in the poem. Motion is associated with sensory imagery: taste, texture, sight, smell, sound. A sense of motion is the sixth sense.

"No Poem" contains sight and a hint of sound: the word "sing" in the eighteenth line, which is marred again by padding and awkward locution. Do she mean, "There is nothing *about* which to sing"?

The author ought to save the imagery she has for the ending, where tension, in a short poem, should generate irony.

The tension in the revised version is heightened by the use of line breaks—to meld and enhance meaning—and stanza breaks, adding to the *motion* of the poem. And, the revision adds only a few words to the original.

In future poems, the author should try to change the gerund form of *verbs—*

```
        Editor's Revision of "No Poem"



        I do not repeat
        Nor remember one line
        To entertain an idea
        Capture it
 ❸
        Track where it went
        Extravagantly into the roaming
 ❹      Place of images like birds
        Still in sight
 ❺
 ❻      But not singing.
```

repeating, remembering, entertaining, tracking, etc.—to the root form. The "-ing" sound can be unpleasant in English.

Finally, the ending in the author's version recaps the beginning, particularly in the next to last line (a mirror of the first), which ends the poem on a trivial note.

Remember that mastering craft will allow you to identify and correct lapses such as the ones described in this critique. And once you're able to do that, you'll be able to push your endings into new and thoughtful territory … and your poems will be stronger for it.

# Your Turn!

Correct the basic flaws in your poems by applying the following tips to your work:

**1.** Start the revision process by underlining each clichéd phrase and padded line in your poem.

**2.** For each underlined phrase or line, write an alternative. Strive for originality by playing with your wording and line length. How many different ways can you rewrite each line and still capture your intended emotion?

**3.** Now, circle each gerund in your poem. How many do you have? Try using the root forms of the verbs. How does this change impact the rhythm of your poem? Is it better or worse?

**4.** Finally, take a look at your poem's length. As demonstrated in the above critique, poems with few concrete images may work better short. How many concrete images are in your poem? How does this compare to your poem's length? Are you using to many? Too few? Try revising with this in mind.

# chapter 19

# Throwaway Lines

Marion Brimm Rewey's poem "Palomino—A Portrait, With Apples" is representative of what you can achieve by tightening and rearranging lines; foreshadowing; and composing a stronger ending.

The title is fine, promising beauty (palomino), portrait (narrator and horse), and archetypal truth (apple). But the first line, which should grab an editor's attention, just isn't strong enough. The line "noon or dusk" is a throwaway. Other beginning lines spend too much time grounding the occasion and/or are poorly positioned. Why not start with action, in keeping with the topic of a horse, a symbol of movement and power? Cut awkward, wordy lines like, "Green pastures were a true domain / and he was king," and break other lines for meaning rather than for breath.

The author also needs to answer this question: Why is the narrator luring the horse with apples if a fruit tree grows in the pasture? That tree is important because the horse is going to die (like a windfall apple) under it in the ending. Why not foreshadow the tree believably from the start as in the second stanza of the revised poem.

**1** The action picks up here with language symbolizing "horse" power. Why not start here?

**2** Here in the third stanza, the pace quickens with the best lines of the poem so far.

**3** This is a "portrait," not a narrative. The author needs to resist the urge to tell a story. As such, her ending should not fulfill any plot—"We buried him / where he died"—but hearken back to the narrator and deepen the meaning of "portrait." (See the revised ending.)

**4** Note the stanza break here. It heightens meaning, associating "deep" with the palomino and, in the stanza below, with the narrator.

**5** The stanza break plays off "just out of reach." The second to last line in that same stanza relates to the narrator and to the horse, foreshadowing the ending. Lines also have been repositioned so that "rose" ends the stanza and echoes in the first line of the next stanza.

"Palomino—A Portrait, With Apples"

Noon or dusk,
I lured him to the stone barn gate
with apples.

Making a flat-palmed platter of my hands,
I offered my bribes in exchange
for a touch of his rough blond coat.

And that was all.
He never broke to halter,
snorted and snapped at hobbles, never carried his load.

Green pastures were a true domain
and he was king. And would remain, year after year
free, untroubled as the air, untamed.
And I, deep in family and routine, plodded on.

The last months saw him falter at the gate,
saw him hunger for the casual stroke
that untangled burrs from mane and coat,
expecting, now, the apples
I gladly gave
for years of grace-filled flight
as he skimmed fields of clover and pink rose,
flanks gleaming gold in slanted light,
charging the wind
with hoof beats that startled my pulse
to a wildness no words would name.

Then,
one fair day,
he bunched his stringy haunches,
folded his stringy legs,
rolled over to rest by a wild fruit tree
in dappled shade.

```
The sun rose
but he did not.

We found him there,
untidy mane tangled in a wild rose vine,
red apples falling, one by one,
on his lion-colored hide.

We buried him
where he died.
```

**❸**

Perhaps the biggest flaw of this poem is that matter-of-fact plotlike ending. The poem needs a more powerful conclusion. To get there, the author should consider using a simple transition based on the first line of the original fifth stanza, and then focus on the tree and narrator.

The ending should refer as much to the poet as to the horse and apple tree. Moreover, the final lines should fulfill the promise of the title, that a palomino—a symbol of beauty—will meld with apples in a meaningful portrait.

As you've heard elsewhere in this book the etiquette of critiques is simple: Keep what you like; like what you keep. And keep revising until you're satisfied. That said, these revisions are meant to emphasize the process: start with a strong opening, cut weak or padded lines, foreshadow effectively, and use line and stanza breaks to augment meaning. Finally, end with universal truth, fulfilling the promise of the title, along with the expectations of readers.

This author's at the gate of breakthrough. She just has to go through it.

# Your Turn!

Rid your poem of throwaway lines by applying the following tips to your work:

**1.** Look at your opening line. Does it grab the reader's attention? Or is it a throwaway line? Does the line hint at what's to come, or does it only ground the occasion—something that can be done later in the poem?

**2.** Next, have a friend or critique group member read the poem aloud. Listen to the rhythm and locution of your words. Can you hear the line breaks? Do portions of the poem drag? Do you spend too much time expressing a single thought or idea?

**3.** Finally, look at your line breaks. Rewrite your poem on a separate piece of paper, and try breaking some or all of your lines at different points. As you're doing this, remember to "break lines for meaning rather than for breath." Do any of the rebroken lines improve the poem?

Editor's Revision of "Palomino—A Portrait, With Apples"


He never broke to halter,
snorted and snapped at hobbles,
never carried his load. Deep

**④**

in family and routine, I plodded on,
luring him to the stone barn gate
with store-bought apples
while the wild tree blossomed in dappled shade.

These, our last easy months.
Summer's fruit ripened and hung
Lower on branches each day,

**⑤**

just out of reach. At the the gate
I'd make a flat-palmed platter of my hands,
remembering years of grace-filled flight,
flanks that gleamed in slanted light
and hoofbeats that kept time
with my pulse—
a wildness no words would name—
skimming fields of clover and pink rose.

The sun rose
but he did not

We found him under the tree,
red apples falling, one by one,
on his gilt mane,
as if set there in still-life
by a gentler essence.

# chapter 20

# Sonnets

I t is difficult to compose a publishable rhymed poem—even more so to publish a sonnet. In addition to rhyme and meter, the form has its own requirements. But the problem with Verna Lee Hinegardner's sonnet, "Standing on the Promises of God," concerns not only form, but foreshadowing, an underemphasized aspect of the craft.

First, let's deal with the major flaw in the sonnet. In this case, the author chose the Shakespearean sonnet, which has three quatrains (four-line stanzas) of alternating rhymes and one ending couplet. Each quatrain develops a theme—in this case, a "promise"—with the third launching the turn, or couplet.

The turn has two prerequisites: It must be foreshadowed, and it needs to startle readers. Think of Shakespeare's famous "Sonnet 130." The first quatrain reads: "My mistress' eyes are nothing like the sun; / Coral is far more red than her lips' red; / If snow be white, why then her breasts are dun; / If hairs be wires, black wires grow on her head."

Some love poem, huh? You bet. Each subsequent quatrain compares his mistress

**1** The use of "solid" is redundant.

**2** There's a subject/pronoun disagreement in line 6; "They" refers to "sins." Also, if "there's much to dread," as stated, then share some of those sins. Otherwise, revise lines 4 through 6.

**3** Don't break lines awkwardly by beginning with a pronoun.

**4** The ending turn doesn't surprise due to a lack of foreshadowing, even though lines 7 and 8 seem to prepare for the ending.

**5** An epigraph enhances foreshadowing and establishes an authority base.

**6** Smooth the meter in the original second line by inserting strong nouns and verbs, and ending the line with a double meaning for "snapped." As it is, there's no sure beat, and read the line as: on PROM-| is-es | but i | THREW BACK | my HEAD.

"Standing on the Promises of God"

I did not know how anyone could stand
on promises, but I threw back my head
**(1)** to sing that song, and hoped for solid land
beneath my feet. At nine there's much to dread.

I knew I did not want to go to hell
**(2)** so I confessed my sins. They baptized me
in all three names. I thought, "A voice will tell
**(3)** me I am loved; a dove, my legacy."

My Mama said she came up clean and pure.
I came up gasping, jerking like a hen
without a head, bone-wet—but I was sure
I heard that organ promising again;

and, as I sang along, dried off and dressed,
**(4)** a sudden gust of August-warmth caressed.

to the artificial standards of love—that's the theme—foreshadowing a startling turn: "And yet, by heaven, I think my love as rare/As any she belied with false compare."

The author's turn in this sonnet is neither startling nor effectively foreshadowed. The poem describes a baptism with background imagery of water and song. The "promise" theme is nicely foreshadowed in the title and in lines 1, 2, 7, 8, and 12. The problem, however, is that the author doesn't fulfill the promise of the foreshadowing in the ending couplet.

To see how powerful foreshadowing can be, reread lines 7 and 8. What if those lines read: "The wind will tell / if I am loved; and warmth, my legacy"? These changes fore-

 **7** The use of "sand" echoes foreshadowing from the epigraph.

 **8** Use enjambment (no ending punctuation mark) in line 12 to parcel the long sentence, to suspend tension with white space, and to launch into turn.

**9** The use of "solo" answers key foreshadowing in lines 7 and 8, completing the turn.

**10** Ending with a slant rhyme creates a slightly off-key effect, enhancing meaning and adding more suspense.

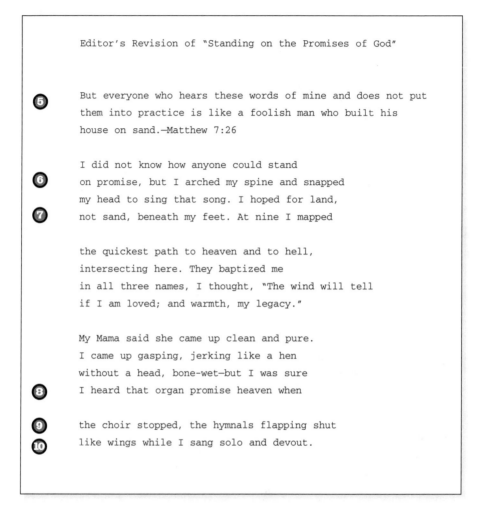

Editor's Revision of "Standing on the Promises of God"

**⑤** But everyone who hears these words of mine and does not put
them into practice is like a foolish man who built his
house on sand.—Matthew 7:26

**⑥** I did not know how anyone could stand
on promise, but I arched my spine and snapped
my head to sing that song. I hoped for land,
**⑦** not sand, beneath my feet. At nine I mapped

the quickest path to heaven and to hell,
intersecting here. They baptized me
in all three names, I thought, "The wind will tell
if I am loved; and warmth, my legacy."

My Mama said she came up clean and pure.
I came up gasping, jerking like a hen
without a head, bone-wet—but I was sure
**⑧** I heard that organ promise heaven when

**⑨** the choir stopped, the hymnals flapping shut
**⑩** like wings while I sang solo and devout.

shadow and strengthen the last line about warm August wind caressing the narrator.

The original ending also is insufficient on formal grounds: It isn't powerful enough to serve as a turn in a Shakespearean sonnet.

In the original version, lines 7 and 8 work well because voices and doves not only are associated with the religious subject matter, but they also provide texture, sound, and motion, enlivening the poem. An epigraph, as seen in the revised version of the poem, can add more foreshadowing.

Epigraphs provide an authority base—an indication that you know your topic. For this sonnet, a quote from the Bible seems appropriate. The line from Matthew in the revised version's epigraph foreshadows the third line—"hoped for solid land"—minus the padding ("solid"). The new word "sand" in the fourth line of the revised poem not only echoes back to the epigraph, but also internally rhymes.

Finally, slant rather than full rhyme in the ending couplet adds more tension via sound and bolsters the independence of the narrator, singing alone and slightly off-key.

The image of hymnals flapping shut like wings is a more effective image, incorporating sound, motion, and sense in a simile. Moreover, the narrator does not hear a supernatural voice, but her own. This generates irony and echoes the epigraph. That's powerful enough to fulfill the requirements of the turn.

No doubt the author could have published this sonnet in a small magazine or even in a Christian one, with a little rewriting. However, the revised version has a chance in any magazine, because of attention to craft and foreshadowing.

# Your Turn!

Add foreshadowing to your sonnet by applying the following tips to your work:

**1.** Sonnets require foreshadowing and a startling turn. But before you focus on foreshadowing, you must have a clear understanding of your poem's theme. For example, Shakespeare's "Sonnet 130" isn't just about love, it's about "the artificial standards of love." What's your sonnet about?

**2.** Once you've identified your sonnet's theme, work on your foreshadowing. Start by looking at your title—what does it promise readers?

**3.** Now read your sonnet with an eye toward imagery and wording. Do the images used support the sonnet's title and theme? Do they work to foreshadow your closing turn? If your poem is lacking in strong imagery, take another look at your theme. On a separate piece of paper, write down any images that come to mind as you're thinking about your theme. Would any of these images work in your sonnet?

**4.** Take a look at your closing turn. Is it properly foreshadowed? Does it incorporate a sense of irony? Would adding an epigraph help to bolster the impact of your ending couplet?

# chapter 21

# Pantoums

The pantoum is a troublesome form that few poets ever master. However, Dorothy J. Stanfill's "In a Quandary Over Form," draws readers in with its playful nature and potential.

The author didn't compose a pantoum, though. She violates the pattern in the last stanza—perhaps intentionally. If so, this is a bad move. Never commit a mistake to show the mistake. You wouldn't write boring prose for an essay titled "Boredom," would you?

Same goes for the pantoum.

Pantoums come in quatrains (four-line stanzas). Each line repeats in a pattern. The second and fourth lines of each stanza become the first and third lines of the next. To end a pantoum, you must repeat the third and first lines of the first stanza as the second and fourth lines, respectively, of the last stanza.

That's where this pantoum attempt misfires technically.

Of course, the author is doing some things right. She expresses one clear idea per line. Her rhyme sounds are rich—yielding many word possibilities to create new meanings in each line. The rhyme is so rich

 **1** Delete this throwaway line. Other throwaways include lines 12, 14, and 16.

 **2** "Met it" doesn't cut it. Hone the rhyme to match "credit it" or insert a new line.

 **3** Awkward meter and locution.

 **4** This violates form. This should mirror the second line of the previous stanza.

 **5** This line also violates form and doesn't repeat anywhere else.

**6** Establish clean pentameter.

**7** Use wordplay to offset repetition of form. Here, "Spoil" means "rot"; in line 5 it means "indulge."

**8** Construct lines that can be separated in different places to attach to lines above, below, etc., providing multiple meanings.

```
"In a Quandary Over Form"

Although mastery of forms could do us credit
do we really need to know pantoum?
Would it be an asset or a debit?
(1) Would it fill my heart with joy or gloom?

Do we really need to know pantoum?
Will it be an easy thing to edit?
Would it fill my heart with joy or gloom?
(2) Would a reader know one if he met it?

Will it be an easy thing to edit?
(3) Is this mastery to be found worthwhile?
Would a reader know one if he met it?
Will my efforts make my readers smile?

Is this mastery to be found worthwhile?
Would I frame one for my trophy room?
Will my efforts make my readers smile?
This may throw me into deepest gloom.

(4) Would it be an asset or a debit?
Would I frame one for my trophy room?
(5) My inactive file is going to get it,
although mastery of forms may do us credit?
```

she really doesn't need to use near rhyme, as she does somewhat awkwardly with "edit" and "met it." Finally, her inquisitive voice tone is good for pantoums.

But this poem has other, more serious problems, chief among them throwaway lines. The throwaway lines here seem inserted mostly for purposes of rhyme rather than meaning, such as "Would it fill my heart with joy or gloom?" and "Will my efforts make my readers smile?" The throwaway line, "This may throw me into deepest gloom," seems padded and re-uses the rhyme word "gloom"; worse, the line doesn't repeat, again violating pantoum form.

The form, however, is relatively simple to fix—as seen in the revised version—suggesting that while these pantoum violations are serious, they're also easy to edit.

Pantoums must scan as fluidly and meaningfully as sonnets or even free verse. In other words, you must transcend the rigors of the form—the most obvious of which here are repeating lines, which bore

Editor's Revision of "In a Quandary Over Form"

**(6)**
**(7)** Mastery of forms could do us credit.
We spoil with free verse. Why not send pantoum?
Would they be an asset, not a debit,
in eyes of literary patrons whom

we spoil with free verse? Why not send pantoum?
Would it be an easy thing to edit
in eyes of literary patrons whom
**(8)** we'd instruct? Assuming they had read it

would it be an easy thing to edit?
Is learning rhyme and prosody worthwhile?
We'd instruct, assuming they had read it.
We're appealing to the bibliophile:

Is learning rhyme and prosody worthwhile?
No one guesses poets in a chat room
were appealing to the bibliophile.
On line we'd better use a nom de plume

no one guesses. Poets in a chat room—
would they be an asset, not a debit,
online! We'd better use a nom de plume.
Mastery of forms could do us credit.

readers if not executed properly.

To do so, formalists typically employ two basic methods: line separation and word play.

Line separation entails constructing a line with phrases that detach naturally and reattach easily to lines immediately above and below the line in question. For example, line 8 in the revised work attaches nicely to lines 7 and 9, sparking new meanings there in addition to another new meaning in the repetition (line 11): "We'd instruct, assuming they had read it."

Word play also is vital in pantoums. You can use homonyms; homophones (two or more words pronounced alike but different in meaning or spelling, such as "days"/ "daze"); homographs (two or more words spelled alike but different in meaning or pronunciation, such as "row"/"quarrel" and "row"/"propel a boat"); and even charades (word combinations that suggest other words or combinations, such as "appear"/ "up here").

Here are two of the word plays found in the revised work:

- lines 2/5, the homonym "spoil" as in "rot" and "indulge";
- lines 12/15, the double word play "We're appealing" and "were appealing," combing a charade ("we're"/"were") and a homonym ("appealing"/"pleading" and "pleasing").

In the end, there's no need to be in a quandary about form. You just have to learn these techniques. In this case, the author should revise her poem using the correct pattern. She also should smooth her pentameter (using five pairs of mostly soft/hard sounds per line), delete her throwaway and weak lines, and replace them with ones using line separation and word play.

Remember, mastery of form is key.

# Your Turn!

Improve your pantoum by applying the following tips to your work:

**1.** First, make sure your work properly adheres to the pantoum pattern outlined in the above critique.

**2.** Once you've got the pattern right, it's time to think about your use of line separations and word play. Do your lines contain phrases that readily transfer from one to the next?

**3.** Now focus on your word play. Circle each homonym, homophone, and homograph. If you don't find any, consider rewriting your pantoum to incorporate such devices.

**4.** As you're working on your word play, keep an eye out for throwaway lines—lines used for rhyme rather than meaning. Can you improve any of those lines with charades?

# Poetry Checklist

Keep these questions in mind as you revise or critique your poems:

## All Poems

✓ Is your first line an attention-getter or a throwaway? Could your poem begin more effectively at a later point?

✓ Have you avoided antiquated language (like "tis")? Have you weeded out clichés and replaced them with fresh language and imagery?

✓ Have you created tension in your poem? Can you improve the tension by playing with line and stanza breaks?

✓ Does your poem contain too many gerunds ("-ing" verbs)? Can you improve the sound of your poem by replacing gerunds with the root forms of those verbs?

✓ Is your poem tightly written or have you padded lines with unnecessary words and images? Is every word carefully chosen for meaning, sound, and impact?

✓ Have you read your poem aloud (or had someone else read it aloud to you)? Do the lines flow the way you want them to? Have you discovered any problems with clarity and sound?

✓ Does your poem simply end or have you crafted the last lines as carefully as the rest of the poem?

## Shakespearean Sonnets

✓ Do your lines scan smoothly or are they awkward and singsongy? Have you chose ineffective words and images for the sake of rhyme rather than meaning?

✓ Have you used foreshadowing to set up the turn effectively?

✓ Is your turn powerful enough (i.e., startling, ironic)?

## Pantoums

✓ Have you adhered to the established pattern of the pantoum?

✓ Have you chosen words to enhance music and meaning, or are you simply trying to make the repetitive rhymes work?

✓ Does every line contribute to the meaning of the pantoum?

✓ Have you avoided boredom in the repetition of the lines by employing interesting line breaks and wordplay (homonyms, homophones, homographs, charades)?

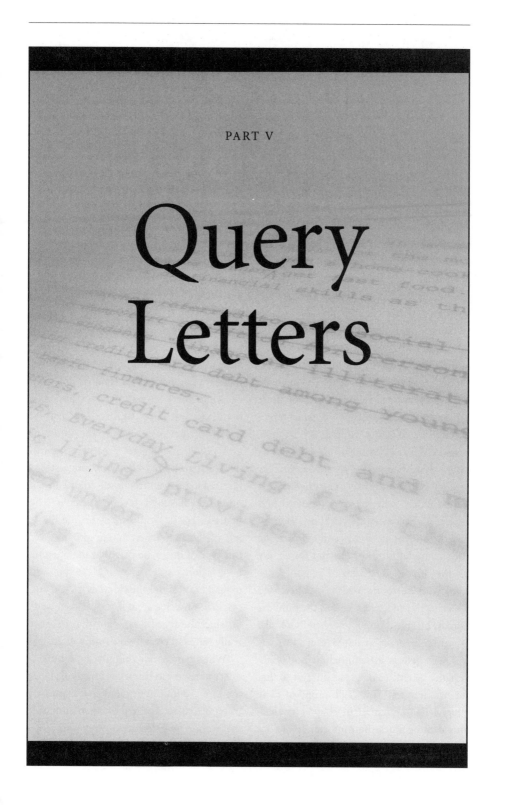

PART V

# Query
# Letters

efore you send in your article, proposal, or synopsis, you must first submit a query letter. The goal of a query letter is to present an article or book topic in a clear and concise manner, thus enticing an agent or editor either to request a complete proposal of the book or to assign the article outright. These one-page letters must be focused, articulate, and intriguing. Each chapter in this section includes a query letter as it was originally submitted by the author, as well as a version of the letter revised by a professional editor.

With magazine query letters, as in chapters twenty-two and twenty-three, you must demonstrate a knowledge of your target publication. Whether your query letter is intended for a well-known national publication like *Woman's Day* or a smaller regional publication like *Texas Highways*, it should address why your proposed article is a perfect fit for the publication. Helpful hint: Before you begin to critique someone else's query letter, ask the writer for a copy of the intended magazine's guidelines (these can be found on the publication's Web site; by sending a SASE to the publication; or by consulting a reference book like *Writer's Market* or WritersMarket.com).

Query letters for nonfiction books are designed to entice an agent's interest so that she will request your full proposal. The query letter presented in chapter twenty-four demonstrates the importance of succinctly summarizing your book's unique benefits into one strong sentence. A nonfiction query also should address why the proposed book is needed in the marketplace, how the book differs from similar titles already available, and why you are qualified to write the book. When you're critiquing this type of query letter for another writer, make sure the author has addressed each of the points mentioned above. Look for ways that the author can validate the need for his book—other than the fact that he really wants to write it, why should the agent ask to see more? Can the author include any facts or figures to support his claims that there is an audience for his book?

While query letters for novels and children's fiction face similar yet distinct demands, the goal remains the same: to grab an agent's interest. Chapters twenty-five through twenty-eight offer suggestions for making an entire novel sound like a must-read in only a few brief graphs. The first paragraph should focus on the book, not the author. When you're looking over this type of query, be sure that the opening hook is doing its job. Does it make you want to read more about the story? Is it vivid and original? Sure, it's great if you've been writing since the age of seven, but what an agent really wants to hear about is your story line.

When you're writing or critiquing a query letter, try to think like an editor: Does the topic sound interesting? Is it expressed in an articulate and confident manner? Is the author qualified to do the work? But also remember to think like a critiquer: What can you do to improve a query?

# chapter 22

# National Magazines

Overall, this is a well-written magazine query from Jean Tennant, but there are a few things she can do to shorten the query and make it more effective.

She begins by addressing Jane Chesnutt, the editor-in-chief of *Woman's Day*. While it's essential that you address your query to a specific person presently working for your target publication, you should always direct queries to the managing editor or articles editor. In this case, while Ms. Chesnutt is the editor-in-chief, she probably doesn't have the time to read general query letters to the magazine—that's why she has a staff. If the query is of interest to *Woman's Day*, then it will be given to the appropriate staff member for follow-up.

The opening sentence of this query is sure to do what all opening lines should do—get an editor's attention. The author alludes to a "promise" that was made between Marie LaPlant and her daughter, Paula, without directly stating the promise. That's an excellent way to pique an editor's interest and force her to continue reading so she can find out what promise was made. As with most query letters, the opening sen-

**1** If you don't have the name of a specific editor to whom to address your query, you should send it to the managing editor or senior articles editor.

**2** The accepted word count for articles appearing in *Woman's Day* ranges from 500 to 1,800 words. In this case, the author needs to adjust the word count for her article.

**3** The author states that she's already interviewed Marie, Paula and Dan Griese, and their doctors. Instead of just mentioning it, the author should slant this sentence so that it conveys to the editor that the article can be written as soon as it's requested.

**4** Unless you're a professional photographer or you know the magazine you're querying accepts photographs with manuscripts, you don't need to mention that you've taken photographs. You can write, however, that photographs are available upon request.

Original Query Letter

April 23, 2002

**(1)** Jane Chesnutt, Editor-in-Chief ) *Address query letters to managing*
*Woman's Day*                           *editors or article editors.*
1633 Broadway, 42nd Floor
New York, NY 10019

Dear Jane Chesnutt:            — *Nice opening line! It will hold an editor's interest.*

More than a decade ago Marie LaPlant made a promise to her
daughter, Paula. Born without a uterus, Paula would never be
able to carry a child, so Marie promised that someday, if Paula
wanted, she would carry a child for her. Last year a newly
married Paula accepted her mother's generous offer, and together the two women set out on a journey that took them from the
Mayo Clinic in Minnesota to *Good Morning America*, and eventually produced not one, but two miracle babies.

**(2)** I'd like to write "Marie's Promise" as a feature article for
*WOMAN'S DAY* magazine, with a proposed length of 1,500 to 2,000
words. The twins, a boy and a girl, were born November 14,
2001; the article could work nicely to coincide with the
babies' first birthday.        *Just say that photos are available.*

**(3)** I've interviewed Marie, Paula and/Dan Griese and their doctors,
**(4)** and <u>have taken dozens of photographs</u>. They've recently appeared
on *Good Morning America*, and an upcoming segment on *48 Hours* is
in the works. They all live in Dolliver, Iowa, just 65 miles
from my home. Best of all, they've agreed to give me an exclu-
**(5)** sive on magazine articles.

I've been writing for almost 25 years. In the late 1970s I had
approximately 35 short stories published by Macfadden Women's
Group, which produces the confession magazines. Then, between
1986 and 1992 I had seven books published. The first was a
romance by Silhouette; the rest were psychological/supernatural
thrillers. For the past few years I've been doing mostly freelance newspaper work. <u>Enclosed please find some recent clips,</u>
**(6)** <u>one of which is about Marie and Paula.</u> *Don't send clips unless the guidelines*
       — *No need to ask this.*        *say that you should.*
**(7)** (May I have the honor of writing Marie's story for *WOMAN'S DAY?*)
Theirs is a unique and heartwarming story, and one I believe
your readers would appreciate learning more about. Thank you
for your consideration, and I look forward to hearing from you.
                                            ↓
Sincerely,                        *Be sure to include a SASE.*

Jean Tennant
Street
City and State
Phone Number
E-mail Address

Revised Query Letter

April 23, 2002

Stephanie Abarbanel
Senior Articles Editor
*Woman's Day*
1633 Broadway
New York, NY 10019

Dear Ms. Abarbanel:

More than a decade ago, the now XX-year-old Marie LaPlant made a promise to her daughter, Paula Griese. Born without a uterus, Paula would never be able to carry a child. So Marie promised Paula that, if Paula wanted, she would carry a child for her. Last year Paula accepted her mother's offer, and on November 14, 2001, she became the mother of twins—a boy and a girl.

According to a study conducted in XXXX by XXXX, X out of every X women are born without a uterus. Of the X women born without a uterus, X of them rely on surrogacy as the only viable alternative to carrying their own child. Of those X women who choose surrogacy, X of them rely on family members to act as the surrogate, and in these cases multiple births occurred X percent of the time.

I would like to write a 1,200- to 1,700-word article tentatively titled "Marie's Promise." I have already conducted interviews with Marie LaPlant, Paula and Dan Griese, and both parties' doctors, so I can provide you with the article at your earliest convenience.

I am a published writer who has been writing for almost 25 years. My credits include 35 short stories published by Mcfadden Women's Group and seven books, including *Title Here* published by Silhouette in XXXX. Recently, I have been doing freelance newspaper work. At your request, I am more than happy to provide clips of my work.

I look forward to hearing from you soon. I have enclosed a SASE for your reply.

Sincerely,


Jean Tennant
Street
City and State
Phone Number
E-mail Address

**5** Cut the last sentence of this paragraph, as it doesn't add to the article. *48 Hours* and *Good Morning America* already have segments in the works, so there is really nothing "exclusive" about the story.

**6** Again, unless the submission guidelines state that you should send clips, don't bother. You can indicate, though, that clips are available upon request.

**7** This last paragraph is unnecessary. The last sentences can be as simple as: "I look forward to hearing from you soon. I have enclosed a SASE for your reply."

tence should be designed and written so it can also serve as the opening sentence of the article.

The author goes on to explain the promise that was made between the two women, noting that Paula accepted Marie's offer to carry her child because Paula was born without a uterus. As interesting as this fact may be, it may not coincide with the editorial slant of *Woman's Day*. According to the publication's submission guidelines, the magazine publishes "dramatic narratives about women who have experienced medical miracles." Is Marie and Paula's situation actually a medical miracle? If the author believes it is, then she should include three or four statistics about women who are born without a uterus. Is it rare? What

number of women experience this type of situation? Note that in the revised version of the query, the letter X is in places where such facts and figures should go.

Once the author's provided this type of information, she needs to pay attention to the submission guidelines of *Woman's Day*. Articles appearing in the magazine range in length from 500 to 1,800 words; so, the proposed length is not appropriate. Instead, she should reconsider the word count and work toward a range of 1,200 to 1,700 words.

One of the easiest ways to lose a potential writing assignment is by not researching the market. Editors know exactly what they want. If you, as potential freelance writer, mention an inappropriate word count, then you may have just given the editor an opportunity to reject your query.

Finally, this author needs to rewrite and condense her last two paragraphs. She simply provides too much information about her publishing background. Also, she doesn't need to include published clips unless the publication's submission guidelines indicate that she should—and the guidelines for *Woman's Day* do not.

One last note: Never end a query by asking for the "honor" of writing the proposed story. In this case, the author's already indicated she wants to write this story by sending in a query letter. You also doesn't need to editorialize your proposed topic by stating how unique and heartwarming the story is—the editor will know this if she's interested in the story.

# Your Turn!

Add heft to your magazine query letter by applying the following tips to your work:

**1.** Is your query addressed to the right person? Check your target publication's masthead or Web site for a current listing of editors. Sending your query to a person who's no longer with the magazine screams, "I didn't do any research, but please buy my work anyway!" If you are unable to identify the appropriate editor from the masthead or Web site, don't be afraid to call the publication and ask.

**2.** If you're proposing an article that can be developed and supported via facts/statistics, go through your query and underline all references to facts/statistics. Can't find any? Try to add at least three facts/statistics to support the content of your proposed story. If you find more than six facts/statistics, try to condense them. You really only need to list three or four of the most compelling.

**3.** If you find that you are a couple hundred words over the maximum word count for a publication, see if the word length includes sidebars or quizzes. If it doesn't, take the extra three hundred words and condense them into an accompanying sidebar or quiz. Be sure to mention in your query, though, that in addition to your article you also have a sidebar or quiz to contribute.

**4.** Now, go through your query letter and underline any place where you ask the editor a question. For instance, do you ask, as the author in this critique does, if you "may have the honor" of writing the proposed article? If so, rephrase it as a statement, something like, "I would like to write this story for *Woman's Day*." Such a statement presents a far more professional tone than a question. You also should use caution when opening your query letter with a question. For example, if you open with a line like, "Did you ever wonder who invented the paper weight?" and the editor's resounding answer is, "No," then you may have just blown your chance. Instead, open with a direct statement that sells your topic.

# chapter 23

# Regional Magazines

This query letter from Linda Akins is very interesting in that the author seems to be proposing multiple articles instead of one focused idea. This is a common mistake, but it's one that a little research and focus can easily fix.

From the bold-faced opening statement, the query seems to be for a story about the Royal Courtesy Mounted Patrol (RCMP) as a Texas corporation and the "only fully operational private mounted patrol firm in North America." But that's not exactly the case. In addition, none of the different articles hinted at in this query truly reflect the type of stories *Texas Highways* publishes.

The writer's guidelines for *Texas Highways* state that "subjects should focus on things to do or places to see in Texas." While the RCMP can be seen in Texas, the group does not meet the above requirements. And, while the RCMP may appear at Texas locations, the proposed article doesn't focus on such places. The author does mention that the RCMP is on patrol at Texas shopping malls, but she doesn't specify which shopping malls, and it's probably safe to assume that the RCMP isn't the main draw to most Texas shopping centers.

**1** This information doesn't need to be here. This is what the query letter will cover.

**2** Spell out the first reference to the Royal Courtesy Mounted Patrol. After that, use RCMP.

**3** This query letter addresses multiple topics that can't all be covered in one article. Be sure your idea is focused and well developed.

**4** Query letters should not exceed one page in length.

**5** The author doesn't need to mention photographs. If her query is accepted, then it's appropriate to mention the certification and training academies that would offer photography opportunities.

**6** The author should include the title of the article and when it appeared in the magazine.

**7** Always include your mailing address in addition to your phone number and e-mail address.

Original Query Letter

January 18, 2002

Jack Lowry, Editor
*Texas Highways*
P.O. Box 141009
Austin, Texas 78714-1009

*Cut—this isn't needed*

**1**

> **RE: "New Millennium Workhorses"**
>
> **A Query about the Royal Courtesy Mounted Patrol (RCMP), a Texas corporation and the only fully operational private mounted patrol firm in North America.**

Dear Mr. Lowry:

*Spell out on first reference.*

**2** Anywhere there is a crowd in Texas, the RCMP is probably clearly in ~~site.~~ *sight*

Red-uniformed troopers sit atop immaculately groomed horses providing crowd management services and weaponless security for shopping malls, sporting events, and special occasions. *Such as?* These horses and their riders create a point of interest for people attending these events. In addition to security, RCMP teams bring color and conversation to every appearance. Horse and rider teams even have their own collectable trading cards, just like the most popular sports celebrities. The "Just Say Neigh to Drugs" program for youth takes RCMP personnel to school and recreation centers nationwide.

Some 250 troopers work in venues across the nation with the majority stationed in Texas. They range in age from 18 to 73 and are 75 percent women. Troopers supply their own horses, trucks, and trailers. Riders like 73-year-old George Richards, whose ancestors worked on an East Texas plantation, have rich, anecdote-filled lives, which they readily share with the people they meet on the job.

RCMP mounts are not born, they are made.
*What will the focus of the article be?*

**3** These highly trained horses and their riders are contracted through Alpha & Omega Services, Inc., based in Southlake, Texas. Frank Keller, president and chief executive officer, founded the family business in 1985. A certified mounted police

**④** PAGE 2 ... ROYAL MOUNTED COURTESY PATROL ... By Linda Akins
*Keep your query letter to one page.*

instructor, Keller trains mounted police units throughout the United States and is the chief training officer for the company. Keller and his staff take their recruits through a rigorous certification class, then each one is required to go to two specially designed training academies in Houston within one **③** year of employment.

RCMP uses Quarter horses primarily. However, they also use Thoroughbreds, Appendix Quarter horses, Warm Bloods, some Clydesdales and other assorted Draft breeds.

I would like to write a story for *Texas Highways* highlighting these new millennium workhorses and how they and their riders strengthen homeland security in public places without the use of weapons. The story would include the history of the company, how the horses and riders are trained, where your readers might encounter the patrol, how riders can apply to become a member of the RCMP, and interviews with riders. I would include quotations from musicians such as the members of PHISH, who use RCMP services at their concerts. I would explain how horse patrols were used at Woodstock '94 and Dallas World Cup Soccer '94, and are currently on patrol at Texas shopping malls.     *Word count?*

**⑤** This year's certification and training academies in February and April will provide a chance for excellent photography. More information can be found at the company's Web site at www.mountedpatrol.com.

*Be specific—when did the article appear and what was the title?*

**⑥** I am an experienced freelance writer and wrote an (article) for your publication many years ago about the centennial celebration of the YO Ranch. I have included a recent sample of my writing. I look forward to your reply.

Sincerely,

**⑦** Linda Akins
Phone Number     *mailing address?*
E-mail Address

Revised Query Letter

January 18, 2002

Jack Lowry, Editor
*Texas Highways*
P.O. Box 141009
Austin, Texas 78714-1009

Dear Mr. Lowry:

Anywhere there's a crowd in Texas, the Royal Courtesy Mounted Patrol is nearby. These red-uniformed troopers sit atop immaculately groomed horses to provide crowd management services and weaponless security for shopping malls, sporting events, and special occasions.

I would like to write a 1,400- to 1,900-word article about XX and XX, two popular tourist locations in XX, Texas. I have chosen these two locations in this exciting city because there is a strong RCMP presence, and I believe that travelers would find the RCMP very interesting. In addition to the historical and cultural aspects of these locations, I would include the historical background about the RCMP and interviews with RCMP riders, like 73-year-old George Richards, on why the RCMP is present in these two locations.

I'm an experienced freelance writer, and in XXXX, I wrote "XXX" for *Texas Highways*, so I'm very familiar with your publication and the type of articles you publish. I've included a recent sample of my writing as requested in your guidelines.

I've enclosed a SASE for your reply. If I haven't heard from you in eight weeks, I'll follow up with a brief e-mail. I look forward to hearing from you soon.

Sincerely,


Linda Akins
Street
City and State
Phone Number
E-mail Address

This query seems to present at least four possible articles. The first is about the general history of the RCMP; two are on personal profiles (one about George Richards and the other about Frank Keller); and the last on the horses used by the RCMP. And these are only four of the many potential topics lurking in this query (homeland security, women in the RCMP, etc.).

Since the author is interested in sending a query that involves the RCMP to *Texas Highways*, she needs to identify one clear topic and express it in her query. Perhaps she could focus on one particular Texas city, and then explore two places in that city where the RCMP is commonly seen. Once she has identified the city, preferably one tourists visit, she should include facts about the location, why she chose it, and what tourists can see—including the RCMP. This is where the author can mention who the RCMP is, why tourists would see the RCMP at this location, etc. (This is the scenario used in the revised query letter.)

The author also may want to consider putting her RCMP information into a sidebar that accompanies the larger article. (First, however, she should confirm that *Texas Highways* does run sidebars with its articles.) Sidebars are the optimal place to include additional information about a topic that's covered within an article.

It's essential to thoroughly research your intended market before submitting a query letter. One look at the submission guidelines for *Texas Highways* shows that this proposed article may be a tough sell for the publication. The guidelines also reveal that articles in the magazine run between 1,200 and 2,000 words. When proposing an article to any publication, you need to adhere to specified word count requirements.

As mentioned earlier, this author touches on a number of potential articles in her query letter that would likely be appropriate for *Texas Highways* and numerous other publications. All she needs to do now is focus her topic and research her market.

# Your Turn!

Keep your magazine topic focused by applying the following tips to your work:

**1.** Using different colored pens, go through your query letter and underline places where you see more than one potential story.

**2.** How many potential topics did you find? If you found more than one, it's time to rethink your intended topic. Remember that your query letter should focus solely on your proposed topic. If more than one topic is presented, editors may think that you haven't taken the time to develop your idea and simply discard your query.

**3.** Now, go through your query and underline any information that does not contribute to the sale of the article you're proposing. As seen in the above query, the author mentions that she would include quotes from the members of the musical group PHISH, who use RCMP services at their concerts. This is information that does not help sell the article. If the author chooses to include such quotes in her article, that's fine, but mentioning it now does nothing to help her sell the idea.

# chapter 24

# Nonfiction Books

No matter how good your book is, you can't sell it if you can't get an agent to read it. But unless you've got a personal contact, getting an agent to read it depends on your query letter. That single page may be the most important piece of writing you'll ever do.

Note: single page. Brevity is the heart of a good query letter. Agents (and this applies to acquisitions editors, as well) have to plow through thousands of queries a year, so yours will probably get skipped if it runs on for more than a page. Within that page, you have to accomplish a lot. Because many agents specialize (medical memoirs, historical novels with a female protagonist, dragon fantasy fiction), you first need to tell them what your book is about. This means you need to boil your rich, complex characters and multilayered story down to, say, two or three paragraphs. That's why the query letter is often harder to write than the book itself.

You also have to establish that you're talented enough to deliver the book you describe. If you have some specialized knowledge or unique experience, say so. If you have publishing credits, mention them.

**1** The agent doesn't really need to know how well Paul Ferris took notes. The agent will assume the book is based on the author's experiences.

**2** Except for the cobra in the backyard, none of these are particularly Burmese details. The birth of a child and a one-engine plane landing are exciting no matter where they happen. The author needs something that brings this specific exotic locale to life (see the revised query for suggestions).

**3** This paragraph repeats that Burma is isolated and mysterious. The author should establish that in the first paragraph, before he introduces his book.

**4** If publishing credits are worth noting, they're worth putting in the main body of the letter.

Original Query Letter

Paul Ferris
Street
Town
Phone

Date
Agent
Street
Town

Dear [Insert Name],

The country of Burma—now called Myanmar—is still a mystery. Few books have been written about it since World War II. I lived there with my family for three years—from 1962 to 1965.

**①** My book is called *Burma Journal* and is based on the 70,000 word journal I kept while working as the communications officer at the American Embassy in Rangoon. It concentrates on the humor, frustrations and joys of living in a country where men wear skirts and women smoke cigars. It also covers my two trips to the fabled city of Mandalay.

**②** Watching my fourth son as he was born in a local hospital was a joy. Not so joyous was a cobra snake in our yard. Or the one-engine landing of a DC-3 on a remote dirt airstrip or having to boil all our drinking water for 20 minutes. Those were just a few of the tribulations that plagued us, not to mention the actual requirement to have current bubonic plague shots for everyone in the family.

Aside from the people who enjoy reading about remote countries and parents who have trouble coping with grass snakes, let alone cobras, there are many who'll recall Dr. Gordon Spifler Seagrave's two books, *Burma Surgeon* and *Return of the Burma Surgeon*. Others will recall the gentle Burmese statesman, U Thant, who was Secretary General of the United Nations from 1961 to 1971.

**③** Recent books about Burma are either travel guides or about the current political situation. Few Americans have lived in Burma since the current government came to power in March of 1962. No one has written about daily life for an American family living there.

Would you like to see a sample chapter? You can read the first 2,500 words by going to: www.writersgalore.com. Click on BOOK GENRE, then on TRAVEL, then on BURMA JOURNAL.

Cordially,


Paul Ferris

**④** PS: I have published short, nonfiction in *GRIT*, *Growing Child*, *Milwaukee Journal*, *American Statesman*, *Tropical Fish Hobbyist*, *Selling Power*, *Lutheran Journal* and other magazines.

Revised Query Letter

Paul Ferris
Street
Town
Phone

Date
Agent
Street
Town

Dear [Insert Name],

Despite a host of available travel guides, the country of
Burma—now called Myanmar—is still largely a mystery. The travel
guides describe routine attractions, but tourists after adventure don't just want a list of landmarks. They're hungry for
what Burmese life is really like—how long to boil the water
before you drink it, where to get your bubonic plague booster
shot, what to do with the cobra in the garden. The truth about
the country is hard to come by, because few Americans have
lived there since the Communists came to power in 1962.

I am one of the few. *Burma Journal* is based on my adventures
while working as the communications officer at the American
Embassy in Rangoon from 1962 to 1965. It chronicles the sights,
sounds and smells of everyday family life—the raucous all-night
party when the next-door neighbor's son entered a Buddhist
monastery, watching my own son born in a hospital while lizards
crawled the walls, a one-engine landing of a DC-3 on a remote
dirt airstrip, the monkeys stealing our lunch during a picnic
in the park.

During the decades of Communist and military rule, the country
itself changed only its name. My Burmese story is also a tale
of modern Myanmar. My visits to the fabled city of Mandalay
will intrigue the adventurous travelers who are currently buying *Lonely Planet: Myanmar (Burma)* by Michael Clark and Joe
Cummings. *Burma Journal* will also attract the armchair travelers who are reading *Myanmar (Burma)* by Caroline Courtauld and
Martin Morland.

I have been publishing nonfiction for fifteen years in periodicals such as *GRIT*, *Growing Child*, *Milwaukee Journal*, *American
Statesman*, *Tropical Fish Hobbyist*, *Selling Power*, and *Lutheran
Journal*. I can send either a sample chapter and synopsis, or
the complete manuscript. Or you can view a sample chapter at
www.writersgalore.com. Click on BOOK GENRE, then on TRAVEL,
then on BURMA JOURNAL.

Yours,

Paul Ferris

And because an agent's time is limited, offer to send either a sample chapter and synopsis, or the full manuscript. Do not send sample chapters with the query. Most agents consider that presumptuous. Also, be careful to raise expectations only as high as your manuscript can deliver. A slick sales pitch can get you read, but a disappointed agent is not likely to sign you.

Finally, if you have space, establish that there are people who will buy your book. The best approach is to compare and contrast your book to a publishing success, and the more successful the better. It's important to contrast as well as compare. Your book needs to be close enough to the successful book to appeal to the same audience ("It's just like Patrick O'Brian—"), but distinct enough not to compete directly with an established product ("—but with an American protagonist").

Writer Paul Ferris is on his way to fulfilling these criteria. The first paragraph of his query letter establishes the greatest strength of his story—showing everyday life in mysterious and exotic Burma/Myanmar. Then, in the next two paragraphs, he hints at some of the intriguing details his book will reveal. He compares his book with Gordon Spifler Seagrave's books but draws the distinction that his is more recent. He also offers the agent a convenient way to read sample chapters and mentions his writing credits. The broad outline is there.

The devil is in the details, starting with his description of the story. He maintains that he's solving the mystery of what Burma/Myanmar is like, but actually he's revealing what it was like four decades ago. This is now far enough into the past to be considered historic, and he needs to take this historic aspect into consideration.

Perhaps the story of his time there could illuminate some of the background to what was happening in the neighborhood at the time—i.e., the beginning of U.S. involvement in the Vietnam War or the turmoil in Tibet. Perhaps Burma/Myanmar, because of its isolation, hasn't changed in the last four decades. (For the sake of illustration, this is the angle presented in the rewrite.) But either way, he's stuck with a historical memoir. He needs to make it work for him.

The author also could more effectively set up his unique access to the mystery of Burmese everyday life. For instance, he mentions in his opening that few books have been written about it since World War II, then later mentions that few Americans have lived there since 1962. Surely these two concepts are related and belong together. He also should add the superficial guidebooks to the first paragraph. This stretches out the mystery enough to give readers' curiosity time to build. Then, he should hit readers with the solution to the mystery—i.e., his book—at the head of the second paragraph. Placing the solution in a separate paragraph highlights it a bit more.

In addition, he should compare himself to a more successful author. He may have been impressed (and justly) by Seagrave's books, but a quick check of the Internet shows that they're currently out of print. Clearly they're not reaching a wide readership today. And few people will remember U Thant. He might do better to focus on the popularity of those travel guides, which seem to be selling well, especially in an era of adventure vacations.

Another important point: The author's writing credits belong in the main body of the letter. Placing them in a postscript downplays them. He also needs to tease readers with more concrete details. For example, witnessing the birth of his son would have been an exhilarating experience even if it had taken place in Teaneck, New Jersey. In addition, the author needs to keep his language sharp and exciting, without slipping over the line into a hard sell.

Finally, referring agents to a Web site can be an effective way to convey sample chapters, but he should offer to mail a hard copy, as well. Many agents still prefer paper—it's easier on the eyes and handy to take to the beach. He should at least give them the option.

# Your Turn!

Improve your nonfiction query letter by applying the following tips to your work:

**1.** Does your query letter exceed one page in length? If so, cut and tighten until you've got it down to a page. Keep in mind that your query letter should ideally consist of only four or five paragraphs.

**2.** Take a look at the details you use to describe your story and yourself. Are they interesting? Evaluate your word choice. As demonstrated in the above critique, even something simple like replacing "experiences" with "adven-

tures" can make a story sound more intriguing.

**3.** Curiosity is key in a query letter. Ask a friend or critique group member who has not read your manuscript to read your query letter. Would he honestly want to read your book based on the letter? If not, try adding more details about your topic and your potential audience. You also should evaluate your word choice—tweaking a few key words could make all the difference.

# chapter 25

# Novels

ummarizing your work and introducing yourself to an agent can be
a daunting task—especially since
you're trying to make a favorable impres-
sion in the process. Writing a query letter to
someone you don't know personally can
feel like an imposition. Keep in mind that
it's part of an agent's job to look for new
clients to represent. She searches through
her mail to find that next great book. Why
couldn't it be yours?

This novel query letter by J. Sheldon Day
has a lot of compelling points: interesting
characters, plot twists, and psychological
suspense. But these elements are buried so
deeply in the query letter that an agent
could have trouble finding them. Also, the
tone of this query feels apologetic, as if the
writer feels he should explain himself or
start a conversation before jumping in and
presenting the goods.

Think of yourself as a salesman. If you're
going to buy a car, you don't want the salesman to spend an hour telling you what *he*
wants in a car. Likewise, you'd probably
become a bit skeptical if he started using big
adjectives to praise the car like "riveting,"
"intriguing," and "mysterious." You'd rather

**1** Addressing an agent by her
first name can seem presumptuous to some agents. It's safer to
stick with "Dear Ms. Smith."

**2** An agent needs to be immediately captivated by your query
letter. Lengthy introductions won't
help you accomplish this. Your compelling story will.

**3** Avoid gimmicks. An explanation of the process you went
through to write the book could
make agents suspicious that you
aren't writing something you're passionate about.

**4** This sounds as if the author
gets preachy in his book and
that his theme won't be subtle. He
should cut the first two paragraphs
and jump right in with the story.

**5** This concept is a little too big
to immediately digest without
first having a basic understanding of
the story line. The author should
begin first with characters and main
conflict.

Original Query Letter

Jane Smith
JANE SMITH LITERARY AGENCY
1234 Writer's Row #500
Del Mar, CA 92014

**(1)** Dear Jane:  *Use the agent's full name.*

**(2)** As a reader, I need to be captivated immediately when I open a book for the first time. I simply don't have the patience to wade through a novel, chapter by chapter, hoping that it will eventually gain my interest. The author is irrelevant to me as long as I'm repeatedly persuaded to move from the bottom of one page to the top of the next.

**(3)** For this reason, I vigilantly laced every paragraph with a  *Watch out for gimmicks* healthy dose of humor, mystery, sexuality, intrigue, romance, adventure, or philosophy. In the unlikely event that these subjects fail to rivet the reader to the back of their chair,

**(4)** I threw in a few illustrations of high moralistic fortitude just to cover the bases.

**(5)** My 60,000-word story is about justice for victims of crime where the perpetrator escapes prosecution because of loopholes in the judicial process. Roth Cameron, a.k.a. Phoenix, assumes various disguises in his role as "vigilante for the people." According to Greek legend, the Phoenix bird consumed itself by fire every 500 years, and a new, young phoenix sprang from its ashes. It was a rebirth of sorts. Likewise, with each killing, Phoenix assumes a new identity. As one identity dies, another

**(6)** is reborn. Kelly Saunders, a journalist for the *Los Angeles*  *Introduce the main character sooner.* *Chronicle*, uses the vast resources of the newspaper to track down the killer for hire. Though Roth and Kelly appear to be at opposite ends of the personality/morality spectrum—the read-

**(7)** er is (stunned) when it is learned that they are the same person.  *Don't presume your readers will be stunned.*

**(8)** I am now actively seeking a contract with a publisher. I have enclosed the first few chapters of my novel in the hope that

**(9)** my writing style will prompt you to turn the pages.  *No SASE?*

**(10)** Thanks for your time and consideration.

Sincerely,

**(11)** J. Sheldon Day  *Include your contact information.*

Revised Query Letter

May 30, 2002

Jane Smith
JANE SMITH LITERARY AGENCY
1234 Writer's Row #500
Del Mar, CA 92014

Dear Ms. Smith:

In his quest to capture a vigilante hit man, Kelly Saunders, a top-notch journalist for the *Los Angeles Chronicle*, fears he is losing his sanity as he tracks down a killer he sees in his dreams. His unsympathetic girlfriend, his overweight dog, and a boss with no sense of humor begin to push him, page by page, right over the edge. As he gets closer and closer to the killer, he begins to question his own identity.

I am currently seeking representation for my 65,000-word manuscript, titled THE PHOENIX PRINCIPLE. I have spent the last several years researching Dissociative Identity Disorder (spending most of my free time with a woman who specialized in ascertaining its prevalence, familial patterns, causes, and treatments). In December of 1999, I signed a book agreement with a reputable publisher, but due to the publisher's failing health, the contract has been cancelled.

Your agency appeals to me because of your interest in commercial thriller/mysteries (my story mirrors the psychological insights of Thomas Harris and the judicial intrigue and narrative style of Scott Turow) and for the reputation you've established for representing authors who have a passion for excellence and commitment.

I would be happy to submit the first of three manuscripts in this series upon request. Thank you for your time and consideration.

Sincerely,


J. Sheldon Day
Street
City and State
Phone Number
E-mail Address

**6** The main character is buried at the bottom of the paragraph. The author should present Kelly first and then state his goal. The character's obstacle is that he's becoming obsessed with the case and losing his sanity. This must be presented clearly and concisely.

**7** Don't presume to know the reader will be "stunned." Simply present the stunning plot twist and allow the agent to decide if it's startling, surprising, or stunning.

**8** If you contact an agent, she'll realize your goal is to get a publishing contract. Instead, explain why you've targeted her for representation.

**9** Don't forget to include a SASE for the agent's reply.

**10** Thanking an agent for her time is always appropriate.

**11** Always include your contact information in your letterhead.

he just presented the facts and then let you take it for a test drive and see for yourself.

Similarly, an agent can only truly judge your work based on your writing. Your query letter's job is to present a quick pitch for your book and yourself—why you're qualified to write it—and to entice the agent to request your manuscript. The best way to impress an agent is to keep the query letter short, professional, and polite.

Be sure to operate from a position of strength and confidence without sounding boastful. To accomplish this, use your first paragraph to introduce your characters and the main story conflict your protagonist faces. Avoid lengthy explanations of the larger social implications of the storyline or excessively playing up the theme. Your story's theme should emerge naturally from the characters and story line. Allow readers to discover the theme without pointing it out. This will prevent your query from becoming bogged down with details.

Notice how the revised query letter cuts right to the chase with no gimmicks: It tells the agent who the protagonist is, what his goal is, and what his obstacles are. It also gives an intensifier—the protagonist's slipping sanity—as well. Note how with three concise sentences, the agent has a much clearer picture of what's going on.

Once you've presented the main idea of your story, give your credentials for writing the book. In this case, the author has left this information out of his query letter altogether. Has he done research about multiple personality disorder? What qualifies him to write about these characters or situations? The revised query tells the agent who the author is and what his qualifications are—and this is all done in two sentences.

Finally, let the agent know why you've chosen to contact her specifically. If you met her at a conference and were impressed by her workshop presentation, or if you read a book by one of the writers she represents, tell her how much you enjoy what she's doing and why.

Compare your work to the type of projects she handles and tell her why you think yours would be a good fit for both of you. In the revised query, the agent knows why the author has contacted her and that he's researched her agency. An agent's job can be thankless; Sincere praise can go a long way.

Now if only car salesmen could be so straightforward!

# Your Turn!

Add confidence to your novel query by applying the following tips to your work:

**1.** Go through your query letter and highlight every "I" or "me." If these appear in the first paragraph, delete or rewrite the sentence. The first part of your query should be about the book, not about you.

**2.** Search your query for any adjectives, and highlight them. Delete any adjectives that are too general. To decide if they aren't specific enough, use this sentence: After reading this book, every reader will be _____. Or: It is a/an _____ book with a/an _____ ending. If you can use the adjective comfortably in either sentence, mark it out. This includes astonished, exciting, beautiful, etc. But words such as overweight or unsympathetic can be left in place. Use your adjectives sparingly. If you have more than five, consider cutting some and keeping only the most essential.

**3.** Check your query for lists. If you have more than three items in succession, the reader will become too bogged down with information. Naming the elements of the story, such as "humor, mystery, sexuality, intrigue, romance, adventure, or philosophy," will weaken your query. Make sure your summary of the book *shows* these elements rather than lists them.

**4.** Check your query for praise or self-deprecation. Putting yourself down won't help your cause, nor will bragging. State the facts as neutrally as possible. Let your work speak for itself.

# chapter 26

# Mystery Novels

When writing genre fiction, it's important to follow the rules of the genre, so be sure you're familiar with the special requirements unique to yours. For instance, this mystery novel query from Thomas Dresser has an amateur sleuth as the main character. The first question an agent will have is, "What qualifies this amateur to effectively investigate a crime?" The agent also will want to know why the amateur sleuth wants to take this task upon herself instead of allowing the police to solve the crime. Anticipate these questions, and be sure to answer them in the query letter.

You can have an original character, a splashy setting, and a roller-coaster plot, but all of those have to fit into the small space of a query letter. To keep your query letter organized, first introduce the character; then the goal she hopes to achieve and why; then the obstacle standing in her way and how she plans to overcome it; and then hint at the resolution or theme.

In this case, the character is Sally. Her main goal is to solve a crime, but her motivation must be equally clear. Just saying that she wanted to have an affair with the mur-

**1** Make the opening sentence is compelling. Don't tell the agent what isn't there; tell her what is there. Delete the first sentence and jump right in with the second.

**2** It's best if you can keep the protagonist to one person. This is far less confusing, at least in the short space of a query letter.

**3** Right away the agent will have trouble sympathizing with the main character and her motivations. Readers are predisposed to dislike a woman considering an affair if they don't know her reason.

**4** The author needs to tell readers why the protagonist wants her goal. In this case, he needs to tell why Sally feels motivated to solve the crime. Did she love the murdered man? Is she just bored? Also, for mysteries with amateur sleuths, it's important to explain why the traditional means of justice won't work. Are the police corrupt? Is there a conspiracy?

```
                    Original Query Letter

May 4, 2002

Literary Agency
2002 Main Street
Anywhere, USA

Dear Ms. Agent,
```

**(1)** (There are few suspicious deaths on Martha's Vineyard.) When the
body of prominent banker Adrian Doyle is found in his bedroom,
Islanders assume an accident or at worst a suicide. No one
wants to think a murderer is loose on this tranquil Island.

**(2)** *Death on East Chop* explores Doyle's death through the eyes of a
neighbor couple, Sally and Bob Carlson. <u>Sally is a frustrated</u>
**(3)** <u>model who fantasized about an affair with Adrian Doyle.</u> When
she learns he is dead, she suspects foul play and (sets out to
**(4)** solve the crime.)
*Keep the focus on the protagonist*                    *Why?*
**(5)** <u>Bob has his own issues.</u> His response to the death is mitigated
by problems in the office. A number of minor characters revolve
**(6)** around one another as they avoid contact/and their own involvement in death.                    *leave out minor characters in a query letter.*

Martha's Vineyard has fewer than 20,000 inhabitants, but our
**(7)** summer population swells to 100,000, ~~many of whom enjoy reading~~
**(8)** ~~mysteries.~~ *Death on East Chop* brings <u>marital challenges</u> to the
murder mystery motif. Tourists, wash-ashores and natives (crave)
**(9)** a local tale that weaves suspense among needy housewives and
Island characters.                    *How does the author know this? Plus,*
*Focus on your experience as a writer.*              *this limits the book's audience.*

Experience as a teacher, health care administrator, bus driver
and freelance writer have exposed me to the vagaries of the
human condition. Previous publications include four non-fiction
**(10)** self-published regional booklets.
                    *Agents don't "publish" anything.*
**(11)** I understand your agency (publishes) local whodunits, a genre
with broad appeal. <u>Hence I solicit</u> you to represent me in the
**(12)** publication of my novel.    *Sounds stuffy.*

*Death on East Chop* is 60,000 words. A complete manuscript is
available.

```
Sincerely,


Thomas Dresser
Street
City and State
Phone Number
E-mail Address
```

Revised Query Letter

May 4, 2002

Literary Agency
2002 Main Street
Anywhere, USA

Dear Ms. Agent:

When prominent banker Adrian Doyle is found dead in the bedroom
of his oceanside mansion on Martha's Vineyard, islanders assume
it was an accident or—at worst—a suicide. No one wants to think
a murderer could be loose on this tranquil island, especially
Doyle's neighbors, Sally and Bob Carlson. Sally is a frustrated
model in a stale marriage and had fantasized about an affair
with Doyle. When she overhears a policeman muttering into his
cell phone that it was probably a murder, but that Adrian had
it coming so they're closing the case, Sally knows she'll never
have any peace until she solves the crime. With this new mission in life, Sally becomes a more passionate, alive person,
and her husband, Bob, isn't the only one to notice. Her new
vocation just might change her life and save her marriage—if
it doesn't get her killed first.

As a Martha's Vineyard native, I know all the most intriguing
island landmarks and types of people who visit and live here.
While there are fewer than 20,000 full-time inhabitants, our
summer population swells to 100,000, making this one of the
most compelling settings for a vacation—and the perfect place
for a murder mystery novel.

*Death on East Chop* is 60,000 words, and I would be delighted
to send a partial sample or the complete manuscript for your
consideration.

Sincerely,


Thomas Dresser
Street
City and Town
Phone Number
E-mail Address

**5** With Sally as the main character, the author should leave Bob's issues out of it, or else show him through Sally's eyes.

**6** It's unnecessary to mention minor characters in the query letter. Readers know that other characters or suspects will be involved.

**7** If you only have vague statistics leave them out. In this case, the population numbers are important, but the "many" who enjoy reading mysteries is not helpful.

**8** The author hints at theme, but he hasn't hinted at a resolution.

**9** This is vague and unsupported. How does the author know what they crave? Also, the author shouldn't limit his audience by supposing all of his readers will be locals. Don't limit a marketing plan to regional interest.

**10** Play up your credentials, but don't add fluff. In this case, the author has things in his favor: He's done freelance writing, and he lives in the region where his book is set—and it's a very popular region. There's no need to mention other occupations.

**11** Agents don't publish books; they represent authors to publishers.

**12** Unless you have a more specific reason for choosing an agent other than the fact that she represents your genre, leave it out.

dered man isn't enough of a reason. An agent needs to see how this passion is part of a deeper issue for the character, that it strikes a chord closer to her heart than a daydream left unfulfilled.

Another element of the plot is the stale marriage. Sally's husband is preoccupied, and she's daydreaming about having an affair. First, Sally's behavior must be justified to the reader in some way in order for her to be a sympathetic character. This plot element also will have to be resolved, so it's important to hint at the conclusion. Will she and her husband part ways amicably? Will she outgrow the marriage? Will they stay together? This part of the plot will play into the book's overall theme. As a subplot, it should reinforce the main plot or act as a counterpoint.

What sort of obstacle does the protagonist face? Are the police trying to stop her? Does the murderer still lurk somewhere on the island? Are the locals refusing to talk to her? Does someone want her dead? The obstacle she faces increases the intensity of her quest and makes the reader worry more about the character, which is a key ingredient for mysteries, thrillers, or horror novels.

To wrap up the plot summary, the author needs to hint at the resolution. Sally must find the killer, but how will she change as a person? How will her life be different once she's been through this experience? She should wiser or better for the experience, more grateful for her husband, or changed in some other personal way. This resolution will illustrate the book's theme.

A theme is not always a conscious choice by the writer, but if Sally and her husband are reconciled, it's an optimistic look at marriage. If Sally outgrows him and moves on to something more fulfilling, the theme involves personal growth and strength derived from independence.

By the time the author has taken all of these elements into consideration, you might expect the query letter to be several pages in length. However, you'll be surprised how at how briefly you can describe the protagonist, her goal, her obstacle, and the resolution. Each element needs only one or two sentences. You don't have to tell the whole plot or introduce all the minor characters. The goal here is to intrigue an agent and make her want to see what the book looks like in the flesh.

Finally, when mentioning your credentials, keep the upper hand by touting your strongest assets as a writer—no other past occupations are of importance here. Play up any knowledge you have that specifically pertains to your subject matter and your ability to write about it. In this instance, familiarity with the setting is a key selling point. But experience with forensic techniques, a family member who is a private detective, a friend on the police force, or other fact checkers who you've consulted for your book can all help you present a more professional, detail-perfect book.

## Your Turn!

Make sure your query is tightly focused by applying the following tips to your work:

**1.** Describe your character in one sentence. This should include her state of mind or situation at the beginning of the novel, before her evolution as a person. For example: Jennifer is in a wheelchair after an auto accident that nearly killed her, and sometimes she wishes she hadn't survived.

**2.** Now it's time to explain your character's goal and obstacle in one sentence. For example: Jennifer just wants to have a normal life, complete with romance, but who'd want to date a girl with her limited mobility

**3.** Give a hint at your character's resolution. For example: When Jennifer meets a special little girl named Alice, who was born without limbs, Jennifer begins to view her situation in a new light. Alice teaches Jennifer how to love and accept love, and gives her a new passion for helping others.

# chapter 27

# Romance Novels

A h, romance! The genre's voracious hunger for new books makes it a compelling choice for new writers. It's a relatively easier market for first-time writers to crack, and it has a strong readership base.

As avid readers of romance novels know, the romance market has different categories within the genre, and it's important to know where your book fits into it. In this case, Dorothy Ellis correctly describes her book as a paranormal romance. Once you know where your book fits into the market, it's time to compose the query letter.

One of the best ways to lay out a query letter's opening paragraph is with the journalist's five questions: Who? What? When? Where? Why? Here, the author's opening paragraph briefly covers the first two, but it doesn't delve into the last three questions. She states that a woman named Sarah Michaels has made a pact with a demon, but that's not enough. Now it's time to divulge a few more of the juicy details.

First, who is Sarah Michaels? How old is she? What occupation does she hold? An agent or editor needs to have an image of the character in order to care about her

1 Who is Sarah? The author needs to provide a short description before she tells the agent or editor more.

2 More details are needed here to prevent the story from sounding like a generic *The Devil & Daniel Webster* story line. What is the pact? Who is the demon?

3 Whoever reads this query will need to know who Sarah's best friend and his little brother are and what danger they're in before he can feel the protagonist's desperation to help them and understand why making the pact is necessary.

4 For the stakes to be high, the author needs to describe what Sarah is risking. Specifically, is Sarah going to hell for eternity if she loses, or is she forced to be the demon's mistress forever? These are two different consequences. Clarity is needed.

5 Joining a networking organization is always a good idea.

Original Query Letter

Dorothy Ellis
Street
City and State
Phone Number
E-mail Address

Jane Doe
[insert name of literary agency]
Street
City and Town

Dear Jane Doe:

*Who is Sarah?*

**(1)** (Sarah Michaels) has impulsively leapt into a year-long pact with

**(2)** (a demon skilled in seduction.) She didn't have time to think of

another, saner, way to save her (best friend and his little

**(3)** brother. Now she must resist the corruption of her body, her

**(4)** soul, and her heart . . . (or lose everything.) *Be clear about what is at stake.*

**(5)** Through my membership in Romance Writers of America, I know

**(6)** that you are looking for a paranormal romance. I have completed

**(7)** the novel described above. It is entitled, THE CORRUPTION, and

**(8)** is approximately 116,000 words long.

**(9)** (I have also submitted a query letter to three other agencies.)

If you are interested, please send your submission guidelines,

or a request to see the novel. Enclosed is a synopsis of the

**(10)** story, as well as a (self-addressed, stamped envelope) for your

**(11)** convenience. Thank you for your time and consideration. *Just use SASE.*

Sincerely,

Dorothy Ellis

*Add more details about these characters.*

Revised Query Letter

October 12, 2002

Jane Doe
[Literary Agency]
Street
City and Town

Dear Ms. Doe:

Sarah Michaels, a high-powered fashion designer in New York
City, doesn't realize how much she cares about her best friend,
Jonathan Smith, until a collapsing balcony leaves both him and
his little brother unconscious in the hospital.

Sitting next to Jonathan, this construction worker she's known
since grade school, Sarah realizes she'd give her soul to save
his life, and she swears this promise under her breath, never
imagining that a demon overheard her vow. When he materializes
in her dreams that night, Sarah keeps the bargain, making a
pact with him: Jonathan and his brother will be spared and will
continue to live if Sarah can resist the demon's seductions for
one year. If not, all of them are destined for an eternity of
hell, and Sarah will be the demon's mistress forever.

Sarah isn't allowed to tell anyone about this pact, and even as
her feelings for Jonathan grow, she can't risk letting him get
too close. Meanwhile, the handsome demon is wearing down her
defenses, sympathizing with her jealousy over Jon's new girlfriend and tempting her to forget him in favor of an eternity
of vengeful darkness.

Through my membership in Romance Writers of America, I know
that you specialize in paranormal romances. My novel, *The
Corruption*, is approximately 116,000 words long, and I would
love to submit it for your consideration. Enclosed are a synopsis and SASE. Thank you for your time and consideration.

Sincerely,


Dorothy Ellis
Street
City and Town
Phone Number
E-mail Address

**6** Knowing that the agent you're submitting to represents the type of work you write is imperative. Knowing where your work fits into the market makes this possible. This will prevent you from making inappropriate submissions.

**7** Don't use commas to offset this title. For books, it's best to italicize your title or underline it.

**8** Word count is important. Be sure yours is the right length for your chosen genre, and include this information in your query.

**9** There's no need to mention a multiple query submission.

**10** No need to write this out; SASE is quicker and takes up less space.

**11** Proofread carefully and check your spelling and grammar. There is no dash in "thank you." This may seem minor, but even the slightest of slips in the short space of a query letter may cause the agent to question your professionalism.

problems. Notice how the revised version of the query letter provides a much clearer picture of who Sarah and her best friend are. This also allows the receiving agent or editor to see exactly what is at stake for Sarah and what the consequences are if Sarah fails.

Once the author has provided this image, she needs to explain what Sarah is up against. There's a pact, but what kind of a pact is it? Does Sarah have to resist the demon's advances for one year? Or does she have to seduce a hundred men in one year?

The pact could be anything, but readers need to know this detail in order to feel the tone of the story. Is it a playful fantasy, or is this a dark, gothic novel?

After the tone has been established, the author can then reveal the world where this novel takes place. Romance novels often take place in the Victorian era or other romantic historical times. Therefore, it's crucial that the author mention if this novel takes place in modern times or in the past. This doesn't have to be stated overtly, but some clues must be given. If Sarah is described as an heiress to the Castle Vondervan, then it will be clear that this is a historical setting. But if Sarah is a copyeditor for one of the busiest magazines in New York City, then the story probably takes place in modern times.

The author then needs to describe where and when the story takes place. Is the setting an old Irish castle or a cramped New York apartment? Locale is one of the ingredients that make romance novels such a wonderful escape from everyday life. Even the time of day can be a key ingredient. Picture New Orleans in the daytime, with bustling crowds and musicians playing on street corners. Now picture the same place at night, with dark alleys and a night-time crowd. Therefore, if the demon appears to Sarah only during the night, this setting immediately becomes distinctive. (The revised query letter paints the novel as a modern-day romance that takes place in New York City.)

Most importantly, the author needs to focus on the why of the story. Sarah makes this pact because she can't think of a quicker, saner way to save two people very dear to her heart. But why is making this pact of any help? How does it save them? How does

Sarah know she can make this pact? (The revised query illustrates why Sarah makes the bargain in the first place and why she might not be able to win it.) Jealousy factors into the equation as a prominent obstacle. This is also likely to make the reader worry for Sarah, to sympathize with the pain she feels while watching someone she loves on his deathbed.

Since this is a romance novel, the author must present a definitive romantic angle. Is the romance between Sarah and the demon, or Sarah and her best friend? This must be very clear in the query letter. The agent or editor needs not only an image of Sarah, but also one of her love interest—all of

them if she has more than one and has to make a choice.

Once the opening paragraph is complete, the credentials should be mentioned. This author may not have any publications to mention, she has the right idea by mentioning her affiliation with the Romance Writers of America.

The final paragraph should be as brief as possible. Thank the agent or editor for her time, but don't disclose that you've sent out multiple queries. Agents know you will and stating the obvious is a waste of space. Only mention multiple submissions on the cover letter of the manuscript itself once a partial or complete sample is requested.

# Your Turn!

Show off your story's romantic side by applying the following tips to your work:

1. Check the opening paragraph of your query letter. Did you cover:
   - Who? Have you included a brief phrase to hint at your character's age or personality?
   - What? Is the main plot twist, the turning point of your story, featured prominently? What obstacles does the protagonist face? What are her goals?
   - When? Is it clear what era your story takes place?
   - Where? Does your setting have a compelling element you can feature in your query?
   - Why? What compels your characters to make the choices they do?

   - How? How does it accomplish their goals? What do they hope to gain? What is at stake?

2. Whether you write genre fiction or not, it's always a good idea to investigate the different guilds and organizations available for writers (see Appendix C for more on this subject). Visit the following Web sites for more information:
   - Romance Writers of America: www.rwanational.org
   - Science Fiction Writers of America: www.sfwa.org
   - Mystery Writers of America: www.mysterywriters.org
   - Horror Writers Association: www.horror.org

# chapter 28

# Children's Fiction

n editor has a few spare minutes to peruse her slush pile. She's got fifty-plus manuscripts on her shelf. She pulls out yours. You have about five seconds to make her want to read your manuscript. If your query doesn't grab her, there are plenty of others to consider.

That said, Meredyth Hiltz's query for *Vinnie's Watering Hole* starts off weak. Remember that you won't make an editor interested in your manuscript by telling her your name. Get right into describing the story. If you do a good job of that, an editor *will* be interested.

When this query letter finally gets into the description of the story—in the second paragraph—it's vague. What's a "flavorful" story? Who gathers at the watering hole? "Everyone" doesn't tell the editor enough. Do children gather there? Are the characters animals? What are the "amusing idiosyncrasies" each animal possesses after emerging from the watering hole? And—an important detail—who is Vinnie?

If the crux of *Vinnie's Watering Hole* is simply that animals visit the watering whole and transform, that's too slight for a publishable picture book manuscript. Do the

 **1** Include your name at the end of the letter. You should start off strong with an enticing description of your story.

**2** "Flavorful" is vague. The author needs to give details of the plot.

**3** Again, this description is vague. Who are the characters? Who is Vinnie? What are their idiosyncrasies?

**4** Don't give personal information that's not relevant to your story. Instead, tell the editor why your book is right for him.

 **5** This sentence doesn't give the editor any information, just the author's opinion.

**6** No need to share your hopes. Wrap up with a simple, "I look forward to hearing from you."

**7** Don't worry about illustrations in your query letter.

Original Query Letter

Street

City and State

Phone Number

E-mail Address

May 10, 2002

Meredith Mundy Wassinger, Editor

Dutton Children's Books

Penguin Putman Inc.

345 Hudson St.

New York NY 10014

Dear Ms. Wassinger,

Subject: Children's Picture Books

**1** My name is Meredyth Hiltz. I write you today about a children's picture book consisting of 537 words: *Vinnie's Watering Hole*.

*The descriptions are too vague.*

**2** *Vinnie's Watering Hole* is a flavorful childlike tale. The story is set, where everyone gathers, at Vinnie's watering hole. The

**3** characters emerge as a variety of unusual animals, each possessing amusing idiosyncrasies.

**4** Having had three children of my own, and five grandchildren; children's books have been a large part of my life. I believe

**5** my story, *Vinnie's Watering Hole*, will bring joy and laughter to any child's life. *Cut—the line doesn't provide any solid information.*

*Keep your closing simple: "I look forward to hearing from you."*

**6** It is my sincerest hope that you will find my story worthy of your time and publication. This picture book is <u>accessible with</u>

**7** <u>or without illustration.</u> I look forward to hearing from you in the near future.

Sincerely,

*— Don't mention illustrations in your query letter.*

Meredyth Hiltz

Revised Query Letter

May 10, 2002

Meredith Mundy Wassinger
Dutton Children's Books
Penguin Putnam Inc.
345 Hudson St.
New York, NY 10014

Dear Ms. Wassinger,

Imagine an elephant who can walk in the clouds; a lion who swims the backstroke; a monkey who uses the spring of his tale to bounce higher than the trees.

When the jungle animals drink from their usual watering hole, they suddenly emerge with newfound talents like these in my 537-word humorous picture book titled *Vinnie's Watering Hole* for readers ages 5 to 8. Vinnie, a trickster jungle snake, has enchanted the animals' favorite watering hole. And while at first the animals have fun with their new skills, the jungle becomes chaotic, Vinnie is stealing their food, and they realize they must come up with a plan to foil the snake and bring things back to normal in the jungle.

As a mother of three and grandmother of five, I've read tons of picture books over the years, including Dutton titles like *Big Bad Bunny* by Alan Durant and *Sun Dance, Water Dance* by Jonathan London. I think *Vinnie's Watering Hole*, full of humor and adventure, would fit well into your line of picture books.

I look forward to hearing from you. I've enclosed a SASE for your reply.

Sincerely,


Meredyth Hiltz
Street
Town and State
Phone Number
E-mail Address

"idiosyncrasies" cause problems for the animals? Does chaos ensue? Is magic involved? Do the animals try to change back to their original forms? Something needs to happen beyond the transforming; there must be a plot. There must be a beginning, middle, and end—even for a story that's only 537 words long.

It's nice that the writer of this query is a mother and a grandmother, but that doesn't qualify her to be a children's writer. If you don't have special qualifications, it's not necessary to come up with something. However, this author's experience reading children's books over the years can be presented as research. It's also a good idea to tell the editor why you chose him for your manuscript. Show him you're familiar with the books his company produces, and tell him why you think yours would fit in.

The third paragraph offers the writer's belief that her story "will bring joy and laughter into any child's life." How? Is it a humorous story? If so, say this in the beginning of the letter. Instead of mentioning "any child," how about giving a specific age level for the story. This is useful information for an editor considering your query.

The final paragraph of the query states the picture book is "accessible with or without illustration." This seems to indicate that the writer is offering to submit the story with illustrations if requested. Stop right there: Unless you are a professional illustrator, you should not try to provide illustrations. The editor and art director takes care of this element after a manuscript is accepted for publication. Writers need not worry about this aspect of their picture books—they should just concentrate on the writing.

# Your Turn!

Animate your picture book query by applying the following tips to your work:

**1.** Start by looking at your first paragraph. Do you dive right into your story, or do you get bogged down in your introduction? If you find that your first paragraph tells more about you than it does your story, try rewriting it. Remember: Your opening paragraph should be brief and intriguing. You can talk about yourself later.

**2.** Next take a look at your second paragraph. Does it paint a vivid picture of your story? Do you hint at plot and conflict? Have you provided detailed information about your characters? The goal here is to be specific. Include story details, but also identify your target age group. You need to provide the agent or editor with a clear understanding of your story. As always, however, brevity is essential.

**3.** Now that you've explained your story, it's time to tell a little bit about yourself. The third paragraph should provide information about your writing background, your qualifications, and why you've chosen to contact this particular agent or editor. Do you cover each of these areas?

**4.** It's finally time for the big sign-off. Resist the urge to plead for a response. Keep it simple—and remember to include a SASE.

# Query Letter Checklist

Keep these questions in mind as you revise or critique your query letter:

### Magazine Articles

✓ Is the letter addressed to a specific editor currently working on the publication?

✓ Does your query letter convey a sense of urgency, making it clear why the topic is important?

✓ Is your proposed topic well focused and concise?

✓ Does your letter state why the magazine is appropriate for an article on the queried topic?

✓ Do you include relevant publishing credits and any special experience or knowledge you may have about the subject?

### Nonfiction Books

✓ Do you describe your topic and its importance?

✓ Do you state why you are the best person to write this book? What is your experience with or background on the topic?

✓ Do you identify the book's target audience and how well competitive titles have sold?

✓ Do you offer to submit sample chapters or the completed manuscript?

### Novels

✓ Do you pique the agent's interest by including your novel's juiciest details? Remember: The *entire* plot is explored in the synopsis—not the query letter. (See Part VI for more on synopses.)

✓ Do you state why you are querying a specific agent or publishing house?

✓ Do you say that the entire manuscript is available upon request?

### All Query Letters

✓ Do you include you contact information (address, phone number, e-mail address)?

✓ Do you include your previous publishing credits?

✓ Do you specify that a SASE is enclosed?

# Novel Synopses

Thanks to that outstanding novel query letter, requests for a detailed synopsis are pouring in, and you're one step closer to fulfilling your dream of becoming a published author. Now all you have to do is iron out a few wrinkles in your synopsis, and you'll be set. A great synopsis, as you'll see in chapters twenty-nine through thirty-two, must do more than describe a story from start to finish. It must sell the story while simultaneously showing off your writing abilities. And, to up the stakes a bit more, all of this must be done in only a few pages.

Properly formatting a synopsis is one of the easiest tasks to master and something you should keep in mind from the outset. Use a one-inch margin on all sides, and align the text to the left. In the upper-left corner of the first page, include your name and contact information. In the upper-right corner, include your novel's genre, a complete word count, and the word "synopsis." Next, drop down about four lines, and center your novel's title. Drop down one more line, and begin the text. On each following page, include a header in the upper-left corner of the page that contains your last name, your novel's title, and the word "synopsis." In the upper-right corner, include the page number. As you'll see, most of the proposals included here deviate in one way or another from this format, but these lapses are easily fixed.

There are other stylistic elements that should be considered as well. However, it is important to remember that most of these points are not as important as the actual content. For example, in chapters thirty-two and thirty-three, the critiquing editor encourages authors to put character names in all capital letters for first references. The editor for chapters thirty-one and thirty-four doesn't specify this. You're seeing two different editorial approaches in action, and either way is acceptable. Will an agent discard your novel synopsis if you don't use all caps? No. But, using all caps for first references does help an agent better recognize when a new character is being introduced. Keep in mind, though, that it won't matter what style you use if the actual content is lacking. Focus on telling—and selling—your story. That is, after all, the purpose of a synopsis.

When you're critiquing a synopsis, it's essential to make sure the opening paragraph is strong. Avoid editorializing the story or offering up an analytical breakdown of the plot—that type of information should be included in your query letter. Instead, the opening paragraph should hook an agent into the story and introduce the main character. Keep an eye out for vague descriptive words that do little to bring the character or story to life.

Remember that a synopsis is your big chance to sell your story—make it count!

# chapter 29

# Purpose

**W**riting a novel synopsis is one of the most difficult tasks a writer faces—much more difficult, most novelists will agree, than writing the novel itself. A synopsis has three important goals: 1) It must sell the story to an agent or editor; 2) showcase the author's writing skills; 3) and lay out the plot in sufficient detail that the reader understands what the story is about—the whole story, including the ending.

In the *Oxygen* synopsis by Karen Kingsley, the story line is a bit fragmented, interrupted occasionally by the author's editorializing. The first and fourth paragraphs should be eliminated altogether. While the author's impulse to include this information is perfectly understandable, this kind of story description belongs in a query or cover letter—not in the synopsis.

Start off strong with the introduction of the protagonist—his name and a few vital statistics—and a succinct statement of the story problem. The author hits most of these points, but someone seeing this idea for the first time will need a clearer mental picture before delving into his story. Tell the agent or editor that "Peter Trotter is a mid-

**1** Write tight. Eliminate redundancies. Question every modifier. "Unthinkingly" is unnecessary here; "leaps headlong" implies the lack of consideration. The characters' nationalities have already been stated; the important information here is their geographic separation. Use active verb forms in the simple present tense instead of progressive forms ("lives" instead of "is living") to give the prose more punch.

**2** The Peter/Trish story line needs to be better supported with a fuller transition here. This also allows the elimination of the awkward transition at the beginning of the next paragraph.

**3** Ruthlessly root out mechanical and stylistic errors, as well as awkward wording. "Kid's" is not only grammatically incorrect (they have two children, so the correct possessive would be kids'), but the word itself is stylistically jarring based on the rest of the narrative. The phrase "which in England displeases both of them" also is awkward.

Oxygen/Kingsley/e-mail

OXYGEN

It's a story about personal responsibility—and the search for its parameters. *Oxygen* asks whether one's obligation to oneself not only supercedes our other obligations, but also provides the only means to deliver on them. *[delete]*

*Start here* ~~The story is about~~ Peter Trotter, *is a middle-aged* ~~an almost-divorced~~ Brit with a demanding job, *a failing marriage and* two children he adores ~~and the realization~~ ~~that~~ he's lived life by rote so far. *but* When he falls in love with an American ~~woman,~~ Trish Rayfield; for the first time, he begins to fall for himself as well. *awkward phrase*

~~As his marriage unravels and he negotiates an appropriate settlement with his~~ *Pete's* wife, Leah Trotter, who is not sure she wants ~~the~~ *a* divorce, although ~~it is equally clear~~ she is *clearly* not happy in the marriage; Peter has to decide whether he can bear to be a part-time parent. Are his children best served by a fractured family or an intact one, even if it is hopelessly dysfunctional? What is his responsibility to his insecure wife who has abandoned her own profession in support of the family? What is his responsibility to unearthing and fulfilling his own personal happiness? *Move this paragraph to the next page.*

The secondary plot looks at how women seek the balance in their lives between work and relationship that men (Peter) seem to take for granted, and discover that, for them balance is nearly, if not impossible, to achieve. So the woman with the strong heart follows her head, and the woman with the fine mind follows her marriage. Peter tries, but ultimately fails, to have it all. *Delete this paragraph. The author should focus on her main plotline.*

Peter meets Trish at a footwear conference. *Where?* They connect immediately, almost chemically. ~~And~~ although, ~~he~~ *Peter* is aware that he is too fragile (emotionally) to pursue a "real" relationship, **①** ~~unthinkingly~~ he leaps headlong into one. It is made all the more challenging by geography—he *lives* ~~is a Brit living~~ in London, she *lives* ~~is an American living~~ in Connecticut and *works* ~~working~~ in New

Oxygen/Kingsley/e-mail

York. ~~But~~ Between ~~his~~ frequent business trips, e-mail and massive telephone use, they forge a powerful attachment, against ~~both of their wishes. /good sense~~ their better judgment.

> Insert paragraph from the previous page here.

At the same time, Leah ~~is trying~~ struggles to manage two distressed children with a largely absentee father, and her own insecurity about how she will ~~manage should she get~~ survive ~~divorced and decide what, if anything, to do with her life.~~

~~At first, Leah clings~~ clinging to the notion that this separation ~~is~~ will be as temporary as the past three ~~were, and~~ Leah plans a family Christmas. Peter plays along, but does not cross the emotional barrier that separates them. His growing relationship with Trish has finally taken precedence; Peter knows he must end his marriage if he ever expects to be happy.

~~As Trish and Peter get closer and Leah and Peter separate further,~~ Peter and Leah begin the tricky negotiation of custody, housing and emotional dissolution, all through the not-so-fine haze of long-held anger and deep-seated resentments. ~~A~~ The one point of agreement between them is the quality of the ~~kid's~~ childrens' education, which in England displeases both of them. ~~The available resolutions to this issue become a major point of contention.~~ rephrase Given the professional opportunities in the US, the superior public school system, and his desire to be closer to Trish, ~~he~~ Peter begins to plant seeds, both at work and at home that he and the family should be reassigned Stateside.

There's only one problem with Peter's plan:
~~However, this requires staying in his marriage since~~ Leah ~~must~~ can only move to the US on Peter's work visa, which means keeping the marriage together. ~~In the meantime, Peter is working double-time trying to excel at the job he loves as he is distracted by his pressing personal concerns.~~ So a new dance is begun as Peter tries to further his relationship with Trish with the understanding that under this plan he cannot leave his marriage for some time; and he tries to separate, both legally and emotionally, from Leah, simultaneously persuading her to move the family to the US. — This doesn't make sense yet.

Peter's scheming ~~This~~ culminates in a Trotter family trip to the US, which proves disastrous, ~~as it~~ It finally dawns on Leah that the purpose of the trip is not rapprochement and a strengthening of the marriage.

Oxygen/Kingsley/e-mail

And Trish realizes that Peter intends to live ~~together as a~~ with his family once he makes the move, at least for a time.

**5** Upon their return to England, Peter and Leah finally confront the end of their marriage, ~~and agree that they will leave~~ After an emotional discussion they agree to leave England, ~~but it will be~~ and move to Dublin, nearer Leah's Irish home and the support of her family. Trish also agrees to make the move to Dublin ~~herself~~ in order to begin a life together with Peter.

~~As Leah is~~ overcome by her fear of being alone and abandoned, ~~she~~ Leah makes a final play to (move to Ireland and) keep the marriage together for the sake of the children. ~~It is at this time that~~ Peter finally tells Leah that he ~~has fallen~~ is in love with someone else and that he plans on bringing her to Dublin to live. Leah loses it entirely and informs Peter that he has just lost all rights to his children, a resolution that is **6** impossible for Peter. Ultimately, he agrees to Leah's threats and chooses to abandon his own wants except the need to be with his children.

*This has already been settled.*

*She can't take his rights away—she can only threaten to try.*

*What about Trish?*

**4** It's more important here to make it clear what Peter's plan is and what it means to both Leah and Trish. His problems at work aren't pivotal unless his job is threatened, which would, of course spoil his plans. If *that's* the case, then that point should be developed more fully here.

**5** This sentence is too long and complicated. It tries to say too much at once and ends up not saying enough.

**6** The author seems to have run out of steam. This unlikely and unappealing ending needs more motivation and a clearer resolution.

dle class, middle-aged Brit," or a "desperately ordinary Brit," or even a "gun-toting, psychotic Brit." Then she'll be a little more interested in his love life and his demanding job. To say that he is an "almost-divorced Brit" tells the reader very little. Plus, it doesn't describe the character; it describes his circumstances.

A synopsis is by definition a summary document. Because it is necessarily short, word choice is crucial. In what would now be the opening paragraph, for example, what does the author mean when she says that Peter has lived life "by rote"? "By rote" conjures up images of multiplication tables and poetry recitals. The reader could make an educated guess as to what the author is trying to say, but she shouldn't have to, and she might guess wrong. The last sentence in that paragraph is bothersome, too—"… he begins to fall for himself as well," is just, well, creepy. Maybe he learns to value himself or finds out what he's been missing. Never sacrifice clarity or risk misunderstanding for a clever turn of phrase.

The rest of this synopsis lays out the main plotline, as it should. There are a few places, though, where the events seem out of sequence. While the novel itself may take some liberties with chronology, the synopsis should follow a logical timeline, showing events—and their consequences—in the order they happen. This assures the agent or editor that the author can construct a coherent story and has worked out the plot "kinks." One potential kink in this story is Peter's "plan." It just isn't clear what he intends. Will he leave his marriage "after some time" in the States? If so, how does that prevent him from losing his children at that point?

The biggest problem with this synopsis is that the author may not be giving his characters a fair shake. When writing a summary, you have to be selective, and it's easy to leave out the wrong things. You need to include enough information to make the characters sympathetic and their actions— if not laudable—at least understandable. There are three main characters in this story, but only Peter comes close to being fully realized. Leah is a weak, shadowy character—making her sudden aggressive behavior at the end unbelievable. Trish is barely a character at all. She's a generic "other woman" willing to go to outrageous lengths to maintain a relationship that offers her very little in return. Peter, while partially redeemed by his apparent love for his children, comes off as a self-indulgent heel who wants to have his cake and eat it too. The story's conclusion—as presented in the synopsis—is hollow and unsatisfying. Certainly a happy ending is not a requirement, but resolution is, and it's simply not clear here how anything has changed for these characters.

The author needs to go back to the novel and extract those details that make the story worth telling and the characters worth reading about. A synopsis should present the best of what the novel has to offer. Don't force an editor or agent to make assumptions. Dig into your manuscript for the gems that are buried there—those are the cornerstones of an effective synopsis.

# Your Turn!

Clear up story line confusion in by applying the following tips to your work:

**1.** Before you start the synopsis, go back through your finished novel and write a one- or two-sentence summary of each chapter. Then, cross out transitions and chapters that deal only with minor subplots. This should leave you with a bare-bones outline.

**2.** Format is important. Unless a market listing specifies otherwise, double-space your synopsis. Indent paragraphs instead of leaving an extra line between them (the latter format is fine for a cover or query letter, but a synopsis should mimic the manuscript's format).

# chapter 30

# Format

efore getting into an evaluation of the synopsis for *As the Sparks Fly Upward*, by Charles W. Blaker, a word about the title. Rather than identifying this work as a suspense novel, *As the Sparks Fly Upward* might lead a bookstore browser to think "romance." Unless the writer can tie some element(s) to the current title early on in the synopsis, a new title should be considered.

The writer also should format his synopsis properly. No contact information other than the writer's name appears on the synopsis. There's also no indication of this manuscript's word count. Length is an important issue when manuscripts are being considered for publication.

This writer provides lots of information in the first sentence: the main character's name, his occupation and former occupation, and his interest in the death of a policeman. From that information-packed first sentence, however, the writer jumps to Ulare being "Rebuffed by the recently-promoted captain of detectives. ..." The receiving agent or editor does not yet know that Ulare starts his own investigation. By ending the first paragraph with the first sen-

**1** A note about format: A synopsis should ideally be kept to one double-spaced page—two or three double-spaced pages at the most. This is especially true for writers trying to get the attention of a busy agent or editor who is unfamiliar with their work. At the top of the first page, flush left, should be the writer's name, followed five or six lines down by the writer's complete contact information: address, phone number, fax number, and e-mail address. At the top of the first page, flush right, should be: the genre (line 1); word count (line 2); and the word "Synopsis" (line 3). The title should be centered in all caps six lines below the writer's contact information. The text of the synopsis begins four lines below the title.

**2** Use all caps as each character is mentioned for the first time.

**3** The "bizarre" nature of this murder seems to be important in Ulare's motivation to solve the murder, so be specific as to what makes this murder bizarre.

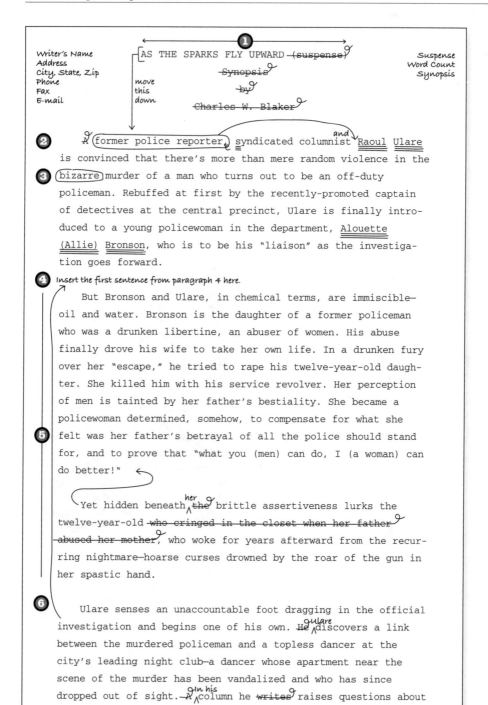

**① AS THE SPARKS FLY UPWARD** ~~(suspense)~~

~~Synopsis~~

~~by~~

~~Charles W. Blaker~~

Writer's Name
Address
City, State, Zip
Phone
Fax
E-mail

move this down

Suspense
Word Count
Synopsis

**②** A (former police reporter,) syndicated columnist *and* Raoul Ulare is convinced that there's more than mere random violence in the **③** bizarre murder of a man who turns out to be an off-duty policeman. Rebuffed at first by the recently-promoted captain of detectives at the central precinct, Ulare is finally introduced to a young policewoman in the department, Alouette (Allie) Bronson, who is to be his "liaison" as the investigation goes forward.

**④** Insert the first sentence from paragraph 4 here.

But Bronson and Ulare, in chemical terms, are immiscible—oil and water. Bronson is the daughter of a former policeman who was a drunken libertine, an abuser of women. His abuse finally drove his wife to take her own life. In a drunken fury over her "escape," he tried to rape his twelve-year-old daughter. She killed him with his service revolver. Her perception of men is tainted by her father's bestiality. She became a policewoman determined, somehow, to compensate for what she **⑤** felt was her father's betrayal of all the police should stand for, and to prove that "what you (men) can do, I (a woman) can do better!"

Yet hidden beneath *her* ~~the~~ brittle assertiveness lurks the twelve-year-old ~~who cringed in the closet when her father abused her mother~~, who woke for years afterward from the recurring nightmare—hoarse curses drowned by the roar of the gun in her spastic hand.

**⑥** Ulare senses an unaccountable foot dragging in the official investigation and begins one of his own. ~~He~~ *Ulare* discovers a link between the murdered policeman and a topless dancer at the city's leading night club—a dancer whose apartment near the scene of the murder has been vandalized and who has since dropped out of sight. ~~A~~ *In his* column he ~~writes~~ raises questions about

SPARKS, Synopsis, Blaker                    page 2

the official investigation and sparks the first of a series of "incidents," one of which touches his daughter, Cara—incidents he feels are subtle warnings to back off.

~~But~~ the column also brings a phone message from the dancer, telling Ulare, she wants to show him something the murdered policeman left with her for safekeeping, ~~and asking Ulare~~ to meet her at a small bar near the dock area. When ~~he~~ Ulare arrives, ~~he finds that~~ the dancer has already left with "the other news guy," according to the bartender. ~~He~~ Ulare wheedles the girl's temporary address—a sleazy hotel room—from the barman, searches it and finds a storage locker key behind a picture taped to the dresser mirror. Taking the key, he leaves just as a couple bouncers from the nightclub arrive and take the room apart.

**7**  (Convinced) that the murdered policeman had been part of a group of other officers involved in some illegal operation associated with the club, and that the evidence is in some storage locker, Ulare intensifies his investigation, (convincing) Bronson to help. The murder and their investigation foul up a [unclear] yearlong Drug Enforcement Agency "sting" as well as the local distributor's unloading operation.

*Reaction from whom?*

(Reaction is swift and violent.) Bronson is shortly the victim of a contrived auto accident ~~leaving~~ that leaves her in a coma; Cara is abducted and taken to a delivery freighter, where she is nearly raped before she escapes overboard as the freighter leaves port and heads for open water; Ulare is taken to an **8** isolated house nearby and tortured for information about the locker, while the "sting" operation goes into high gear (to salvage whatever of plans and people can be salvaged.) [unclear] In the end (they manage;) and Ulare, Cara, and Bronson recover health and *Who manages what?* sanity while discovering a new and (more mature relationship) *Be more specific.* with each other, a relationship that intensifies in the second novel of the trilogy, and creates its own problems as the trio are thrust into the middle of a case involving serial child abuse while getting some R&R in a Maine fishing village.

*While it's good to mention a series, this sentence needs to be reworked. As it's written, it implies that the serial child abuse also involves getting some R&R in a fishing village.*

**4** The hook, the most important element of the novel synopsis, is a succinct, compelling statement of who and what the novel is about. It should be contained in the first few sentences of the synopsis. Although this beginning is good, pulling the sentence from paragraph 4 makes it clear that the main character takes it upon himself to investigate.

**5** Tighten and combine paragraphs 2 and 3 into a one-paragraph character sketch of Bronson.

**6** Insert a one-paragraph character sketch of Ulare here. In this synopsis, the reader knows almost nothing about the main character or about his motivation.

**7** Since the synopsis is a short document, repetition of words becomes very obvious.

**8** It is unclear here who the bad guys are, and why. The plot must be laid out as succinctly and clearly as possible for the editor or agent reading the novel synopsis.

tence of the fourth paragraph, the agent or editor will get a more complete picture of what happens in the novel:

Syndicated columnist and former police reporter RAOUL ULARE is convinced there's more than mere random violence at play when an off-duty policeman is found murdered (what makes the murder "bizarre"?). Rebuffed at first by the recently-promoted captain of detectives at the central precinct, Ulare is introduced to ALOUETTE (ALLIE) BRONSON, a young policewoman who becomes his police liaison as the investigation continues. When Ulare senses an unaccountable foot dragging in the official investigation, he begins one of his own.

Notice that this slightly rewritten version of the hook is more specific about what makes the murder "bizarre." Was there a purple ribbon tied around the murdered officer's toe? Was a cryptic note written in lipstick found on his chest? The editor or agent reading the synopsis should have this type of information.

With all the information given in the first paragraph, there is nothing to indicate Ulare's motivation for wanting to solve this crime. Why is he so driven to get involved in the investigation, even after "incidents" become "subtle warnings to back off" and place his daughter in harm's way? The writer also needs to provide more information to round out Ulare's character. Is he single, divorced, widowed? Other than Ulare's being a man, what specifically makes him and Bronson so "immiscible"? One short paragraph should be room enough to give the agent or editor a better picture of this novel's main character.

The second and third paragraphs provide a good character sketch of Bronson, especially the motivation for the conflict between her and Ulare. What the reader learns about Bronson's relationship with her father and his brutality sets up reader expectations for her actions throughout the novel. However, the information in these paragraphs could be combined and tightened into one paragraph.

A little more information about Cara, including her age, will provide the reader with a more concrete image of the character. It is not altogether clear if the incident that "touches" Cara in the fourth paragraph is an early one in the action and happens before she is abducted in the last paragraph. It is also difficult to determine how important a role Cara plays in the novel.

Plot highlights must be presented in a concise, facts-only manner while including some interesting details. The plot is easy to follow until the sixth paragraph. Here, what happens and why things happen become unclear. It would appear that Ulare believes the murdered policeman was involved in an illegal operation. Are the "sting" and the "local distributor's unloading operation" connected? If so, how? And who is the "local distributor"—distributor of what?

In the last paragraph it is still not clear what is going on. Why and from whom is reaction "swift and violent"? Is the police department so upset that their sting operation has been foiled that they try to harm or even kill Ulare, Bronson, and Cara? Is the police department corrupt? If it is not the police, then who are the people trying to kill Bronson in a car accident, abduct Cara, and torture Ulane? In a one- or two-page synopsis, an editor or agent must get an accurate picture of hundreds of manuscript pages. A synopsis should be short, but it also must be clear about what happens.

Also for clarity's sake, the author should be more specific about the "more mature relationship" that develops between Ulare and Bronson. Are there romantic implications, or is it just platonic friendship or mutual professional admiration?

It's good that the author mentions this is the first book in a trilogy. With mysteries, especially, most editors and agents like a manuscript with series potential.

# Your Turn!

Develop your plot points by applying the following tips to your work:

**1.** Write a one- to three-line "hook" for your novel. This will become or at least begin the first paragraph for your synopsis. Answering the following questions will help you create your hook:

- What is the title of your novel? Does it reflect what your novel is about?
- What is your main character's name?
- What is your main character's goal?
- What thing(s) and/or person(s) stand in the way of your character achieving that goal? (This is the conflict integral to your plot.)

**2.** Identify the primary "plot points" in your novel. Start with three: the first major action, the last major action, and the most important point of action or change between the beginning and the end. Then include only those additional points necessary to tell your story. These major plot points are essential to your story and become the ones that must be included in your synopsis.

**3.** Ask a friend or critique group member who has not read your novel to read your synopsis. Then ask him to tell you what your story is about. This will let you know whether an agent or editor reading your synopsis will get an accurate picture of what your novel is about.

# chapter 31

# Length

lthough the author of *Slightly Imperfect*, Dar Tomlinson, has included a cover page with her work, she should also include her contact information, the genre category, and the word count on the first page of her eleven-page synopsis ... which leads to the much debated subject of length. A synopsis should ideally be one to two pages in length, five pages at the most. Based on the first two pages of her synopsis that appear here, this author is a fine writer and should be able to condense her synopsis into no more than two double-spaced pages.

If *Slightly Imperfect* gets published and someone tries to pitch the movie rights in Hollywood, a one- to three-sentence "hook," also known as a "pitch," will be used to describe it to producers. While there are some people who suggest as much as one page of synopsis for every twenty-five pages of novel manuscript, most editors and agents just do not have time to read long synopses.

Also, as mentioned in chapter thirty, capitalize all names of characters when they appear for the first time, even those who are mentioned but deceased. There are a lot of

**1** The writer's name and contact information, the genre, and word count should be included in the correct format on page one.

**2** That Zac is Hispanic plays an important part in the plot of this story. This information is easily included in the first sentence of the "hook" of the first paragraph.

**3** The first paragraph should only include essential information. State the story in one to three compelling sentences.

**4** Always type character names in all caps the first time they are mentioned in the synopsis.

**5** Avoid ambiguous pronoun references. Easy character recognition is essential to understanding the plot.

Writer's Name
Address
City, State, Zip
Phone
Fax
e-mail

①

Suspense
Word Count
Synopsis

Synopsis

SLIGHTLY IMPERFECT

② ③ ④  ZAC ABRIENDO, a thirty-two-year-old Hispanic shrimp fisherman by trade, has sailed the world on a freighter for a year, mourning his divorce and the death of his young son, <u>Allie</u>. Zac's goal is to restore his marriage. ~~One month before his tour of duty ends~~, he meets VICTORIA MICHAELS, a ~~twenty-nine-year-old~~ mother of three, ~~in a Portofino piazza.~~

Victoria is sailing the Italian Riviera on a friend's yacht, rethinking her troubled marriage. Zac is jolted by the resemblance of her six-year-old son, MARCUS, to his dead son, Allie. Marcus is Hispanic. Victoria's other children, twins, blond Anglos like her, cast a mysterious slant to Marcus and Victoria's relationship. Victoria is spellbound by Zac's resemblance to someone she loved and lost, Marcus' father, <u>Tomas</u>

④ <u>Cordera</u>.

Plagued by a sense of knowing Victoria, Zac learns her home is Puerto San Miguel, Texas, a Galveston Bay fishing village neighboring his hometown of Ramona. Zac considers this a coincidence, as well as his resemblance to Cordera and Marcus' striking resemblance to Allie, and deems the meeting fate.

At dinner that night Zac learns why Victoria looks familiar. She was involved in a scandal in Puerto San Miguel five

⑤ years ago in which her cousin, in a jealous rage, murdered (her)
Victoria's?

SLIGHTLY IMPERFECT/Tomlinson

Hispanic lover, and attempted to murder her husband. Due to the scandal, Victoria's father, <u>Pierce Chandler</u>, withdrew from a lay-down senatorial race, her husband <u>Christian</u>, an Episcopal minister, lost his church, and Victoria and Christian separated. They reconciled after two years, but the marriage is in turmoil. The dead lover was the father of Marcus, whom <u>Victoria</u> adopted after the murder. ~~She has lived i~~ ̖*After her* self-imposed exile for five years, ̖*and* ~~but~~ hoping the scandal has waned, her goal is to return to Texas with Marcus to acquaint him with his Hispanic heritage.

Is Victoria Marcus's biological mother?

In turn Zac shares with Victoria the tragedy of his son being hit by a car when he chased a puppy into the street. (5) While recovering from his injuries, *the boy* ~~he~~ died of pneumonia. Zac has a seven-month-old daughter, <u>Angel</u>, whom he has never seen. Drawn to Marcus, Zac encourages Victoria to contact him upon her return to Texas and allow him to help impart Marcus's Hispanic heritage. Through Marcus, Zac hopes to amend past transgressions.

Back aboard the yacht, Victoria's hostess confronts her, reminding her she came on the cruise hoping to salvage her marriage, also warning her against a relationship based on Zac's resemblance to her dead lover. Victoria insists she is interested only in Zac befriending Marcus.

Victoria terminates the cruise and meets Christian in London, informing him of her decision to end the marriage. She returns to Puerto San Miguel to establish herself, Marcus, Alexander and Ariana in a historic hotel Marcus inherited from his father, Tomas Cordera.

Once home, Zac contacts his wife, <u>Maggie</u>, seeing Angel for the first time. He seeks forgiveness for his affair with a wealthy Anglo journalist, now dead, and absolution for Allie's death. The puppy Allie chased into the street was a gift from Zac's lover, <u>Carron</u>. Maggie still loves Zac, but based on pride, distrust, and scars from his former betrayal, she rejects reconciliation. Because of their mutual love for Angel, she agrees to an amicable association.

characters—both alive and deceased—in this novel, and the agent or editor reading this synopsis may have a difficult time remembering who each is. If each character is introduced in capital letters, it's easier to look back and be reminded of who they are.

Like many authors, this writer has found it necessary to include every little thing that happens in the novel. Anything other than the most important skeletal parts of the story is best left for the manuscript text. At best, what the author has now is a good outline of the novel, a chapter-by-chapter account of what happens. Some agents and editors might ask for an outline; some may ask for an outline to accompany the synopsis. But first they want to read a short synopsis.

As the "hook" in the first paragraph is now, it gives information the editor or agent does not need to know and leaves out information important to the plot. For instance, Zac's wife's name, MAGGIE, is not mentioned until the second page of the author's current synopsis, even though reconciliation with her is Zac's goal in this novel. Also, the author does not mention in the hook that Zac is Hispanic, a fact that plays prominently in the novel. The hook should include each of the following: the main character(s); what the main character wants to achieve; and what stands in the way of the main character's goal. Here's the basic information for this synopsis:

- Main Character: Zac Abriendo, a Hispanic shrimp fisherman.
- What Zac wants: to restore his marriage with his ex-wife, Maggie.
- What stands in Zac's way: his relationship with Victoria Michaels, whose marriage is also crumbling, and his feelings for her son, Marcus.

Based on this information, here's a three-sentence pitch:

ZAC ABRIENDO, a thirty-two-year-old Hispanic shrimp fisherman, has sailed the world on a freighter for a year, mourning his divorce and the death of his young son, ALLIE. His goal is to restore his marriage with his wife MAGGIE. Then he meets VICTORIA MICHAELS, mother of three, whose youngest, MARCUS, is the illegitimate son of her murdered lover and the image of Zac's dead son.

One final technical note: As the author condenses the synopsis for *Slightly Imperfect*, she should watch out for vague pronoun references. There are a lot of characters mentioned in this synopsis, and the agent or editor may not always recognize which pronoun refers to whom.

Condensed, however, this will be a strong synopsis to represent what promises to be a publishable manuscript.

# Your Turn!

Keep your synopsis tight by applying the following tips to your work:

**1.** Condense, condense, condense when writing your synopsis. After you write the first draft of your synopsis, go through and highlight each phrase or sentence that absolutely cannot be left out in the telling of your story. Then go through that highlighted draft and condense at least one more time until your synopsis is as tight and compelling as it can possibly be.

**2.** Once you've condensed as much as possible, go through your synopsis and highlight every pronoun you find. Is the character to whom each pronoun refers perfectly clear? Are there places where you should include a character's name instead to avoid any chance of mistaken identity?

**3.** Before you send your synopsis out, make sure it includes:

- A strong lead sentence that begins the hook of the first paragraph.
- Logical paragraph organization with smooth transitions between paragraphs.
- Concise expression of ideas with no repetition. Make sure you say exactly what you mean to say.
- Only those plot highlights necessary to tell your story. Try leaving out every plot point in your synopsis one at a time to see how much each deletion changes the telling of your story. If a deletion doesn't change the story, leave it out of the synopsis.
- Narrative writing in the present tense, even if your novel is told in past tense.
- Strong verbs. Use a noun, action verb format wherever possible.
- Minimal use of adjectives and adverbs.
- Correct punctuation, grammar, and spelling.
- The story's conclusion. The synopsis, although short, should always include how the story ends. Without that, a novel synopsis is incomplete.

# chapter 32

# Story

Overall, the synopsis for *The Losers Club*, by Lisa Schulman, is nicely written and professionally presented. It starts off strong, introducing the two main characters and hinting at the story problem. At the end of the second paragraph, though, the author includes descriptive material that should be cut and moved to a query/cover letter. Included here, it interrupts the flow of the story before it even gets properly started.

The author has employed a clever device to introduce her cast of characters while simultaneously giving clues about how the story will develop. It's not uncommon to include a separate "Cast of Characters" in a novel proposal, but the author has done a fine job of incorporating this cast into the synopsis itself. Not every story will lend itself to this approach, of course, but it works well here since it serves as Jared's "recruitment" list as well.

That said, however, more clarification of *The Losers Club* is needed before the characters are introduced. The author's original wording of "willing members include" makes it sound as if there are members other than the ones on the list. Plus, *willing*

**1** Dangling modifiers—both marked as point 1—need to be fixed. The first one, "Living on his own since he was 14," requires the subject of the following clause to be "Jared," not his "freedom from rules." Since his freedom is implicit in his living alone, it's easy to eliminate the offending phrase. The second one, "Without a … witness," followed by "Charlotte" as the subject of the main clause, implies that Charlotte—not the evidence—requires the witness. (In fact, the opposite is true—the last thing Charlotte needs is a witness.)

**2** There is no logical connection between these two sentences. A transition is needed; otherwise the reader may think Jared takes the group to the cemetery because of his lack of success with Charlotte.

members begs the question of *un*willing ones. Actually, including a character who turns down Jared's invitation is worth the author's consideration. It would crank up the conflict to have a character who recognizes something not so savory about this

Lisa Schulman

Street

City and State

Phone Number

E-mail Address


Synopsis


( **The Losers Club** ) *Title?*

by Lisa Schulman


When Charlotte Brody, a naive and lonely seventeen-year-old at Kennedy High, receives an invitation to join The Losers Club, she signs on for the "instant friendship" promised by the group's *charismatic* organizer, Jared Howe.

The Losers Club offers its members many benefits: companionship, an escape from boredom, and the unique opportunity "to teach a lesson" to those who have wronged them in the past.

In the name of justice, acts of resentment spiral into schemes that humiliate and terrify the bullies of their insulated world.

Friendships are born, enemies are identified, and love is ignited—all within the confines of The Losers Club itself. Charlotte struggles with a need to belong, the addictive lure of power, and a longing for someone who might not have her best interests at heart. She must control the course of her life before events take her down a path of remorse.

*This material belongs in the query or cover letter.*

*cut*

Jared selects four teenagers, more for their vulnerabilities than their strengths, to join him in The Losers Club. Willing members include: *The*

*This line, as it's worded now, implies that there are unwilling members, but there's no evidence of this in the synopsis.*

- JARED HOWE: A natural leader, Jared is intelligent, charming, and manipulative. Living on his own since he was 14, Jared's freedom from rules has led to a disregard for boundaries. He has had a few run-ins with the law, result-

*Fix dangling modifier.*

**1**

Schulman, synopsis for THE LOSERS CLUB, page 2

*This is redundant. Where else would he be the principal?*

*Make the threat stronger.*

ing in a ~~recommendation~~ *warning* by the principal ~~at Kennedy High~~ that Jared be ~~transferred~~ *will sent* to juvenile detention at the next sign of trouble. To keep his hands clean, Jared ~~unites the Club to do~~ *intends to coerce club members into doing* the dirty work for him in a dangerous *secret* plot he ~~keeps private.~~

- CHARLOTTE BRODY (POV): *overly* ~~P~~rotected by her adoptive parents, Charlotte has yet to *fully* experience ~~what~~ life ~~has to offer.~~ She holes up in her bedroom with her only friend, a viola that promises her a future far away from Kennedy High.

- ZOE CARPENTER: With a dad ~~that~~ *who* is black and a mom ~~that~~ *who* is white, Zoe doesn't fit into the racially-divided world of Kennedy High. Beautiful, funny, and defensive, she marches through life, dressed in army fatigues, with the hope that everyone will believe she prefers to be alone.

  *Be careful to avoid stereotypes.*

  *Does she just anticipate cruelty or has she experienced it? If she has, explain it.*

- NORA WALKER: Nora shields herself from (peer cruelty) with a self-righteous attitude that (deters) *deflects?* potential friendships. She has spent her life trying to please her parents after the suicide of her sister, ten years earlier. On track to be the class valedictorian, Nora won't let anyone get in her way.

- RICHARD MORRIS: Gay and painfully shy, Richie ~~Morris~~ is an outcast ~~with~~ *from* the homophobic ~~population at Kennedy High.~~ *student body* He is devoted to Jared, who has protected and listened to him for the past four years. His ~~ill-gotten~~ *unfortunate* nickname, "Psycho," comes from a misunderstood episode involving his father's gun collection and an alleged plan to obliterate a classroom of students.

At first, Charlotte's self-assigned role is to monitor ~~the "weakest link" among~~ the Club's members to prevent a breach of confidentiality. Each of ~~their livelihoods is~~ *them has something important* at stake, especially Charlotte~~'s.~~ She won't get an audition at the prestigious Barrymore School of Music if a single blemish appears on her record. Ironically, she ~~is~~ *becomes* the leading candidate for ~~the notorious label,~~ "weakest link," *herself* as her compassion makes it difficult *for her* to inflict (increasing) acts of cruelty on fellow students. Nevertheless, she continues to participate, high on a newfound sense of belonging.

Schulman, synopsis for THE LOSERS CLUB, page 3

*Under Jared's direction,*
The group quickly and flawlessly executes detailed plans against their foes. They vandalize the ~~gym~~ office of Madame Porova, a modern dance teacher who refused to give Nora better than a C-. Charlotte's own nemesis, Tiffany Miller, faces public humiliation on a Homecoming float. Dave Harper, a senior *Why else?* who tormented Richie ~~because of his sexuality~~, is attacked by fellow jocks after they find a love letter "proving" the *starting* ~~football~~ quarterback is a homosexual. *"football" is redundant here; why not pick a more descriptive modifier?*

But something is awry in the group's infrastructure. Jared detects Charlotte's discomfort with the goals of the Club. *Be more specific.* Their relationship (proceeds to the next level,) more out of Jared's desire to keep a close eye on Charlotte than his growing feelings for her. Despite a gut-level reluctance, Charlotte can't help but fall into Jared's trap of seduction. She faces a critical decision: will she blindly pursue what feels good, even if it means ignoring her conscience? When she uncovers a (dark secret in Jared's past,) Charlotte is forced to question his trusthiness. *Great hook! An agent will want to see more to find out what happens!*

*physical attraction?* *aren't*
**2** Charisma and (experience) ~~isn't~~ getting Jared as far as he had hoped with Charlotte. He leads the group to a local cemetery, supposedly for retribution against Zoe's worst enemy, a boy who taunts her about an embarrassing incident she would like to forget. Instead, The Losers Club comes face-to-face with Jared's secret plot. *There needs to be a transition between these two lines.*

The group discovers Principal Reid tied to a gravestone. A blindfold and earplugs prevent Reid from seeing or hearing the *explains that he* *and tries to convince* teenagers. Jared wants Reid dead, urging Richie to do the deed *But as Richie works up the courage to carry out Jared's revenge,* **3** with a large rock. ~~At the climax of the story,~~ Charlotte finds her voice, at last abandoning the passivity that has led to this moment. She persuades Richie to drop the weapon and abandon the crime in progress. ~~(Score one for Charlotte, but we aren't on the last page yet.)~~ *Pick a more descriptive verb—this one seems too casual.*

Zoe, Richie, and Charlotte (walk) away, informing the police of Reid's whereabouts from a cell phone. When sirens approach, Nora and Jared scatter, leaving Reid behind.
*evidence of*
Although the group meticulously buries ~~clues to~~ their *apparently* involvement, someone has figured it out. Principal Reid

*very nice introduction of additional conflict.*

Schulman, synopsis for THE LOSERS CLUB, page 4

receives an anonymous letter implicating Charlotte in the kid-

napping. Reid knows that more students ~~are~~ involved and tries
*[above: must be ~~g~~]*

to force Charlotte into a confession. When Charlotte reads the

letter, she discovers an alarming hint to the informer's iden-

tity. Only one person has a specific piece of knowledge
*[left margin: Nice!]* *[right margin: This should be stated earlier in the synopsis.]*

revealed in the note: Jared Howe.

Charlotte has little to lose if she admits guilt. (She has

**④** abandoned her dreams of Barrymore, after Jared astutely

observes that music is not her passion.) Still, if she confess-

es to her role, Reid won't stop until he has the names of

every involved student. ~~Charlotte is~~ haunted by a promise to
*[above: g]*

protect her friends through silence, ~~She~~ steadfastly denies all
*[above: = g Charlotte]*

**①** charges. Without a ~~physical~~ witness, Charlotte succeeds in hav-
*[inconclusive?]* *[above: corroborating g]* *[right: Watch dangling modifiers.]*

ing the (elusive) "evidence" thrown out. The case is dropped, and
*[above: must be]*

the members of The Losers Club will graduate as planned.

It is a shallow and painful victory for Charlotte. She must

end a burgeoning friendship with Nora Walker, who remains

unswervingly committed to the Club's mission—and to Jared. And

Charlotte can't forgive herself for being the instrument that

freed Jared from the consequences of his own actions. She fears

Jared's potential in society, as his powers of manipulation

grow unchecked.

The last chapter reveals a changed Charlotte. Although she

must live with the guilt of her actions, she has stood up for

her beliefs and prevented a violent crime. At last, it is grad-

uation day for the self-assured young woman, but her happiness

is tempered by a public display of affection between Nora and

Jared. Their passionate kiss is an unnerving reminder of a

longing ~~she~~ had to refuse.
*[above: Charlotte g]*

As Nora gives the valedictori~~an~~ address, Charlotte spots
*[above: y g]*

Jared, slowly stroking his chin a (physical sign) that she knows
*[above: gesture?]*

all too well: Jared Howe has already ~~left~~ the graduation cere-
*[above: forgotten]*

mony, ~~as~~ his mind races ahead, planning for another time.
*[below: g]*

*The ending doesn't satisfy.*

**3** This pivotal scene needs fleshing out (then the author wouldn't have to *say* it's the climax!). *Why* does Jared want Reid dead? There's got to be more to it than a vague threat. *How* does Jared get Richie so close to doing the deed? *How* does Charlotte convince him not to? Actually, this scene is not the novel's climax; the climax comes when Charlotte is forced to decide whether she will protect Jared or expose him.

**4** Parenthetical remarks have no place in a synopsis—the information is either important enough to include or it isn't. This bit, since it refers to something that happened earlier, should be moved to the place in the story where it actually happened. In fact, it might be appropriate material for the transition mentioned in point 2.

charismatic young man. Such a character might also come in handy later, when Charlotte needs an ally.

The author also should give some more thought to the club's name, especially since it doubles as the novel's title. Even if these characters have such low self-esteem that they think of themselves as "losers," wouldn't Jared try to build them up by giving the club a more inviting name? Clearly Jared (and the author) intends the name to be ironic, but that irony is perhaps too subtle to be implicit in the title. There's a risk that readers just won't connect with the word "loser." Words such as "outcast" or "outsider" have a certain rebel cache that teen readers might find more appealing. Or consider a name that more directly reflects the

club's ultimate mission—The Payback Club, for example.

The character list is strong, and the short descriptions are sufficient for a synopsis. There are enough supporting characters to generate subplots and conflict, but not so many that a young reader will become overwhelmed trying to keep track of everyone. There are serious and volatile themes evident here—racism, homophobia, suicide, seduction, violence. They must be handled with subtlety and sophistication. Stereotypes must be avoided at all costs.

The rest of the synopsis moves along smoothly, laying out the escalating events of the plot as well as developments in Charlotte's character and her relationship with Jared. The editorial suggestions made throughout these paragraphs are primarily related to tightening the prose and fine-tuning the language.

Diction—word choice—is especially important in a synopsis, where every word has to be as specific and forceful as possible. For example, a number of words appearing in the manuscript are circled—these are all words where the author just needs to be more specific or original. The teens wouldn't just "walk" away from the horrific scene in the cemetery—they'd run and stumble over fresh graves. Evidence that *eluded* the authorities wouldn't be available to throw away. The speech given by the valedictorian is a *valedictory* address; a "physical sign" is a *gesture*. Small tweaks in word choice, phrasing, and sentence structure can go a long way toward making a synopsis the succinct, compelling document it needs to be.

The author falls just short of selling this story in the last couple of paragraphs. This isn't a fault of the synopsis itself, but of the way the author intends to end the novel.

Charlotte's "shallow and painful" victory isn't a positive enough resolution, especially for a young adult story. It's fine for the ending to have some unhappy elements—Charlotte has made a difficult choice, after all, and sacrificed personal happiness for her convictions; all is not rosy.

But the story would be much stronger—and much more appealing to an editor or agent—if Charlotte found a way to bring Jared to justice without compromising her commitment to her friends. Surely she is clever enough to trip him up, make him reveal himself. At the very least, Jared should be exposed, even if he manages to evade prosecution and avoid punishment (setting up, as the author presumably intended, the *next* Jared story).

Young adult readers, a primarily female audience, will expect Charlotte to be—or become—a strong, smart, and resourceful heroine, someone they can admire and emulate. There's just no satisfaction in having her stop short of giving Jared his due, especially when she "can't forgive herself" for letting him get away—almost literally—with murder. Charlotte's regret at losing Jared's affections also is questionable. She should have grown enough to realize what a heel Jared is; she should feel sorry for Nora, not envy her. Girls will cheer at the end of this novel if Charlotte walks away with no regrets, leaving a diminished (if still dangerous) Jared in her wake.

# Your Turn!

Tighten up your young adult synopsis by applying the following tips to your work:

**1.** Ask a friend or critique group member who has not read your manuscript to read your synopsis and underline any lines that lack clarification. As in the above critique, vague points that evoke unintended questions in readers are distractions. Oftentimes, these small questions can be addressed by adding a single sentence.

**2.** Watch out for redundancies. Look over your synopsis, and highlight repetitive words or descriptions. In the preceding synopsis, for example, notice how many times the author repeated "Kennedy High" while describing her characters. By cutting down on such repetitions, the material stays fresher. Do you have similar redundancies in your work? If so, try replacing some or all of them with fresher words.

**3.** Next, make sure you have solid transitions in place. Don't jar an interested agent or editor out of your story by failing to properly link your scenes. Read your synopsis once again, this time focusing only on transitions. Are your sentences logically connected?

**4.** Finally, it's time to check the order in which you describe the events of your story. Again, as in the preceding synopsis, a sudden shift to an earlier incident can slow readers. If you find any events described out of sequence, move them to their proper places with the synopsis. You may even find that you can cut the material altogether.

# Novel Synopsis Checklist

Keep these questions in mind as you revise or critique your novel synopsis:

✓ Does the hook contain the core conflict of the novel?

✓ Does the synopsis include a character sketch for each of the main characters? Remember, these sketches should concentrate on characters' motivations, especially those that bring the characters into conflict with one another.

✓ Does the synopsis state the main character's goal? What does the main character want to accomplish? (This provides the motivation behind the character's actions.)

✓ Does the synopsis explain what is keeping the main character from achieving his goal? (This is the conflict integral to the plot.)

✓ Does the synopsis identify the novel's plot highlights? Hint: Begin by detailing the beginning and ending scenes, and one or two in the middle. These plot points should include only those necessary to make the primary plot hang together and conclude with a logical, even if unexpected, ending.

✓ Does the synopsis succinctly examine the novel's core conflict?

✓ Does the synopsis adequately explore the novel's conclusion?

# PART VII

# Nonfiction Proposals

**Y**our nonfiction query letter did its job, and an agent has requested a full proposal of your book. Now, before the panic sets in, take a deep breath, relax, and look over the next four chapters. You'll see that while a proposal may at first seem daunting, it's nothing a little research and development can't conquer! Because they require so many different components, nonfiction proposals can seem overwhelming—to both the writer and the critiquer. Once you recognize, however, that each section complements the one before it, you'll be able to improve your proposal with ease.

Here, you'll see several different sections of actual nonfiction proposals. Chapters thirty-three and thirty-four take a more comprehensive view, exploring how the cover page, overview, marketing analysis, author information, chapter outline, sample chapter or chapters, and relevant attachments come together to make up a complete proposal that supports and sells a book's unique topic. Proposals also are formatted in such a way as to provide a harried agent or editor with all the information she needs at just a glance. Each one-page section is short, focused, and direct. Use a one-inch margin on all sides. Starting with the overview, include a page number in the upper-right corner and a header in the upper left-corner. The header should consist of "Proposal: Your Book's Title."

Chapters thirty-five and thirty-six focus more on refining individual sections, like the specifications or marketing analysis sections. These last two chapters also include revised versions of the critiqued material. Here, you'll see how a section is developed to stand alone while simultaneously accentuating the proposal as a whole. By writing and/or revising each section with this in mind, you'll find it easier to develop a complete proposal that effectively pitches your book *and* demonstrates your writing ability.

When you're critiquing a proposal, remember to look for a sense of continuity as you move from section to section. Each part should be as specific as possible. Every sentence should offer concrete evidence of the book's need, its audience, its originality and marketability, and your ability as the author to produce the work. Use facts and figures to back up your claims—this is the ideal place to show off your business savvy. Research competing titles on the Internet. How are they selling? How will your book be different? This also isn't the time to be bashful about your prior writing achievements and other related work experience. Always remember that in the publishing business you're selling yourself as well as your idea.

# chapter 33

# Organization

ynne Weinberg and Marge Pellegrino, the authors behind *Inner Journeys: Writing Exercises for Personal Growth and Community Building* may have a salable book. But first they need to put their proposal into a form that can be easily digested by busy agents and editors.

Every proposal needs a cover letter; overview; marketing analysis; competitive analysis; author information; chapter outline; sample chapter or chapters; and attachments that support your case.

Each of these elements should start on its own page, with the name of the proposal in the upper left-hand corner and the pages numbered in the upper right-hand corner. That way, if the proposal gets circulated around the office, people can easily get things back into order or look at the section they need (the competitive analysis, for example). It's also best to double-space a proposal. That also leaves room for the editor or agent to make notes. Has a single-spaced proposal without numbers ever sold a book? Of course. But why start the game with a strike against you?

A proposal's cover letter simply reminds

**1** This section, along with those titled Value, Intended Audience, and Benefits, should be combined into one-page, double-spaced page—the overview. Author information should go here too.

**2** Provide more information. How many chapters are in Section One? What will they accomplish? In Section Two, list the short chapters by title and explain what rationale/theory, background, and material each will include.

**3** The Intended Audience section gets overly broad at the end. Check with professional organizations, government Web sites, and trade associations to get figures and statistics of people in the categories.

**4** When this section is moved into the overview, it needs to better explain how *Inner Journeys* helps accomplish this goal and how the book will reach its audience.

the editor or agent that she requested the proposal based on your query.

**Inner Journeys:**

**Writing Exercises for Personal Growth and Community Building**

**Purpose**

① *Inner Journeys* provides teachers, group facilitators, parents, and other professionals with an easy-to-use book of writing exercises. These dynamic techniques and activities:

- emotionally empower participants
- build teams
- increase a sense of community.

Clinical studies support the health benefits of writing about the negative as well as the positive. This book offers facilitators a step-by-step approach to stimulate the group process and participants' growth and insight.

*explain further*

**Table of contents**

② **Section One: Writing Exercises**

- Each exercise contains everything a facilitator needs to guide a group or individual through the writing exercises.
- Each group-tested experience includes the purpose, educational standards, step-by-step directions, essential and optional supplies, samples of participants writing, and bibliographical information.
- Whenever appropriate, suggested workshop combinations are noted and supplemental materials, handouts, and templates included.
- Organized by time, the exercises begin with short warm-ups and are followed by longer exercises like the enclosed *Heroes*.

This material comes from more than 48 years of combined experience of the authors' work with a variety of groups that include agency, corporate, private practice, school, and community set-

tings and groups as diverse as caregivers, at-risk youth, fos-
ter children, survivors of trauma and torture, writers, and
those interested in personal growth.

**② Section Two: Want More?**

Within this section readers will find short chapters discussing:

- Rationale and theory
- Background and development
- Material to build effective groups
- Journaling techniques
- Additional resources

**Value**

*This seems to over promise.*

Projecting our lives in writing provides a powerful tool to
nurture psychological and physiological health. This book
offers facilitators what they need to know to approach a group
confidently ~~with the exercises~~. Facilitators will experience
success in guiding participants through these tested activities.

The exercises will appeal to people who like to write as well
as seduce the reluctant writer.

Facilitators will learn simple ways to help everyone write suc-
cessfully and to develop:
- Strategies to strengthen their relationship with partici-
  pants
- New ways to encourage groups to think together
- Leadership skills
- Confidence in using writing as an adjunct therapeutic tool

Participants will thank facilitators for:
- Self-expression
- Insights
- Tools for change

- Validation
- Coping strategies

Teachers will discover that when students write about their own material, the conventions of writing are strengthened.

**3** ### Intended Audience

Social workers, therapists, school and community counselors, teachers, group facilitators, librarians, journal workshop leaders and individuals.

### Benefits

*vague*

**4** Journaling helps people cope, heal, deal, and push themselves forward. Professionals without the background and a comfort *awkward* level hesitate to use writing as a tool. This clear guide will bridge the gap for those without experience and help professionals already using journaling to broaden their repertoire.

Practical and easy to use, with step-by-step instruction, *Inner Journeys*'s group-tested workshops integrate powerful techniques into existing groups, classrooms and practices.

### Contemporary Theory, Research, and Application

*cited*

**5** A study ~~sited~~ in the April 14, 1999, *Journal of the American Medical Association* discussed scientific findings demonstrating the link between physiological health and writing. The power of writing for psychological health is well documented. Many psychotherapists already use journaling as an adjunct in their practices. Teachers and group facilitators know how writing builds self-esteem and a feeling of community. As a tool, writing helps people move and grow. Writing helps reveal and empower.

---

### Major Selling Points

*Inner Journeys* presents easy-to-use activities that include
tips to deal with challenges that crop up and bilingual samples
of writing from workshops, which broadens the audience base.   *too broad*
The examples and ideas <u>represent people as young as preschool-
ers, on up to seniors</u>. A proposed <u>spiral binding allows the
book to lie open which makes it comfortable to refer to</u> during
use.
                                            *awkward*

### Why Consumers Will Purchase This Book

                                    *What are they? How have they sold?*
While there are <u>books that offer journaling exercises</u> available, *Inner Journeys* is simple, easy to use and offers fresh,
new exercises developed through years of experience.

**Length:** Approximately 200 pages   *Give a word count instead.*

**Anticipated First Draft Completion Date:** September 2002

---

**5** This study focused specifically on journaling and arthritis. Look for newer, broader research.

**6** The authors should list journaling books that are similar to that being proposed and explain what makes *Inner Journeys* unique.

**7** Give a word count rather than a page length for your manuscript.

The actual overview should be no more than a page, double-spaced, beginning a third of the way down the page. It gives the big picture—what need the book meets, who's going to read the book, and why the author is the one to write it. The authors of *Inner Journeys* have included this information, just not in the right format. For example, the Purpose, Value, Intended Audience, and Why Consumers Will Purchase This Book sections should be incorporated into an overview page. A brief mention of the authors' credentials also should go here.

The marketing analysis describes the audience and outlines special sales opportunities. It's also the place to explain unique facets as worksheets or exercises. For *Inner Journeys*, the intended audience section begins very specifically, then becomes a bit too broad at the end. The authors should outline how many workshops they present each year and the average attendance at those workshops. The agent or editor also may find it helpful to know how many social workers, therapists, and counselors there are in the country (trade associations, magazine media kits, and the U.S. Labor Department would be sources for this information). The more quantifiable the size of the target audience, the better your chances for selling your work. Never say your book will appeal to everyone; that's just not possible.

The competitive analysis lists four or five books similar to the one you're proposing. You can find these at your local bookstore or an online bookstore. Avoid books listed online as out of print, or books that haven't been revised for five or more years. List each competitive book's title; the author; the publisher; the year it was first published; and what makes your book different.

The author information is all but absent from the *Inner Journeys* proposal. The authors should include the names of the groups with which they have worked. The authors also should include how and why they started the workshops, and how successful the workshops are today. Previous publishing experience and other speaking credentials should be listed here as well.

The chapter outline is just that: an explanation of what each chapter will contain.

The outline can be prepared as a single document or one page per chapter. For each chapter, explain what will be included—narrative, exercises, handouts, key benefits, etc. The agent or editor needs to see how the author's vision for the book will be carried out, even though that vision may change.

The sample chapter should read as you would expect it to read in the book itself. Although it's not reproduced it here, the *Inner Journeys* sample chapter consists of virtually no narrative, only sections of bulleted points such as Purpose, Time, Discuss, etc. An agent or editor is likely to find this approach choppy and jarring. The key is to make sure the sample chapter is complete, not simply an outline.

Finally, the attachments section is ideal for supporting material—columns written by the author(s), research buttressing the need for the book, and so on. Endorsements also belong under attachments in the back.

Remember that you know your book and its value more than any editor or publisher. If you want to see your book published, you need to communicate that value in a language and form any editor or publisher can understand.

# Your Turn!

Perfect each section of your proposal by applying the following tips to your work:

**1.** Based on the information above, create a four-chapter outline for *Inner Journeys*. The experience will help in crafting your own chapter outline.

**2.** Next combine information from the Value, Intended Audience, and Benefits sections, along with some author information, and create a one-page overview. Then, write the overview for your book.

**3.** Finally, visit an online bookstore and find four or five books on the topic of journaling that seem similar to *Inner Journeys*. Based on the information provided, explain how *Inner Journeys* differs from those books.

# chapter 34

# Overviews

hen putting a book proposal together, you want to try to get into the head of the agent or editor. What is he looking for in a proposal? In a nonfiction book, there are two things: 1) a marketable subject with a unique angle, and 2) a writer who can pull off not only the book but the promotion of the book once it's released.

The overview is the part of the proposal that will influence the sales and marketing people to give the editor the thumbs-up or thumbs-down. That said, it's crucial that author Karen Shepherd create an overview for *Buttons to Budgets, Everyday Living for the Microwave Generation* that promises specific reader benefits, and endless and tireless author promotion.

The author's subject hook is a grabber—readers will identify with the characters in the anecdotes. The purpose of the grabber is to quickly get readers' attention and then move on. In this case, the grabber goes on for four pages. The author should cut this at least in half. Most of this information will be covered in the first chapter anyway. Remember, the purpose of the overview is not to describe your book (you do that in

 This anecdotal lead works well for a subject hook, but the paragraph that follows seems out of place. It's merely restating the problem that the author already showed.

 Identifying the seven headings is good enough. An agent or editor can find the topics in the chapter outline.

 Combine this section with the examples that follow and shorten by at least half. This is all still subject hook, and if goes on too long, it's no longer a hook.

**4** Too verbose. Each should be one concise, clear statement.

**5** The selling handle should focus on content and format.

**6** If these teaching guides are separate from the book itself, list them under Spin-offs.

**7** How long will the book be? How long will it take to complete the manuscript?

*Buttons to Budgets, Everyday Living for the Microwave Generation*

Introduction

Overview

• At a business dinner in Charleston, South Carolina, a saleswoman invited her very sophisticated client and his wife to dinner to celebrate the signing of a large construction contract. The owner of the construction company insisted on going to dinner with the saleswoman. The saleswoman watched her commission disappear while her boss picked his teeth with fish bones, used a common expletive as five different parts of speech and used his napkin to wipe his mouth and blow his nose. The following day the contract was rescinded.

• Sean, a national merit scholar and junior at the University of Oklahoma, managed to obtain eleven credit cards despite his minimum wage, part-time job. Sean was finally forced to drop out of school and attempted to pay back his debts. A short time later, after telling his mother he felt like a failure and could not see a way out of his financial situation, he committed suicide.

• Lennie, one of twelve young men living at a Safe and Sober House—transitional housing for recovering alcoholics—waited eagerly for the monthly meal prepared by members of a nearby church. "It's the only time I get a home-cooked meal," he said. "I don't know how to cook, so I either microwave dinner or get fast food." Other house members agreed and cited the inability to cook and lack of financial skills as their biggest obstacles to living independently.

A noted etiquette teacher referred to the social graces of young Americans as "McManners," while the *Jump$tart Coalition for Personal Financial Literacy* labeled the majority of high school students "financial illiterates," and points to the rise in bankruptcies and overwhelming credit card debt among young people as evidence of their inability to handle their most basic finances.

What boorish table manners, credit card debt and microwaved meals have in common is the subject of *Buttons to Budgets,*

*Everyday Living for the Microwave Generation.* This book—a quick
reference guide for basic living—provides rudimentary information on a wide range of subjects. The subjects are grouped
under seven headings: kitchen tips, household tips, health
tips, skill tips, finance tips, safety tips and automotive
tips. The topics include buying pots and pans, planning to use
leftovers, shopping for grocery bargains, keeping ahead of the
daily clutter, how to sort laundry, performing CPR and the
**2** Heimlich maneuver, selecting a doctor, mealtime etiquette, making your time count, the true cost of installment buying, fire-
proofing your home, what to do in case of a natural disaster,
minimizing the damage from identity theft, limiting impulse
buying, understanding car insurance terms and automotive safety
tips.

Is this information needed? According to an article in the
*Detroit News*, "Many, many teens don't understand even the
basics of money management, from living within a budget and
using credit wisely to saving for the future." Pam Baugher, a
home economics teacher for 30 years, wrote for the *California*
**3** *Educator* that she is concerned about her sixth-graders' social
skills. Baugher has seen a dramatic change in her students.

"The knowledge base they used to have is not there,"
observes Baugher. "Even simple things—like manners—I have to
teach them to say 'please' and 'thank you' today, which I did-
n't have to do in the past."

According to Baugher, there was a time when teens—particularly girls—learned simple home management techniques, like how
to create a budget and how to shop wisely, in a home economics
class. The lessons would be practiced by doing household chores
and during weekly grocery shopping trips with their mothers.

Times have changed and in some schools home economics is no
longer taught, nor is it any easier for a teen to learn home
management at home. Today's parents are more likely to grab a
few grocery items on the way home from work rather than schedule a weekly shopping trip. Dinner is often fast food or ready-
made meals, time is considered more important than money, and
table manners don't really apply to a burger and fries.

For many older Americans the idea that anyone living in

modern times would lack basic social skills is unthinkable, but for the younger generations it is reality. Generation X, the children of the baby boomers, were the pioneer "latchkey kids." Many were raised in single-parent homes or with two working parents where time and interaction between the parent and child was at a premium. Often these children came home to an empty house and ate fast foods or ready-to-eat frozen foods or microwaved meals. Their entertainment focused around TV, the computer and video games—forms of solitary entertainment that did not require social skills.

Generation X'ers are now grown up and the parents of a new generation. Their children, labeled as "Generation Next," are second-generation latchkey kids and are learning the life skills, social graces and financial knowledge from their parents. In other words, modern parents are now not teaching their children the same life lessons that were not taught to them.

Some examples:

• According to recent studies, 81% of college freshmen have at least one credit card, with balances ranging from a low of $1,000 to over $10,000 and little knowledge of how to budget money. A University of Indiana administrator said, "We lose more students to credit card debt than to academic failure." A Georgetown University student complained, "We don't need another AIDS awareness program, but credit cards—that is the information that we need and don't get."

• Etiquette classes are experiencing a huge resurgence as young people lacking basic social skills enter a workforce demanding good manners during business meetings and meals.

• A recent study found the fastest growing segment of the grocery industry is the ready-made or quick-fix meals, even though the cost is prohibitive, savings in preparation time is minimal and the food is loaded with preservatives.

• Employers are faced with a young workforce believing they should have the same benefits and pay range as their parents. While minimum wage employers lament the lack of students willing to work summers, a college sophomore was quoted as saying his time was worth much more than the going rate. "I don't mean to be arrogant," he said, "but my time is worth more than nine or ten dollars an hour."

• Road rage and identity theft, two crimes virtually unknown even five years ago, are now major threats, yet few people have the knowledge of how to prevent or avoid these crimes, or what steps to take if they are victims.

• In 1997 the Louisiana legislature passed a bill designed to "help stem the drop-out rate, violence, rudeness and guns in public schools." The bill, authored by a state senator whose wife had quit her job as a schoolteacher, requires all public school students in the state to address public school employees as "Mr.," "Mrs.," or "Miss." They also must respond to adults with "yes sir," "yes ma'am," "no sir," "no ma'am." While many agree it is impossible to legislate manners, the fact that this bill was considered necessary highlights the widespread lack of social skills among school-age children.

**⑤** While it is obvious a book can never take the place of human contact or parental involvement, *Buttons to Budgets* provides a "first step" in some innovative ways. *Buttons* will be the first book to include:

• Expert advice from a variety of sources
• Short, bulleted information in an easy-to-read format
• Additional resources for further information on each subject
• One-liners to lighten the serious tone and connect with the reader
• Tabbed and spiral-bound pages for ease of use
• Erasable back cover for emergency and important numbers
**⑥** • Optional teaching guides for use in a classroom setting

This book is unique because it can be used not only for individual quick reference, but also as part of a broader learning experience. The 45-page teaching guides will be offered in versions appropriate for secular community education and for Christian outreach. **⑦** They will include suggestions and hands-on exercises for most of the subjects, particularly those dealing with job skills and finances. Since the information provided in *Buttons* is basic, the teaching guide is also simple and requires no special skills to be effective.

the outline), but to convince the sales and marketing committee that there is a need for your book and that you will work to make sure it sells once it's published.

If you had to state the subject of your book in one sentence, what would you say? In this case, the author claims that what "boorish table manners, credit card debt, and microwaved meals have in common is the subject" of her book, but she doesn't specify what that subject is. A "quick reference guide for basic living" is too broad and too vague. In addition, the author's selling handle includes a number of questionable items. For example, will her book really be the first to include "expert advice from a variety of sources" or "short, bulleted information in an easy-to-read format." Lots of books do this. Most of the items on the author's list also focus on format. While format is important, the selling handle should focus on content. For example:

My book is the first book to combine physical, emotional, financial, and household living skills into one volume with a referencing system that puts the information at the reader's fingertips.

The last item on the selling handle list is "optional teaching guides," but this is confusing. Aren't these guides separate from the book? This information should fall under a separate section called Spin-off Projects. What is needed here is the proposed length of *Buttons to Budgets*, as well as an estimate of how long it will take the author to finish the book. Usually, six to nine months should be enough time to complete a manuscript.

This book also lends itself to a special features section, which would follow next. This would include any sidebars, exercises, quizzes, charts—anything that would make your book more visually appealing.

When you write your overview, think like an editor. If you diligently keep the editor in mind as you go about your polishing and tweaking, you may have a contract in your future.

# Your Turn!

Enhance your overview by applying the following tips to your work:

**1.** Highlight your subject hook—the opening graphs of your overview that grab an agent or editor's interest. Do your opening lines sound interesting? Are they specific to your book's focus?

**2.** Now take a look at your selling handle. Do you offer any expert advice? Life lessons? Project instruction? Be specific—and honest.

**3.** New writers can gain credibility by getting an expert to write a foreword for their books. Is there anyone who can endorse your book? For *Buttons to Budgets*, the author should seek out a humanitarian, someone who is working to help single parents, former prisoners, immigrants—anyone in the book's target market—get his or her life on track. Make a list of possible experts who work in fields relevant to your book. Perhaps someone on your list would write a forward for your book.

# chapter 35

# Target Audience

While the *Follow Your Gut* proposal by Laurel A. Nelson needs help in several areas—for example, double-space everything, and don't tell a publisher to format the book in a certain way or to buy magazine ads to promote the work—amplification of two elements in particular is crucial to the proposal's success. The first is the need for the book. The second is why this writer is the person to write it.

The world is full of guidebooks with broad information and those that deal with restaurants on a regional basis. Is slicing the niche even further to vegetarian restaurants in Great Britain and Ireland feasible?

To prove it is, the author must buttress the proposal with facts and figures. How many vegetarians are there in the United States? The magazines listed as places to advertise the book may have such figures in their media kits. The author should call and ask for them. How many Americans travel each year to the countries in the book? Travel associations should have this information. (See how the revised overview and marketing analysis examples illustrate this. Also, note how this new information builds

**1** Show the breadth of ground covered in the book by listing the number of reviews, and show you've got some knowledge of the geography involved.

**2** Help the publisher or agent understand the size of the potential market. The more of this work that the writer does, the easier it is to sell a book.

on the author's original overview and target audience sections.)

The author is a self-described freelance writer, but she isn't specific about where she's been published. She may want to consider proposing an article on the best vegetarian restaurants in London, for example, to one of the magazines listed under her Suggested Marketing section. A track record of published magazine articles all relating to the proposed topic will make book publishers more comfortable with a project. Also, the author may want to consider teaming with a nutritionist or someone else on this book proposal in order to strengthen her credentials. If she does have signifi-

Proposal: Follow Your Gut                                        1

Original Overview and Marketing Analysis

**FOLLOW YOUR GUT:**

*The Ultimate Vegetarian Eating in Europe*

**OVERVIEW**

*Proof? Any numbers?*

These days, <u>more Americans than ever before</u> are on the right track to getting and staying fit. We are beginning to chuck our couch potato ways and are living our short lives to the fullest—which may include eating well and seeing the world before we die. Consequently, eating well may make it harder to see the world before we die.

While going abroad, today's modern travelers are (increasingly) finding it difficult to balance cultural experience and good food choices. For most vegetarians, a trip to Europe means art, culture, and a bag of chips (I mean, crisps) for dinner. Healthy ~~and~~ *or* vegetarian dining has been a staple of many European diets for centuries. Most guidebooks have yet to highlight this and continue to herd tourists into overrated, overpriced restaurants that cater to bland taste buds and fat wallets. Sure, most run-of-the-guidebook-mill restaurants may have one or two edible items on the menu, but why should anyone have such limited choice*s* while on the road?

The proposed work could not be more suitable for today's modern traveler. With many Americans weary of international travel, this special guidebook can make them feel more comfortable by providing unimaginable access to their favorite cuisine. Also, most seasoned travelers who are cashing in on low airfares want (and should have!) a complete, updated, and comprehensive guide during their visit.

*A marketing analysis should come next—not the "Competition" section. How many Americans are vegetarians? How many of these vegetarians travel abroad? Prove there's a need for this title.*

Proposal: Follow Your Gut                                    page 2

## COMPETITION

Right now, whole series of food travel guides are being developed. These range from nuts-and-bolts facts to essay collections. But they don't combine these styles to create a thorough guide with a humorous eye (or should I say stomach?) for gourmet travel that emphasizes vegetarian restaurants and local farmer's markets. It's time to develop (a series with Guts.)  *What other books would be included?*

Several books are riddled only with dry facts and restaurant reviews of countries or regions, such as Lonely Planet's two series, "Out to Eat" (reviews) and "World Food" (facts about regional food, but no restaurant reviews). Also, there are books that are city-specific, like Food Guides for Europe: the Food Lover's Guide to Paris by Patricia Wells. Although these are great food guides, they seem to include every kind of restaurant imaginable and are not marketed toward those who follow a vegetarian or even healthy lifestyle.

*Who published these titles? How successful are the titles?*

A guide that covers a lot of ground, like Europe on 10 Salads a Day by Mary Jane Edwards and Greg Edwards, does a good job concentrating on vegetarian travel, but it doesn't have mainstream appeal to people who may not fully subscribe to that way of life. Also, it does not provide enough detail on the food or restaurant selection of any one country in particular.

At the other end of the style spectrum are travel essays and memoirs, which don't specifically review restaurants and markets, but concentrate on European eating as an experience in itself. These include the Traveler's Tales series "Food," "The Adventure of Food," and "Her Fork in the Road." Even memoirs such as Frances Mayes' Under the Tucson Sun and Peter Mayle's French Lessons emphasize food as a main component of travel and cultural experience, ~~and are an enjoyable read~~ or but again they are not health-specific and lack restaurant information.

My guide would include both—a restaurant review that is disguised as an entertaining essay, with important facts that follow, such as price, location, etc. The Hamburgers' Paris Bistros is by far the most accessible guide to food and travel. It recounts each restaurant so thoroughly, I might later wonder if I've been there. Now if it only catered to vegetarians ...

Proposal: Follow Your Gut                                    page 3

## TARGET AUDIENCE

*Based on what?*

I believe this guidebook series will appeal to a wide range of travelers. Vegetarian eating doesn't just apply to the young backpacker crowd anymore, as it's becoming widely accepted as a beneficial lifestyle change that crosses socioeconomic boundaries. But I have yet to find a complete, updated, and comprehensive guide that appeals to everyone. I seek to fill this niche.

*This should be more specific.*

## SUGGESTED MARKETING

1. Print advertisements placed in travel and health magazines
   - Vegetarian: *Vegetarian Times, Veggie Life*
   - General health: *Health, Natural Health, Self*
   - Upscale travel: *Conde Nast Traveler, Travel & Leisure*
   - Budget travel: *Transitions Abroad, Big World, Frommer's Budget Travel*
   - Inflight magazines
2. Submit book for review
3. Place in regular bookstores, travel stores, natural food stores, travel agencies such as Council Travel that sell books
4. Press releases to health and vegetarian organizations
   - EarthSave, peta, North American Vegetarian Society
   - American Medical Association, Physicians Medical Research Council
5. Promote at travel, book and health fairs
6. Subsidiary rights potential
   - Selected essays excerpted in magazines or through newspaper syndicates

To coincide with the book's publication, book signings should be scheduled at mega bookstores and independent ones, such as Elliott Bay Books in Seattle, along with travel bookstores and possibly health stores.

Proposal: Follow Your Gut                                    1

### Revised Overview and Marketing Analysis

#### Overview

Imagine this: You don't eat red meat, and you find yourself
in Manchester, England, on a business trip. Do you tell your
dinner appointment that you're a vegetarian and ask him to pick
an appropriate restaurant, putting a chill on the meeting
before it starts, or do you pick through the edible parts of
yet another kidney pie?

**1** There's a third option. *Follow Your Gut: The Ultimate
Vegetarian Eating in Europe* provides reviews and listings
information for xxx restaurants from the tip of Scotland to the
cliffs of Dover (not to mention Wales and Ireland) at which
vegetarians can eat without apology or remorse.

The guidebook business is changing. While 40 years ago
there may not have been much out there beyond Michelin,
Fodor's, Frommer's, and AAA, today a plethora of special-inter-
est books are succeeding on topics ranging from traveling with
kids to food lovers' guides for specific cities to gay and les-
bian travel. Yet, to date, no major publisher is addressing the
special needs of vegetarians traveling in Europe. *Follow Your
Gut* will resonate with that audience.

## Marketing Analysis

**2** Vegetarians aren't just longhaired commune dwellers these days. *Vegetarian Times* magazine estimates XX percent of American adults consider themselves at least sometime vegetarians, eschewing red meat, all meat or dairy products. Membership in the National Association of Vegetarians in 2001 was at XXX,XXX, the highest ever with an increase of XX percent in the past XX years.

Vegetarians have disposable incomes and are likely to spend at least some share of their incomes on travel. The average subscribers to *Vegetarian Times* and *Veggie Life* have annual household incomes of $XX,XXX. The International Travel Association reports XX million Americans visited Great Britain and Ireland in 2000, the latest year for which figures are available. If *Vegetarian Times* is correct and XX percent of Americans consider themselves vegetarians, that means XX million American vegetarians annually travel to Great Britain and Ireland and could use the help *Follow Your Gut* will provide to identify acceptable dining experiences before they ever leave home.

cant experience in the restaurant review, cooking, or vegetarian community, then she should say so it in her proposal.

This is an intriguing idea, but it's important to keep the cart behind the horse. If the author is willing to establish some personal credentials in her subject area and do additional research to prove there's a viable market for the book, she'll be able to enhance her proposal.

# Your Turn!

Focus in on your target audience by applying the following tips to your work:

**1.** Make a list of the magazines that serve your book's target market. Call the ad sales departments and request media kits. Use the demographic information (market size, income, education level, and so forth) in the kits (with attribution) to bolster your case that there's a market for your book.

**2.** Take a hard look at your credentials to write your book. If you do not have a degree or extensive, credible experience in the area, write down five types of people who have those credentials. For example, if you wanted to write a book about angels, your list might read "theologists, mystics, artists, philosophy professors, people who've had near-death experiences." Learn more about these types of people via the Internet or library research. Determine the best fit for your book, and then begin looking within your chosen group for a potential co-author.

**3.** Put together a list of three magazines that would be appropriate for excerpts of your book once it is published. Query those magazines about writing an article on the topic, noting you are working on a book as well. Such contacts may help down the road with getting the book excerpted or reviewed by the publications.

# chapter 36

# Cover Letters

*he Poppie Book*—the story of a child who loses her grandfather and how she and her mother work together to honor the grandfather's memory—is a terrific idea and comes packaged in a professionally written proposal that demonstrates the book's marketability. Kudos to author Cindy B. Johnson!

Several elements make this proposal stand out: The author's credentials as a licensed clinical social worker; the information for parents, which offers activities to help a child understand and deal with grief; and the idea of creating a memory book for a departed loved one.

Notice how the revised cover letter is slanted a bit to play up those strengths. The revised cover letter also has some of the information that originally appeared in the Market section.

Here are a few additional suggestions for improving proposal cover letters:

- Each section—such as Specifications, Market, and Competing Titles—should appear on a separate piece of paper. Individual pages make it easier for an editor or agent to leaf through the package. You should put your name and your

**1** The number and the statement are striking. They represent the hook that should sell your book.

**2** The author's credentials for writing this book are excellent and need to be stated sooner.

**3** The author can sharpen the book's added value by emphasizing various ways parents can use it to help their children beyond reading them the story.

book's title on each page, and number the pages.

- Skip the Specifications section. Once the book is sold, you can share your ideas for illustrations and discuss ways to send the manuscript. There's no need to do so now.

- In the Market section, this author should get 2000 census figures for the number of children in the United States under the age of five. Unless she can better extrapolate the number of men who lose fathers to the number of men who have children in this age range, she may

Original Cover Letter and Overview

CINDY B. JOHNSON

May 15, 2002

Mr. Willem Meiners, Publisher
Erica House
P.O. Box 1109
Frederick, MD 21702

Dear Mr. Meiners:

*ital.* *The Poppie Book* is a story for children 3-8 years old, dealing with one of life's most difficult problems — death. Written in the first person, this story presents a child's experiences as she gets the news of her grandfather's illness, flies to the hospital with her mother, and then attends his funeral. After her grandfather's death, she struggles with her feelings regarding her loss. Her mother helps her create a *Poppie Book* *ital.* from old pictures of her and her grandfather together. This special book allows her to hold the memories of her grandfather and comfort her during the grieving process.

I wrote the story for my daughter, Erica, following the death of her grandfather. As a mother and a licensed clinical social worker, I wanted to help my daughter with her grief. The *ital.* *ital.* *Poppie Book* relates funeral details, as well as, emotional specifics I observed in my daughter following the death of her grandfather. I couldn't find these items in the children's books on death and dying presently available.

Many baby boomers have chosen to delay the birth of their children as I did myself. Our children face the death of their grandparents at a much earlier age than previous generations. *ital.* *The Poppie Book* is a tool other parents can use to help their own children deal with this loss.

My freelance writing has appeared in local and regional publi-*ital.* cations. *The Poppie Book* won second place in the 1999 Children's Inspirational Nonfiction Contest. I would like to send you a proposal and the complete 1,134-word manuscript. I look forward to your response. Thank you for your consideration.

Sincerely,

Cindy B. Johnson

Street • City and State • Zip
Phone • E-mail

Cindy B. Johnson, R. Ph., LCSW
Proposal: The Poppie Book

### OVERVIEW

An article in the May 16, 1999, edition of the *Denver Post* indicated that "many parents find it harder to talk to their children about death than sex, but a good picture book or novel can help." Stories about death and mourning can offer comfort to children not ready to talk. They can also open the doors to communication between children and their parents. I wrote *The Poppie Book* for my daughter following the death of her grandfather. As a licensed social worker, I wanted to help her process her grief. Written in the first person, *The Poppie Book* presents a child's experience as she gets the news of her grandfather's illness, flies to the hospital with her mother, and finally attends his funeral. After her grandfather's death, she struggles with her feelings regarding her loss. Her mother helps her create a *Poppie Book* from old pictures of her and her grandfather. *The Poppie Book* describes funeral details and recounts the emotions—sadness, anger, jealousy—the same feelings exhibited by my daughter following her grandfather's death. According to Mary Ann and James Ernswiler, the authors of *Guiding Your Child Through Grief*, approximately 3.5 million children are presently grieving the death of a parent. Even more are grieving the death of a grandparent. Millions of parents could use books like *The Poppie Book* to help their children make sense of the loss and move through the grief process.

*[Handwritten margin note: "Great information!"]*

Cindy B. Johnson, R. Ph., LCSW
Proposal: The Poppie Book

## SPECIFICATIONS

The Poppie Book is a picture book with 1,575 words for
children 3-8 years old. An illustrator could develop pictures
for the book from photographs that make up the actual Poppie
Book I created with my daughter. You can find a sample of
these photographs on page 16 of this proposal. The book begins
with a "Letter to Parents," written by the author, to explain
the contents and uses of the book. It ends with "Information
for Parents," that lists the signs and symptoms of grief in
children and ways to help. You can find the complete manuscript
on pages 9-15 of this proposal. The author typed The Poppie
Book in Microsoft Word 95. She can transfer the manuscript to
you through an e-mail attachment.

## MARKET

The Poppie Book is aimed at children 3-8 years of age
and their parents of all socioeconomic groups. At sometime during their lives, all children will have to deal with one of
life's most difficult problems—death. The Poppie Book can
help during their time of mourning.

According to the 1990 US Census Bureau, there are
approximately 29,498,195 baby boomer families. Many of these
baby boomers have chosen to delay the birth of their children.
Now our children face the death of their grandparents at a much
earlier and vulnerable age than previous generations.

*Great info.!*

Cindy B. Johnson, R. Ph., LCSW
Proposal: The Poppie Book

More than 1.5 million American men lose their fathers to death each year. Their children lose their grandfathers. These parents can use "The Poppie Book" as a tool to help their children deal with these losses.

## COMPETING TITLES

The Family Christian Bookstore's online inventory failed to provide any books on the subject of death, dying, and bereavement in children. A search through the stock of a local Family Christian Bookstore revealed the book *Balloons for Trevor* by Anne Good Cave. The author wrote the book when her son's best friend died.

The non-Christian book market produced only 11 books about a grandfather's death. Three of these books appeared similar to "The Poppie Book." *The Granddad Tree* by Trish Cooke relates the seasons of nature and the passage of human life.

After Granddad's death, this African-American family plants and nurtures an apple tree in his memory. In *Pearl's Marigold for Grandpa*, by Jane Breskin Zalben, Pearl keeps her grandfather's memory alive by growing marigolds as he did every year. *Gran-Gran's Best Trick* by Dwight Holden, MD, follows a young girl's experience with her grandfather's illness and death from cancer, and her struggle to gain something positive from the loss.

*How do these other books rank on Amazon? Who published them?*

"The Poppie Book" book differs from these three books because it is useful to both parents and children. The story describes funeral details. It recounts the emotional days following the death. Most important, it provides a tool—making a memory book—which parents can do with their children to help them deal with the loss of a loved one.

*Nice job of explaining how your book is different.*

Revised Cover Letter

Mr. Willem Meiners
Publisher
Erica House
P.O. Box 1109
Frederick, MD 21702

Dear Mr. Meiners,

**①** More than three million U.S. children [*What age?*] today are mourning the death of a grandparent [*In the past how many? Is the number higher now than it was ten or twenty years ago?*]. With baby boomers having delayed the start of their own families, more young children are losing their grandparents. Yet there's little information to guide parents on how to help their children at this difficult time.

**②** As a licensed clinical social worker, I looked without success for books to help my four-year-old daughter Erica through this time when my father died. That's why I've written *The Poppie Book*, written through Erica's eyes.

**③** *The Poppie Book* is more than a story. It provides a means by which parent and child may work through their grief via the creation of a memory book with photos of their lost loved one. It also includes a list of additional tools parents can use to help their children deal with loss.

*The Poppie Book* won second place in the Colorado Writers Fellowship's 1999 children's inspirational nonfiction writing competition. My work also has appeared in local and regional publications.

I look forward to your response. A self-addressed stamped envelope is enclosed.

Sincerely,

Cindy B. Johnson
Street
City and State
Phone Number
E-mail Address

want to skip that number. She's made an interesting point on children losing their grandparents at a younger age since many baby boomers delayed becoming parents.

- In the Competing Titles section, you always should include the name of each book's publisher, the year the book was first published, and it's rank at an online bookstore. This information helps the

publisher see that you understand the books yours will be up against. One special note about this particular proposal—the word the author wants is *secular*, not *non-Christian*.

Please do understand these are tweaks. The proposal as a whole is strong and well organized, and makes a good case for publication. Other writers should emulate it.

---

# Your Turn!

Perfect each section of your proposal by applying the following tips to your work:

**1.** List the ways in which readers will benefit from your nonfiction book. Select the two or three most compelling, and make sure they are stated clearly and concisely in your cover letter. If you can't come up with two or three direct benefits, it may be time to rethink your book's direction.

**2.** Think of five ways to quantify the number of people in your target audience. Magazine media kits and government Web sites, such as that of the U.S. Census Bureau, are gold mines for this sort of valuable information.

**3.** Go to the bookstore and buy three books that will appear on the same shelf as yours. Read them. What makes your book different and better? Write down the ways in which your book is superior to each of these three. Be specific—don't just write, "My book is better," or "That book is lousy." In what ways does your book better or uniquely meet the target audience's needs?

# Nonfiction Proposal Checklist

Keep these questions in mind as you revise or critique your nonfiction proposal:

✓ Does your proposal include all of the following sections: a cover letter; overview; marketing analysis; competitive analysis; author information; chapter outline; sample chapter; attachments?

✓ Does each section start on a new page?

✓ Does your overview address what need the book meets, who's going to read the book, and why you're the right person to write it? Does the overview exceed one-page in length?

✓ Does your marketing analysis identify realistic sales opportunities? Does it use concrete figures to portray the size of the target audience?

✓ Does your competitive analysis identify at least four or five competing titles? Does it include each competing title's author, publisher, date of first publication, and primary focus? (Remember not to include titles that are out of print in your list.) Does it address how your proposed title differs from—and is better than—the competition?

✓ Does your author information section address why you are the best person to write this book? Are your previous publishing credits included? Do you list your relevant work experience?

✓ Does your chapter outline offer a succinct explanation of what each chapter will address?

✓ Do your attachments provide adequate supporting material for the proposal?

# Appendices

# Critique Etiquette

He was nineteen years old, perhaps a bit young and no doubt too thin-skinned for the workshop. Here, after all, were veterans of the Iowa Writers' Workshop, faculty members from several prestigious creative writing programs, and published poets. But, having paid the price of admission, Brian had every right to be there, and he had every right to a supportive or at least considerate response to his work.

Instead, the workshop leader, after listening to one short poem, laid Brian flat. There was, in that critic's opinion, not a single redemptive word in that or any other of Brian's offerings, none of which the critic had seen. A few feeble attempts were made by other participants to save the situation, but the workshop leader cut them short, and Brian could not hear them anyway. He left the session, his thick manuscript in his sweating hand, and burned the notebook—all the poems he had ever written. Word has it that he has not written since.

That workshop leader should have been the one to be laid flat. Who knows what Brian, with a little encouragement, may have been capable of writing? Who knows what positive comments could have—and should have—been made?

Next time you are in a workshop or class and another writer is reading, think about this: What are we looking or listening for? What are we doing here anyway?

Unless the entire purpose of the gathering is to form a circle and pat each other on our backs, we are here to bring out the best in each of us. We are here to solve problems, to get feedback that will develop our ability to move from good to better to best. What should Brian's workshop colleagues have said? What can we say? Here are a few practical suggestions.

**1. Listen to the work.** Listen or look for words or phrases that catch your attention, that truly work in the poem or story being presented; look for words and phrases that serve as psychic adrenaline. Point them out to the writer; describe your reaction to those words or phrases or the whole piece. What mood did the piece create? What could you see, hear, smell, feel, taste, or sense? What was your general reaction; how do you feel about the piece?

**2. Ask questions.** Don't hesitate to ask questions or admit that you don't know quite how to feel or what to say. Confusion is a legitimate reaction, just the same as no reaction at all. In fact, a negative response may be just what the writer was longing for. Or you may ask to respond later, after you've heard what others have to say. Someone else may speak for you, or you may decide that you really didn't have anything to say anyway. Better any of these responses than to leave the writer wondering where everyone went.

**3. Listen to the group.** At some point, do listen to what other participants have to say, and do not argue if they have reactions different from yours. Reactions are bound to vary, and the writer has a right to know about those variations. Many theoreticians would say that a writer's goal should be to draw forth as many different and personal reactions as possible. That's what deliberate ambiguity is all about.

**4. Be specific.** If the piece triggered your imagination, suggest any ideas that were prompted—similar poems or stories, personal experiences of your own, analogies that the piece brought to mind. Refer to specifics that elicited these responses. If you have advice to offer, base it on something specific. For example, if the writer intended the poem to convey a soft, gentle tone but used the word "garbage," you might suggest that the word be changed to "litter" or even "debris," both of which sound softer. Or if you assumed that the main character was a twenty-year-old college student and she turned out to be a seventy-year-old male valet, you might suggest a little clarification or a few words of characterization.

**5. Paraphrase the point.** Paraphrase the point you think the writer was trying to make. It may even be effective to do this in the form of a question. This will allow the writer some wiggle room. It may also prevent you from sounding like you were absent when the message was delivered.

**6. Honor the owner.** Finally, it is always wise—and encouraging to the writer—to be reminded that the piece ultimately belongs to the writer, that critics' words should not be taken personally. You may not like the elastic bow encircling the poor little baby's head, but you know very well that the baby does not belong to you. The same goes for the "babies" presented by writers. The writer's name will appear as the author. You won't have to take the blame. Nor will you get the credit. Remember that old cliché: As you treat your fellow workshop or critique group members, so will you (usually) be treated. In short, show some respect.

## When Your Work Is Being Critiqued

Writers want to be read. Face it, with the possible exception of those late-night journal entries, you crave feedback on your writing efforts. Your first audience is likely to be a friend, spouse, or well-meaning neighbor. But as morale lifting as these early "critics" are likely to be, they're not going to contribute to your growth as a writer (unless you happen to live next door to, say, John Irving). At some point most writers will seek peer and/or professional feedback on their work. When you reach that point, here are some things to consider—before, during, and after the critique—in order to make sure that your experience is positive, productive, and (reasonably) pain-free.

**Before you submit your work for critique:**

✓ Assess your goals. Do you aspire to commercial publication? Are you preparing a manuscript for a contest entry? Or do you want to finish a draft of your novel?

✓ Assess (honestly) what kind of feedback you're looking for: gentle encouragement; peer support and motivation; or no-holds-barred, give-it-to-me-straight-doctor-I-can-take-it professional editing.

✓ Find a group or individual to meet your needs and goals. If you're paying for the service, look for publication credits, genre experience, testimonials and/or references. If you're joining a critique group, consider the frequency and location of meetings; composition of the group (published vs. unpublished, genre vs. mainstream, fiction vs. nonfiction, etc.); number of members; and amount of work read.

✓ Prepare yourself and your work. This means not only bringing your best efforts to the table, but also preparing yourself mentally for the process. Leave your ego at the door, and open yourself to the possibility that you might learn something.

**While your work is being critiqued:**

✓ Listen/read carefully; take notes if the presentation is oral. Depending on the venue, you may or may not have a chance to go back and revisit previous comments or critiques, so don't just sit there and nod your head. And don't stop listening/reading when you encounter something negative. If you discount an entire critique because you don't agree with one or two points, you're throwing out the baby with the bathwater.

✓ Resist the temptation to defend your work, and don't argue with the critic. If you spend all your energy justifying your choices or challenging the critic's opinions, you won't benefit from the advice you're being given. To put it brutally, shut up and listen. You don't have to agree with everything the critic says, but you do have to hear and understand the critique in order to evaluate it.

✓ Ask for clarification. This is the only exception to the "shut up and listen" rule. If you don't understand a comment, can't read a reviewer's handwriting, or aren't sure how to implement a suggestion, ask the critic to explain further.

✓ In a group situation, pay special attention to areas where there is a consensus among members—if only one of the ten readers "gets it," you probably haven't made "it" clear enough.

✓ If you are part of a critique group, be a responsible member: Show up; bring your best draft (this doesn't mean *final* draft, just the cleanest, best draft you can produce at this point); abide by the Golden Rule.

**After your work has been critiqued:**

✓ Set the criticism aside and let the work "cool." You need to get past the natural inclination to react emotionally and get to a place where you can objectively consider all comments—positive and negative—before you can assess their value.

✓ Discard suggestions that are at odds with your vision of the work. Only you can decide what's right for your story. If you've paid for a professional edit, you're probably smart to follow advice on grammar, composition, and even structure. But beyond that, suggestions on style, word choice, plot direction, character development, etc., are just that—suggestions. Granted, if they are suggestions from a well-informed, highly credentialed, and better-educated source, they should be given appropriate consideration. Still, it's your name in the byline; you have to be able to live with your decisions.

✓ Selectively implement those suggestions that feel right. Once you've discarded anything you feel is blatantly unusable, look carefully at what's left. Even if the recommendations are on target, you'll need to make sure they blend with the rest of the piece. If you've been given specific revision suggestions, don't necessarily graft them wholesale into your story. Experiment with word choice and sentence structure until you're comfortable that you've incorporated the essence of the suggested improvement without compromising your voice or style.

✓ Seek additional help if you need it. If your work comes back with so many red ink marks on it that you can barely read the original text, chances are you may need additional practice and/or instruction on the basics of the craft. Look for a class, a tutor, or at least some good how-to books to help you hone your skills. Ideally, you shouldn't submit your work to critical scrutiny until you feel solidly grounded in the basics. But if you've jumped the gun, don't be embarrassed about getting the instruction you need to polish up your writing.

## When You're Critiquing Someone Else's Work

Critiquing another writer's work can be difficult, especially if you're not sure what to look for in terms of possible areas for improvement. Should you focus on flaws in character development, unnatural dialogue, awkward pacing, grammatical gaffes, etc.? It's important for you to analyze the work and develop your own opinions before taking part in the group's critique of the manuscript. If your group consists only of you and another writer, it's especially important to give the manuscript a careful read. Use the following list of questions as a guide as you read over your fellow writer's work:

✓ Does the title complement the content and tone of the piece?

✓ Did the writer use the most appropriate form (poetry, fiction, nonfiction, drama) for the subject matter and theme?

✓ Is the opening of the piece seductive?

✓ Is the "problem" of the piece clear (character conflict, conveyance of beauty/ugliness, mystery, etc.)

✓ Is the writing style appropriate in terms of variety, consistency, diction, voice?

✓ Is the pace of the piece appropriate for the subject matter and overall tone?

✓ Does the dialogue/voice ring true? Does it seem natural and appropriate?

✓ Is there a clear moment or line or event of truth, a point in the piece when all elements make sense and complement each other?

✓ Is there a good reason behind every line, every word, every scene?

✓ Is every portion of the piece absolutely necessary to the overall effect? Are there sections that seem unrelated to the rest of the work?

✓ Does the piece communicate a universal truth, something that makes sense and adds to the experience of readers of various cultures, locations, and values?

✓ Is the piece well focused? Can you describe the essence of the piece in a few words or sentences?

✓ Is the ending appropriate, or is it inconclusive or redundant or too obvious and predictable?

✓ Have you been involved in the piece; has a change occurred in you for having read this piece?

✓ Is this piece memorable? Would you recommend it to others? Would you reread it with equal or renewed interest?

✓ Has the writer respected the principles of the form chosen for the piece (e.g., for poetry, such elements as imagery, sound, lining, and metaphor).

✓ Does the piece have definite strengths? What are they?

✓ Does the piece have conspicuous weaknesses? What are they? Can they be corrected? How?

## When You're Taking Part in a Group Critique

The group members have arrived. Everyone has read the same manuscripts. It's time to get the critique ball rolling. Instead of opening with the standard, "So, what does everyone think?" line, use these questions to help focus your group's critique.

**For the author:**

✓ Don't go into a lengthy explanation of how you came to write this piece.

✓ Do be specific about what you want from the group—you need help with the dialogue, you wonder if your villain is believable, you want the local newspaper to accept your witty letter to the editor, you are determined to see your poetry published in a national magazine, etc. If you don't tell them what you want, they can't give it to you.

✓ Do honor the group's rules. If your reading is supposed to average about five minutes, don't take thirty seconds—or thirty minutes. If manuscripts are to be e-mailed to the other members three days in advance, don't show up with copies in hand at the meeting.

✓ Do honor your prose. Whether it's a query letter or a short story, stand up and read clearly. If the character you've written about is upbeat and excited, your voice should be as well.

✓ Do remind the group about the type of help you're seeking.

✓ Do take notes and remain quiet until a member has finished his comments about your work. Don't interrupt or become defensive. If the person finishes and you don't understand his comment, ask for clarification. Don't immediately explain why what he said is wrong.

✓ Do remember that this is your work. Listen carefully to everyone's comments, and when you get home, analyze whether a suggested change would improve your article, letter, or novel. If you honestly feel it wouldn't be an improvement, don't make it—and make no apologies to the group member for not using his suggestion.

### For the group leader:

✓ Do remind members to focus their comments on the areas the writer wants addressed. For example, if the writer is primarily looking for help with setting, it's not appropriate to talk about how stiff her characters are.

✓ Do keep the discussion constructive. When you hear comments such as, "I just don't believe it," respond with, "What do you find unbelievable in that passage and how could it be written more believably?" If the comment is, "I think she should throw it away and start over," say, "Mary has asked us whether the story should be told from Jane's viewpoint or Jane's sister's viewpoint. Which do you think would work better and why?"

✓ Do encourage all members to participate. If someone is monopolizing the session, when he stops to take a breath say, "And thank you, Frank. I'm sure Mary finds those points very helpful. Mary has asked us to help her find the right point of view. Susan, what do you think the right point of view for this story is?"

✓ Do honor the nitpickers, but move on. For example, "Frank notes that there are some grammatical problems with Mary's narrative, and it certainly is important to make sure your query letter/proposal/manuscript is as error free

as possible before you send it out. But tonight, Mary's asked for help with her dialogue. Jane, what sort of phrases and idioms could her protagonist use so that we understand more quickly that she is a newly arrived Swedish immigrant?"

✓ Don't put the responsibility for focusing the discussion totally on the reader or the other group members. Sometimes, a reader will say she just wants to know what everyone thinks. It's your duty then to focus the discussion. Jot down possible questions during the reading. Some examples of general questions:

• What was Jane trying to accomplish with this scene? How might she have used her dialogue or narrative to better move the story forward?

• Jane has asked us if there's a better way to show what her character looks like than to have her stand in front of a mirror. What are some other things she could do?

• Jane has set her novel in seventeenth-century England but worries that she hasn't done enough research on the period. What are some resources she could consult? How do you know when to stop researching and focus on your writing?

• Jane's query letter is for an essay about a Christmas memory, and it is now Halloween. How can she find out how far in advance she needs to query editors about seasonal articles?

• Based on the chapter Jane has shared with the critique group, where do you think the story goes from here? What happens next and why?

# Critique Groups

ou know all those goals you set for your writing? Write ten pages a day, write ten hours a week, make *The New York Times* best-seller list, send out fifteen article queries per month? You need to do the same thing with your critique group. If you're not learning and improving your writing directly or indirectly at every meeting, you're losing time you might be spending more productively at the computer.

## Forming a New Group:

- **Determine your goals.** If everyone's not on the same page, this isn't going to be a useful experience. Is the common goal working on query letters? Trying to improve the members' novel-writing craft? Serving as a cheerleading or support network? Your group will be all these things and more at one time or another, but the members must agree on the key purpose.

- **Limit the size.** Keep the group to somewhere between six and twelve members. Much smaller and you run the risk of quickly losing freshness; much bigger

and there won't be an opportunity for healthy interaction.

- **Set a meeting place and time upon which everyone agrees.** You can rotate among each others' homes, meet at someone's workplace, or get together at the local coffeehouse. The starting and ending time should work for everyone— it's aggravating to wait for someone who's consistently late, or to lose feedback from someone who always has to leave early. Set a regular meeting schedule (preferably twice a month; certainly no less frequently than once a month).

- **Set ground rules and follow them.** This doesn't have to be a dictatorship, but an effective critique group has to have some order. What will the standard agenda be? Will all members share work at each meeting? Will manuscript copies be distributed prior to each meeting? Who's responsible for copying and/or distributing the manuscripts? What happens when a member doesn't show up or has nothing new to read for two or three sessions?

- **Determine the form for critique.** Agree that when members don't like something about another writer's work, they will offer solutions instead of negative comments that offer little or no constructive advice. "The first page seems to run a bit long. How would it read if you eliminated paragraphs one through three and started with the fourth paragraph?" is much more helpful—even if the advice ultimately isn't followed—than "I thought the whole thing was boring. Have you thought about just starting over?"

## Joining an Existing Group:

- **Just as in setting up a group, be sure that members share your goals.** Do their ground rules and usual agenda mesh with what you hope to achieve? If not, keep looking at bulletin boards at area bookstores or local colleges and universities until you find a group more to your liking—or start putting up your own notices to start a group.

- **Ask about the experience level/publication record of the members.** It can be fun to join a group made up of only new writers, but you won't necessarily learn very much. At least one member of the group should have achieved your goal (finishing a novel, finding an agent, getting a magazine article published) in the past year. While you may not want to be in a critique group with five National Book Award finalists if you're still on the first chapter of your first novel, it's better for you if the others in your group are a bit more advanced than you are. That way, you can learn from them.

## Switching to a Different Group:

- **You've got the most impressive credentials of the group.** If you wish to stick around, consider this more of a social gathering. If you really want to improve your writing, get into a group that will challenge you and make you stretch your writing skills.

- **Your goals change.** Your initial goal may be to get published, and you may decide that's too ambitious. Maybe what you really want is a half dozen people to meet with once a month to gossip or talk to about books, not a session designed to get feedback on your writing. Or, you may decide your focus for the year will be on finding an agent rather than spending more time perfecting your novel. In either case, find a group whose members share that goal.

- **The people are mean-spirited.** If members are telling you where to put commas or smugly noting that you mistyped *the* as *teh* on the second page, then you may want to move on to a new group. Or, if their comments repeatedly consist of, "I don't understand it," or, "I don't like it," with no explanation of the problems they found in your work, then it's certainly time to get out.

- **The people are too nice.** If all you (and all the other members) hear and say are phrases like, "That's really nice," or, "I wouldn't change a single word," then it may be time to find a new group of writers who will help you improve your work, not just make you feel good about yourself.

# Established Writing Groups

Belonging to a major writing organization can provide you with education about technique, expose you to new markets, and give you a sense camaraderie. Many writing associations also offer awards, insurance, conferences, and networking opportunities. Some groups also publish newsletters to keep members apprised of what's happening within their areas of specialization.

But, before you sign that check or credit card form to join a writing association, determine what benefits you're seeking. Some organizations excel at education, others at networking and still others at providing market information. Next, consider the credentials for acceptance.

We've gathered information on a number of the leading organizations to get you started. (Note: The dues listed do not include additional fees. For example there may be a one-time membership processing fee; for more information, visit each organization's Web site.)

**American Society of Journalists and Authors**

1501 Broadway, Suite 302
New York NY, 10036
Tel: (212) 997-0947
Web site: www.asja.org
Founded: 1948
Number of Members: More than 1,000
Dues: $195
Focus: Peer exchange of confidential information about markets, contracts, fees, and editors.
Membership Criteria: Minimum of six full-length (1,000 words or more) freelance articles; submit more than six if your articles are shorter freelance articles published in major consumer magazines or two nonfiction books. Also accepted: freelance TV, film, and radio scripts, and some material written for major Web sites.
Benefits: Annual conference; monthly newsletter; writer referral service; private online discussion forums; profes-

sional resource lists; discounts on magazine subscriptions, insurance.

## Authors Guild

31 E. 28th St., 10th Floor
New York NY, 10016
Tel: (212) 563-5904
Web site: www.authorsguild.org
Founded: 1919
Number of Members: More than 8,000
Dues: First year $90. After that, dues are based on earnings.
Focus: Professional services, including a well-organized and experienced contracts department, and seminars on topics such as contract negotiation and publicity.
Membership Criteria: Regular members must have published at least one book or three articles with general circulation periodicals within the last eighteen months; an associate must have a contract for a forthcoming book.
Benefits: Quarterly journal; e-mail alerts and bulletins; professional seminars; contract services department; group insurance; advocacy on e-rights, copyright, and taxes.

## Canadian Authors Association

Box 419, 320 S. Shores Road
Campbellford Ontario K0L 1L0
Fax: (705) 653-0593
Web site: www.canauthors.org
Founded: 1921
Number of Members: 700
Dues: $125 (Canadian)
Focus: Aims to assist writers in all aspects of their careers.
Membership Criteria: Open to Members (Published) and Associate Members.

Benefits: Conference; newsletter; awards; mentorship; seminars; grievance and contract assistance.

## Horror Writers Association

P.O. Box 50577
Palo Alto CA 94303
Tel: (650) 322-4610
Web site: www.horror.org
Founded: 1987
Number of Members: 950
Dues: $55 ($65 outside North America)
Focus: Advancing the horror and dark fantasy genre.
Membership Criteria: Active members are published writers (see Web site for criteria); affiliate and associate members are genre enthusiasts and nonwriting industry professionals.
Benefits: Conventions; awards; marketing reports; career help; meetings; regional chapters; newsletter; handbook.

## Mystery Writers of America

17 E. 47th St., 6th Floor
New York NY 10017
Tel: (212) 888-8171
Web site: www.mysterywriters.org
Founded: 1945
Number of Members: 2,400
Dues: $80
Focus: Emphasizes networking, access to research materials and enhancing the genre's stature.
Membership Criteria: Active members have published mysteries in any medium; additional categories for unpublished writers and those who live outside the United States.
Benefits: Annual meeting; national and chapter newsletters; discounts on maga-

zines, books, car rentals, hotels; insurance; mentor program; annual literary awards.

## National Federation of State Poetry Societies

2736 Creekwood Lane
Fort Worth TX 76123
Web site: www.nfsps.com
Founded: 1959
Number of Members: More than 6,000
Dues: Varies by state
Focus: Emphasizes national cultural heritage, educational aspects; furthers poetry and promotes fellowship and understanding among poets.
Membership Criteria: Varies by state
Benefits: Convention; newsletter; contests; workshops; awards; annual anthology.

## National Writers Union

113 University Place, 6th Floor
New York NY 10003
Tel: (212) 254-0279
Web site: www.nwu.org
Founded: 1982
Number of Members: More than 7,000
Dues: $95 to $260, depending on income
Focus: A labor union improving economic and working conditions for freelance writers.
Membership Criteria: Must have published a book, a play, three articles, five poems, a short story or an equal amount of other types of copy. Accepts unpublished writers actively trying to sell their work.
Benefits: Magazine; grievance and contract advice; discounts on magazines; delivery services; car rentals and theme parks; list servs; insurance; job hotline;

agent database; e-mail bulletins; local chapters.

## Outdoor Writers Association of America,

121 Hickory St., Suite 1
Missoula MT 59801
Tel: (406) 728-7434
Web site: www.owaa.org
Founded: 1927
Number of Members: 2,100
Dues: $30 to $1,000, depending on level
Focus: Provides mentorship, education about outdoor communications and preservation.
Membership Criteria: Six categories of varying expertise for writers, artists, and photographers (see Web site or call).
Benefits: Conference; scholarships; contests; grievance services; monthly publication; seminars; equipment loans.

## Periodical Writers Association of Canada

54 Wolseley St., Suite 203
Toronto Ontario M5T 1A5
Tel: (416) 504-1645
Web site: www.pwac.ca
Founded: 1976
Number of Members: More than 500
Dues: $240, plus chapter dues (Canadian)
Focus: Promote higher industry standards and share market and other information; vocal proponent for writers on copyright issues.
Membership Criteria: Publication of and payment for at least one 300-word article within the last twelve months (see Web site for details).
Benefits: Conference; mentoring; insurance; market guide; discounts; newsletter; discussion forums; seminars.

## Poetry Society of America

15 Gramercy Park
New York NY 10003
Tel: (212) 254-9628
Web site: www.poetrysociety.org
Founded: 1910
Number of Members: 3,500
Dues: $45 ($25 for students)
Focus: Challenging and inspiring readers and writers of poetry.
Membership Criteria: Open to poets and literary enthusiasts.
Benefits: Biannual journal; seminars; readings; competitions; discounts; event calendar.

## Romance Writers of America,

3707 FM 1960 W., Suite 555
Houston TX 77068
Tel: (281) 440-6885
Web site: www.rwanational.com
Founded: 1980
Number of Members: 8,400
Dues: $75
Membership Criteria: Open.
Focus: Dissemination of market and craft information at the national level; chapters provide support and mentoring to writers in the same geographical area or those working in the same subgenre.
Benefits: Newsletter; annual conference; e-mail lists and bulletins; professional seminars; contests and awards; mentoring; publisher and agent lists.

## Science Fiction and Fantasy Writers of America

P.O. Box 877
Chestertown MD 21620
Tel: (410)778-3052
Web site: www.sfwa.org

Founded: 1965
Number of Members: More than 1,200
Dues: $50
Focus: Craft and contract information.
Membership Criteria: Three published short stories or one published novel or dramatic script; associate membership is available to those who have had one piece of work published in a recognized publication.
Benefits: Conference; awards; magazines; insurance; grievance committee; bulletin; handbooks.

## Sisters in Crime

Box 442124
Lawrence KS 66044-8933
Tel: (785) 842-1325
Web site: www.sistersincrime.org
Founded: 1986
Number of Members: 3,300
Dues: $35 ($40 outside United States)
Focus: Promotion of women mystery writers.
Membership Criteria: Open.
Benefits: Newsletter; publications; support of special interest groups, minorities, and new writers.

## Society of American Travel Writers

1500 Sunday Dr., Suite 102
Raleigh NC 27607
Tel: (919) 787-5181
Web site: www.satw.org
Founded: 1956
Number of Members: More than 1,300
Dues: $130 to $250
Focus: Promote professional journalism and encourage preservation of historical sites.
Membership Criteria: A year's experience

in travel writing and sponsorship by two members.

Benefits: Newsletter; awards; contract dispute resolution; tax and legal advice; insurance; hotel and book discounts; new markets.

## Society of Children's Book Writers and Illustrators

8271 Beverly Blvd.
Los Angeles CA 90048
Tel: (323) 782-1010
Web site: www.scbwi.org
Founded: 1971
Number of Members: More than 18,000
Dues: $50
Focus: Sharing resources and information for children's writers and illustrators.
Membership Criteria: Full membership open to anyone who has published work for children; associate—open to anyone interested in children's literature.
Benefits: Annual conference; bimonthly newsletter; awards; grants; insurance; manuscript/illustration exchange.

## Society of Professional Journalists

3909 N. Meridian St.
Indianapolis IN 46208
Tel: (317) 927-8000
Web site: www.spj.org
Founded: 1909
Number of Members: 9,500
Dues: $35 to $90
Focus: Preserving freedom of the press and educating journalists.
Membership Criteria: Must spend half of each year working as a journalist or journalism educator; associate and student levels available as well.

Benefits: Conference; magazine; directory of sources; insurance; awards; discounts on office services, telephone, travel, car rental, and hotels.

## Western Writers of America

1012 Fair St.
Franklin TN 37064-2718
Tel: (615) 791-1444
Web site: www.westernwriters.org
Founded: 1953
Number of Members: More than 500
Dues: $75 to $150
Focus: Aggressive promotion of the literature of the American West.
Membership Criteria: Publication in the genre (see Web site for details).
Benefits: Convention; magazine; networking; awards; seminars.

## Writers Guild of America,

West: 7000 W. Third St., Los Angeles CA 90048
East: 555 W. 57th St., New York City NY 10019
Tel: (800) 548-4532
Web site: www.wga.org
Founded: 1912
Number of Members: 11,000
Dues: $2,500
Focus: Labor union representing the professionals who write films and television shows. Contract negotiation and review, and credit for members' work.
Membership Criteria: A specific amount of work within film, television, or radio (see Web site for details).
Benefits: Contract negotiation assistance, review and arbitration; copyright protection; newsletter; insurance; awards; conferences.

## Writers' Union of Canada

40 Wellington St. E., Third Floor
Toronto Ontario M5E 1C7
Tel: (416) 703-8982
Web site: www.writersunion.ca
Founded: 1973
Number of Members: More than 1,350
Dues: $180 (Canadian)
Focus: Fellowship among Canadian
authors of books; contract advice and
grievance assistance.
Membership Criteria: Open to Canadian
citizens; one published trade book.
Benefits: Conference; newsletter; e-mail
lists; manuscript evaluation; contract
evaluation and negotiation; grievance
committee.

## Other Writing Groups

If you're looking for a local or regional
group beyond chapters of the associations
listed:

- Visit the Writer's Digest/ShawGuides
  Directory at www.writersdigest.com to
  learn about more than 1,000 different
  conferences—including groups that
  sponsor conferences in your area. You'll
  also find fee and contact information.
- Check local bookstores for announce-
  ments of writing group meetings or ask
  the store if any groups meet there.
- Call your local college or university's
  English or communications department
  and ask if it has any information on
  writing groups.

# Resource Directory

## Getting Published/
## Fiction and Nonfiction

*Agents, Editors and You: The Insider's Guide to Getting Your Book Published*, edited by Michelle Howry (Writer's Digest Books). This collection of articles and interviews with industry insiders helps demystify the process of getting published.

*The Forest for the Trees: An Editor's Advice to Writers*, by Betsy Lerner (Riverhead). As a former editor with Houghton Mifflin, Ballantine, Simon & Schuster, and Doubleday, Lerner brings years of experience to her reflections from the editor's side of the desk.

*Guide to Literary Agents*, edited by Rachel Vater (Writer's Digest Books). An annual directory of some 600 literary agents, with contact information and specialty areas included. Also features articles on the business of getting an agent and interviews with industry experts.

*How to Write a Book Proposal*, by Michael Larsen (Writer's Digest Books). A com-

prehensive guide to creating a successful nonfiction book proposal, from content to structure to pitching editors. Helps writers negotiate contract, royalties, and advances.

*How to Write Attention-Grabbing Queries and Cover Letters*, by John Wood (Writer's Digest Books). As both writer and editor, Wood brings broad knowledge to this subject and covers magazine queries, as well as fiction and nonfiction book proposals. Also includes samples of queries and cover letters that work and those that don't.

*Novel & Short Story Writer's Market*, edited by Anne Bowling (Writer's Digest Books). An annual directory of some 1,900 places to get fiction published, from literary magazines to online markets to book publishers. Also includes listings of conferences and contests, and features instructive articles and interviews with writers and editors.

*Poet's Market*, edited by Nancy Breen (Writer's Digest Books). An annual directory of some 2,000 places for poets to get their work published, from literary magazines to small presses and more. Also includes feature articles on the business of publishing poetry, and interviews with poets and editors about the craft.

*Thinking Like Your Editor: How to Write Serious Nonfiction—And Get it Published,* by Susan Rabiner & Alfred Fortunato (W.W. Norton & Co.). The husband and wife team show nonfiction writers how to take a book from idea to publication, and include information on the submission process, instruction on craft, and insider views on the writer/editor relationship.

*Writer's Market,* edited by Katie Struckel Brogan (Writer's Digest Books). An annual directory of more than 4,000 markets for writers' nonfiction and fiction. Includes contact information and editorial needs for book publishers, consumer magazines, and trade, technical and professional journals, and more. Also includes agent information, instruction on submissions and craft, and interviews with noted writers and editors.

*The Writer's Market Companion,* by Joe Feiertag and Mary Carmen Cupito (Writer's Digest Books). This handbook covers the waterfront of writing for pay, from coming up with an idea to pitching it successfully, and writing an effective piece to getting paid for the work. Also includes information on writer's groups and self-promotion, and a pricing guide.

## Inspiration

*The Artist's Way, A Spiritual Path to Higher Creativity,* by Julia Cameron and Mark Bryan (J.P. Tarcher). Cameron and Bryan's classic guide to creativity takes readers through a twelve-week program designed to help them overcome the barriers to expression and free the artist within.

*Becoming a Writer,* by Dorothea Brande and John Gardner (Jeremy P. Tarcher). This classic was first published in 1934. It offers advice, exercises, and techniques for cultivating the writing life.

*Bird by Bird: Some Instructions on Writing and Life,* by Anne Lamott (Anchor). Part essay and part how-to guide, this book inspires and entertains while delivering practical advice on craft.

*Fiction Writer's Brainstormer,* by James V. Smith (Writer's Digest Books). Smith supplies strategies, tools, exercises, puzzles, graphs, and checklists to guide the reader to more powerful writing.

*If You Want to Write: A Book About Art, Independence and Spirit,* by Brenda Ueland (Graywolf Press). A best-selling classic series of essays that help writers and other artists stay motivated and find their personal sources of creativity.

*Lessons from a Lifetime of Writing, A Novelist Looks at His Craft,* by David Morrell (Writer's Digest Books). The creator of the Rambo character popularized in his novel First Blood, Morrell discusses his philosophy and techniques of writing.

*Living the Writer's Life*, by Eric Maisel (Watson-Guptill). As a therapist and writer, Maisel helps readers negotiate the obstacles and challenges that come with the writing life.

*On Becoming a Novelist*, by John Gardner and Raymond Carver (W.W. Norton & Co.). Gardner reflects on his twenty-year career as a novelist, offering the reader insight into what to expect from the work and the writing life. Introduction by Raymond Carver.

*On Writing, A Memoir of the Craft*, by Stephen King (Scribner). The master of horror covers both autobiography and instruction for aspiring novelists, with specific examples on how to and how not to approach dialogue, characterization, and more.

*The Right to Write: An Invitation and Initiation into the Writing Life*, by Julia Cameron (J.P. Tarcher). In more than forty brief personal essays, Cameron instructs readers on how to integrate their passion for writing with the demands of daily life. Includes creativity exercises.

*The Writer's Idea Book*, by Jack Heffron (Writer's Digest Books). A jump-start for the creative process, this book offers guidance in generating ideas specifically and the writing process in general. Includes more than 400 writing prompts.

*Writing Down the Bones: Freeing the Writer Within*, by Natalie Goldberg (Shambhala Publications). Goldberg coaches writers on how to tap into their creativity and develop powerful writing by working without the rules.

*Writing from the Inside Out: Transforming Your Psychological Blocks to Release the Writer Within*, by Dennis Palumbo (John Wiley & Sons). Screenwriter turned psychologist Palumbo helps writers handle the downsides of writing life—writer's envy, loneliness, fear of rejection, doubt, procrastination—and offers new and positive ways of regarding the writing art.

*Zen in the Art of Writing: Essays on Creativity: Expanded*, by Ray Bradbury (Joshua Odell Editions). A series of inspirational essays on craft.

## Craft and Technique/Fiction

*The Art of Fiction: Notes on Craft for Young Writers*, by John Gardner and J. Laslocky (Vintage Books). For the serious literary fiction writer. Gardner covers character building, plotting, vocabulary, sentence structure, and style in this comprehensive classic.

*Beginnings, Middles & Ends*, by Nancy Kress (Writer's Digest Books). Part of the WDB Elements of Fiction series.

*Characters & Viewpoint*, by Orson Scott Card (Writer's Digest Books). Part of the WDB Elements of Fiction series.

*The Complete Guide to Editing Your Fiction*, by Michael Seidman (Writer's Digest Books). In an easy-to-reference format, *The Complete Guide* shows readers how to approach fiction editing from three angles: macro editing, style editing, and market editing.

*The Complete Handbook of Novel Writing,* edited by Meg Leder and Jack Heffron (Writer's Digest Books). A series of articles and interviews broken into categories on The Art, The Craft, The Genres, The Marketplace, and so on, giving readers an insider's look at writing and getting published.

*The First Five Pages: A Writer's Guide to Staying Out of the Slush Pile,* by Noah Lukeman (Fireside). Literary agent Lukeman teaches readers how to identify and avoid bad writing.

*How Fiction Works,* by Oakley Hall (Writer's Digest Books). Advice on all forms of fiction, including short stories, short-short stories, and novellas, covering every fictive technique, from plot and characterization to word choice, voice and style.

*How to Grow a Novel, The Most Common Mistakes Writers Make and How to Avoid Them,* by Sol Stein (St. Martin's Press). A novelist and fiction editor, Stein walks readers through the process of writing a novel with an eye on satisfying the reader.

*How to Write a Damn Good Novel,* by James N. Frey (St. Martin's Press). Basing his instruction on the Three C's—character, conflict, and conclusion—Frey leads readers through writing the novel from the beginning to the end in this informative and authoritative volume.

*How to Write & Sell Your First Novel (Revised Edition),* by Oscar Collier with Frances Spatz Leighton (Writer's Digest Books). Newly revised and updated, this guide reveals the keys to writing and publishing a successful novel in today's complicated market. Collier and Leighton combine their years of publishing experience with the success strategies of twenty-two accomplished authors.

*How to Write Funny, Add Humor to Every Kind of Writing,* by John Kachuba (Writer's Digest Books). A humor writing workshop for fiction and nonfiction writers, including original articles from Dave Barry, P.J. O'Rourke, Jennifer Crusie, Tom Bodett and more.

*Immediate Fiction, A Complete Writing Course,* by Jerry Cleaver (St. Martin's Press). Crafting a story from idea through marketing takes skill, discipline, and talent. Cleaver, like so many of his ilk, encourages the development of all three through practice and daily writing exercises. He also discusses self-editing, rewriting, time management, and the basics of plot and story.

*The Marshall Plan for Novel Writing,* by Evan Marshall (Writer's Digest Books). This sixteen-step program takes readers from idea to completed and ready-to-submit manuscript. Includes instruction on how to find a hook, create conflict, and develop a protagonist.

*The Marshall Plan Workbook,* by Evan Marshall (Writer's Digest Books). This companion volume to *The Marshall*

*Plan for Novel Writing* details the process of building a novel's plot, with more than one hundred pages of fill-in sheets that become a blueprint for any novel.

*Mastering Point of View*, by Sherri Szeman (Writer's Digest Books). Guides writers through the difficult process of choosing point of view and provides straightforward instruction for using it well. Includes examples from notable writers.

*The Plot Thickens, 8 Ways to Bring Fiction to Life*, by Noah Lukeman (St. Martin's Press). A follow-up volume to literary agent Lukeman's *The First Five Pages*, this book offers readers insight into character and plot development.

*Self-Editing for Fiction Writers*, by Renni Browne and Dave King (Harper Collins). Two professional editors provide solid instruction for writers on how to tighten, revise and polish fiction.

*So You Want to Write: How to Master the Craft of Writing Fiction and the Personal Narrative*, by Marge Piercy and Ira Wood (Leapfrog Press). Based on years of workshops conducted by Piercy and Wood, this book offers instruction in craft, technical exercises, and insight into the writing life.

*Steering the Craft: Exercises and Discussions on Story Writing for the Lone Navigator or the Mutinous Crew*, by Ursula K. Le Guin (Eighth Mountain Press). Instruction and inspiration in a classic from a master of the craft.

*20 Master Plots and How to Build Them*, by Ronald B. Tobias (Writer's Digest Books). Presents twenty fundamental plots that recur throughout all fiction— with analysis and examples—outlining the benefits and drawbacks for writers to consider in their own fiction.

*The Weekend Novelist*, by Robert Joseph Ray and Jack Remick (Dell). Ray and Remick take readers from idea to completed mystery manuscript in one year, writing only on weekends.

*What If? Writing Exercises for Fiction Writers*, by Anne Bernays and Pamela Painter (HarperCollins). Bernays and Painter offer seventy-five exercises for beginning and experienced writers.

*Word Painting, A Guide to Writing More Descriptively*, by Rebecca McClanahan (Writer's Digest Books). Engaging word exercises challenge writers to elevate their writing to new levels of richness and clarity.

*Writing Fiction: A Guide to Narrative Craft (Fifth Edition)*, by Janet Burroway (Addison-Wesley). A guide for writers that focuses on the writing process from inspiration to final draft. Includes practical techniques and concrete examples.

*Writing the Blockbuster Novel*, by Albert Zuckerman (Writer's Digest Books). Covers the subject thoroughly, from creating outlines and building larger-than-life characters to injecting suspense and more. Uses examples from the fiction of Ken Follett.

*Writing the Breakout Novel*, by Donald Maass (Writer's Digest Books). Maass explains the elements that all breakout novels share, and shows readers how to write a novel that has a good chance of succeeding in a crowded marketplace.

## Craft and Technique/Nonfiction

*The Art of Fact: A Historical Anthology of Literary Journalism*, edited by Kevin Kerrane and Ben Yagoda (Touchstone Books). A compendium of more than three hundred years of literary journalism, from Daniel Defoe to Jack London, from Lillian Ross to Hunter S. Thompson. Traces the evolution of the form from style to content.

*The Art of Creative Nonfiction: Writing and Selling the Literature of Reality*, by Lee Gutkind (John Wiley & Sons). For the beginning creative nonfiction writer, this book covers interview skills, fact checking, focusing the piece, what editors expect, and what qualities good writers of this form should have.

*Follow the Story: How to Write Successful Nonfiction*, by James B. Stewart (Touchstone Books). Pulitzer Prize-winning Stewart uses example and instruction to teach readers to craft compelling nonfiction.

*The Fourth Genre: The Contemporary Writers of/on Creative Nonfiction*, by Michael Steinberg, et. al. (Longman). Provides readings in essay, memoir, literary journalism, and cultural criticism as models for writing creative nonfiction. Also includes articles about nonfiction forms and writing strategies.

*Literary Journalism, A New Collection of the Best American Nonfiction*, edited by Norman Sims and Mark Kramer (Ballantine). A selection of fifteen pieces from the best literary journalists writing today.

*On Writing Well: The Classic Guide to Writing Nonfiction (25th Anniversary Edition)*, by William Knowlton Zinsser (Harper Resource). For writers of any form of nonfiction, this book teaches readers to write strong, streamlined prose. Zinsser also provides instruction on science and technical writing, business writing, sports, and humor.

*Writing Creative Nonfiction: Instruction and Insights from Teachers of the Associated Writing Programs*, edited by Carolyn Forché and Philip Gerard (Writer's Digest Books). Thirty outstanding nonfiction writers present essays that cover every key element of the craft.

*Writing for Story: Craft Secrets of Dramatic Nonfiction by a Two-Time Pulitzer Prize Winner*, by Jon Franklin (Plume). A pioneer in style and technique, Franklin offers instruction on applying traditional fictional techniques to creative nonfiction.

## Crime/Mystery/Suspense

*The Criminal Mind, A Writer's Guide to Forensic Psychology*, by Katherine Ramsland (Writer's Digest Books). Forensic psychologist Ramsland gives readers a detailed primer on the science by using case studies from history, as well as accurate and inaccurate depictions from pop culture.

*Howdunit, How Crimes are Committed and Solved*, by John Boertlein (Writer's Digest Books). Includes the best of the Howdunit crime series as well as thirteen new chapters on key topics such as gangs, hate crimes, street cops, the drug trade, terrorism, surveillance, and forensic psychology.

*Urge to Kill, A Writer's Guide to How Police Take Homicide from Case to Court*, by Martin Edwards (Writer's Digest Books). With a mix of text, case studies and photographs, Edwards explores this subject in a step-by-step manner that empowers writers to create engaging and believable scenarios.

*Writing Mysteries*, edited by Sue Grafton (Writer's Digest Books). In this revised edition of the Mystery Writers of America classic, Grafton weaves the experience of today's top mystery authors into a comprehensive how-to guide that instructs and thrills.

## Science Fiction/Fantasy & Horror

*Aliens and Alien Societies*, by Stanley Schmidt (Writer's Digest Books). Teaches writers how to use scientific knowledge of the universe to create more convincing portrayals of extraterrestrial life forms in their science fiction or fantasy novels.

*How to Write Science Fiction and Fantasy*, by Orson Scott Card (Writer's Digest Books). Card's Hugo Award-winning classic teaches how to produce market-ready stories based on worlds readers will want to explore.

*Monsters*, by John Michael Greer (Llewellyn Publications). A comprehensive look at things that go bump in the night.

*Worlds of Wonder, How to Write Science Fiction & Fantasy*, by David Gerrold (Writer's Digest Books). Hugo and Nebula Award-winning author Gerrold charms and challenges readers with his detailed instruction for creating compelling tales of fantasy and science fiction.

*Writer's Complete Fantasy Reference*, from the editors of Writer's Digest Books (Writer's Digest Books). Featuring an introduction by Terry Brooks, this book is an A to Z coverage of the realm of the fantastic.

*Writing Horror*, by Edo van Belkom (Self Counsel Press). A thorough guide to writing for and getting published in the genre.

## Romance

*The Complete Writer's Guide to Heroes and Heroines*, by Tami D. Cowden, et. al. (Lone Eagle Publishing Company). A comprehensive guide for creating compelling characters for writers in any genre.

*How to Write a Romance for the New Market and Get It Published*, edited by Kathryn Falk (Genesis Press Ltd.) From the founder and owner of Romantic Times Magazine, this book provides in-depth instruction in craft and getting published, with a focus on emerging subgenres in romance.

*The Romance Writer's Handbook*, by Laflorya Gauthier (iUniverse). For the beginner, this book instructs in the process from initial idea to plot development to satisfying conclusion, with examples.

*Writing Erotica*, by Edo Van Belkom (Self Counsel Press). Defines erotica, outlines its elements, and dissects how it works. Also includes instruction in how to get published.

*Writing the Romance Novel*, by Leigh Michaels (PBL, Ltd.). The author of sixty romance novels, Michaels presents a workbook approach to the craft.

## Essay and Memoir

*The Art of the Personal Essay: An Anthology from the Classical Era to Present*, edited by Phillip Lopate (Anchor). Includes more than seventy-five personal essays from such writers as Virginia Woolf, Michel de Montaigne, Edward Hoagland, and F. Scott Fitzgerald.

*Modern American Memoirs*, edited by Annie Dillard and Cort Conley (Harper Perennial). A sampling of memoir excerpts from a wide range of writers.

*Write from Life*, by Meg Files (Writer's Digest Books). Supplies writers working in any form with the inspiration and practical instruction they need to get their experiences and emotions on paper and into print.

*Writing Life Stories*, by Bill Roorbach (Writer's Digest Books). This book helps writers see their own lives more clearly while learning that real stories are often the best ones.

*You Can Write a Memoir*, by Susan Carol Hauser (Writer's Digest Books). Passionately encouraging readers to reclaim the precious moments of their personal histories, Hauser shows how to transform life stories into intimate, compelling narratives.

## General Reference

*The Associated Press Stylebook and Briefing on Media Law*, edited by Norm Goldstein (Perseus Publishing). This revised and updated edition covers the style, grammar, and punctuation rules used in news writing. Also includes advice on libel issues and copyright infringement.

*The Chicago Manual of Style: The Essential Guide for Writers, Editors and Publishers (14th Edition)*, The University of Chicago Press. In print since 1906, the *Chicago Manual* is a thorough desk reference for style matters in journalism, fiction, and nonfiction.

*The Creative Writer's Style Guide, Rules and Advice for Writing Fiction and Creative Nonfiction*, by Christopher T. Leland (Writer's Digest Books). A resource for writers who want to write with precision and passion or just need to fine-tune their work. Addresses issues of grammar, punctuation, and usage, specifically in the context of writing short stories, novels, poetry, screenplays, and creative nonfiction.

*The Elements of Style (Fourth Edition)*, by William Strunk Jr. et. al. (Allyn & Bacon). The classic reference for standard punctuation, word usage, grammar, and style.

*Fiction Dictionary*, by Laurie Henry (Writer's Digest Books). With more than six hundred literary terms, this is a browsable reference for writers, teachers, students, and language fans. Includes examples of terms such as conspiratorial mystique and deconstructive fiction from a wide assortment of literature.

*Flip Dictionary*, by Barbara Ann Kipfer, Ph.D. (Writer's Digest Books). A huge reference that offers cues and clue words to writers, students, crossword puzzlers, and logophiles to the exact phrase or specific term they need.

*The MLA Style Manual and Guide to Scholarly Publishing (Second Edition)*, by Joseph Gibaldi (Modern Language Association of America). Offers basic information on writing and source citation, copyediting, proofreading, index preparation, etc.

*Roget's Superthesaurus (Second Edition)*, by Marc McCutcheon (Writer's Digest Books). With more than 400,000 words, including more than two thousand new and expanded entries, this reference guide offers more features than any other word reference on the market.

*The Writer's Guide to Character Traits*, by Dr. Linda Edelstein (Writer's Digest Books). Profiles the mental, emotional, and physical qualities of dozens of different personality types. Mix and match traits to create original characters.

# Contributors

## Critiquers

**Paul Bagdon** is a Writer's Digest School instructor and a contributing editor for *Writer's Digest* magazine. He has a four-novel action/adventure contract with Baker House Books for a series titled "West Texas Sunrise." *Chapter 6.*

**James Scott Bell** is a contributing editor for *Writer's Digest* magazine and the author of several thrillers, including *Blind Justice, Final Witness*, and *The Darwin Conspiracy: The Confessions of Sir Max Busby* (all published by Broadman & Holman). *Chapter 8.*

**Anne Bowling** is the editor of *Novel & Short Story Writer's Market. Appendix D.*

**Katie Struckel Brogan** is the editor of *Writer's Market* and coeditor of WritersMarket.com. *Chapters 22, 23.*

**Michael J. Bugeja** is the author of *Living Without Fear: Understanding Cancer and the New Therapies* (Whitston Press), and *The Art & Craft of Poetry* (Writer's Digest Books), *Poet's Guide:*
*How to Publish and Perform Your Work* (Story Line Press), and *Millennium's End: Poems* (Archer Books). *Chapters 18, 19, 20, 21.*

**Caroline Crane** is the author of more than twenty published novels, including *Summer Girl, The Girls Are Missing, Trick or Treat*, and *Wife Found Slain* (all published by Dodd Mead). She is a former Writer's Digest School instructor. *Chapters 4, 17.*

**Jennifer Crump** is a freelance journalist and the author of *Frommer's: Toronto With Kids* (CDG). *Appendix C.*

**Geoff Fuller** is a book editor in Morgantown, West Virginia. He has won numerous awards for his writing and is a contributing editor for *Writer's Digest* magazine. His work has appeared in such publications as *Mindprints. Chapter 12.*

**Steven Goldsberry** is a professor at the University of Hawaii and a contributing editor for *Writer's Digest* magazine. He is the author of several books, including *Maui the Demigod*, *Luzon*, *Over Hawaii*, *Sunday in Hawaii*, and *The First 16 Secrets of Chi*. His poetry has appeared in *The New Yorker*. *Chapter 13.*

**Gloria Kempton** is a freelance writer, a writing coach, and an instructor for the Writer's Digest School. She has written seven nonfiction books, two novels, and numerous short stories and articles. *Chapters 10, 14, 15, 16, 34.*

**David King** is an author and book editor based in Shelburne Falls, Massachusetts. *Chapters 1, 3, 5, 7, 9, 11, 24.*

**Barbara Kuroff** is editorial director of Writer's Digest Books. *Chapters 30, 31.*

**Kelly Nickell** is an editor with Writer's Digest Books and the former features editor for *Writer's Digest* magazine.

**Alice Pope** is the managing editor of Writer's Digest Books and the editor of *Children's Writer's & Illustrator's Market*. She regularly speaks at children's writing conferences and is a former regional advisor for the Society of Children's Books Writers and Illustrators. *Chapter 28.*

**Melanie Rigney** is editor of *Writer's Digest* magazine. *Chapters 33, 35, 36, Appendix A, Appendix B.*

**Barbara Smith** has published more than three hundred poems, short stories, essays, and features, and she is the author of seven nonfiction books and two novels. *Appendix A.*

**Stephenie Steele** is the former director of Writer's Digest School, as well as the former the program director for WritersOnlineWorkshops. Her work has appeared in *Writer's Digest* magazine and *Cincinnati Magazine*. *Chapters 2, 29, 32, Appendix A.*

**Joe Stollenwerk** is the manager of educational services for Writer's Digest School. He also is a former editorial assistant for *Writer's Digest* magazine. *Appendix C.*

**Rachel Vater** is an editor with Writer's Digest Books, and the former editor of *Guide to Literary Agents* and *Guide to Talent & Modeling Agents*. *Chapters 25, 26, 27.*

## Fiction Contributors

**Jay Heininger** (*The Cylinder*) has finished writing one novel and is currently at work on his second.

**Heather Myles** (*Haven*) has been writing fiction since she was a child. This is her first attempt at novel writing.

**Tony Colatruglio** (*The Thunder, the Ballet, and Her Perfect World*) has been writing fiction for more than five years. He's currently working on his first novel and screenplay.

**David M. Ryan** (*Ride of the Valkyrie*) is a sergeant in an airport police department. This is his first attempt at a novel.

**George Onstot** (*Rash Acts*) is a former public relations consultant. He now writes for *The Other Press*.

**Adrian M. Tocklin** (*Murder on a Sunday Afternoon*) lives in Florida and is the CEO of Tocklin & Associates.

**Ruth M. McCarty** (*Preston Point*) is a member of Sisters in Crime and Mystery Writers of America. The pages critiqued here are from the subplot of *Preston Point*. She's currently working on the novel's rewrite.

**Angela Fox** (*Fowl Play*) is an award-winning advertising writer. Her clients include such companies as Hallmark, Holiday Inn, and Minute Maid. She's a fan of mystery novels, and *Fowl Play* is her first attempt at fiction.

**Charles Scott** (*Fever Spike*) is a cattle rancher and senior member of the Wyoming senate. This is his first attempt at fiction.

**June F. Forte** (*Texas Teardrops*) has worked as a journalist for both daily and weekly newspapers. Her work has appeared in *Midstream, Washington Golf Monthly*, and *Women's World*.

**Katherine Harvey** ("Mona on Darkening Ground") is a student at the University of Hawaii.

## Nonfiction Contributors

**Pamela Moore** (*The Pieces of My Heart*) has worked as a freelance writer for a health care foundation and children's hospital since 1991.

**Mindy Halleck** (*Mr. Ed*) is a freelance writer who currently writes a column for an online bridal magazine. She is working on a how-to credit repair book and her first novel.

**Kathy Walker** ("The Belly Dances") has been a book editor, and a copy editor and writer for twenty-two years.

**James Elmore** ("Schizophrenia: Faulty Parenting or Faulty Neurology?") is a clinical psychiatrist who has written papers for psychiatric journals.

## Poetry Contributors

**Wendy DeWachter** ("No Poem") has been writing poetry seriously for the past several years. Her work has appeared in numerous anthologies.

**Marion Brimm Rewey** ("Palomino—A Portrait, With Apples") has been writing for more than twenty years. She has won several awards, and her work has appeared in numerous publications, including *Anthology of American Poetry, McCall's, Good Housekeeping*, and *Madison Magazine*.

**Verna Lee Hinegardner** ("Standing on the Promises of God") is the poet laureate of Arkansas and has written ten volumes of poetry. The poem critiqued here placed fifth in the rhyming poetry category of the 2000 Writer's Digest National Writing Competition.

**Dorothy J. Stanfill** ("In a Quandary Over Form") is a lifelong poetry lover. Her work has appeared in *Rural Heritage*.

## Query Letter Contributors

**Jean Tennant** (*Woman's Day*) has been writing for more than twenty-five years.

She has had more than thirty-five short stories published by MacFadden Women's Group. She also has published seven books, including a romance novel published by Silhouette.

**Linda Akins** (*Texas Highways*) has worked as a freelance writer, PR consultant, and corporate communications executive. She has published more than three hundred articles in trade journals, travel publications, and regional magazines.

**Paul Ferris** (*Burma Journal*) has been working on *Burma Journal* since the 1960s. His work has appeared in *Grit*, *The Milwaukee Journal*, *Lutheran Digest*, and other publications.

**J. Sheldon Day** (*The Phoenix Principle*) began his writing career more than four years ago. He's actively looking for an agent for his novel, *The Phoenix Principle*. Using the revised version of his query letter, Day already has received several positive responses from different agencies.

**Thomas Dresser** (*Death on East Chop*) spent thirty years working in education and health care before becoming a freelance writer. He has self-published four regional booklets.

**Dorothy Ellis** (*The Corruption*) is currently attending the Georgetown University Law Center. Her poems have appeared in such publications as *Papyrus* and *Simple Vows*.

**Meredyth Hiltz** (*Vinnie's Watering Hole*) is a novice writer.

## Novel Synopsis Contributors

**Karen Kingsley** (*Oxygen*) has been writing for more than twenty years. She's written for more than six trade publications. She's currently working on her novel, *Oxygen*.

**Charles W. Blaker** (*As the Sparks Fly Upward*) is the editor and publisher of several monthly and quarterly newsletters and has published more than one hundred magazine articles. He has written a suspense novel, a collection of short stories, and a collection of essays. He also has self-published a poetry chapbook.

**Dar Tomlinson** (*Slightly Imperfect*) has been writing full time for eight years and is now concentrating on writing mainstream women's fiction novels. She won a Hemingway First Novel award in 1994 for her literary novel *Broken*.

**Lisa Schulman** (*The Losers Club*) has been a freelance writer for Kidshealth.org, iVillage, and other Web sites. She recently sold her first national magazine article to *Parents*. She's currently working on her first young adult novel on which the synopsis appearing in this book is based.

## Nonfiction Proposal Contributors

**Lynne Weinberg** (*Inner Journeys*) has written for numerous publications, including *Sunset Magazine*, *Tucson Lifestyle*, and *Puerto del Sol*.

**Marge Pellegrino** (*Inner Journeys*) writes nonfiction, fiction, and poetry. Her children's books include *Too Nice, My Grandma's the Mayor,* and *I Don't Have an Uncle Phil Anymore,* all published by Magination Press. Her nonfiction has appeared in such publications as *Catholic Digest* and *American Libraries.*

**Karen Shepherd** (*Buttons to Budgets, Everyday Living for the Microwave Generation*) lives in Washington and has been an active writer for six years. Her work has appeared in *Sew News* magazine and several community newspapers.

**Laurel A. Nelson** (*Follow Your Gut*) is a freelance writer based in Seattle. She has written for various newsletters and online magazines that cater to travelers.

**Cindy B. Johnson** (*The Poppie Book*) has written for numerous regional publications, including *The Denver Post* and *Alaska Parenting.* She is a member of the Denver Woman's Press Club.

# Index

# Get more of the best writing instruction from Writer's Digest Books!

**The Creative Writer's Style Guide.** Textbook rules about punctuation and grammar can be difficult to apply to your novel, short story, personal essay, or memoir. There are special considerations that normal style manuals just don't address. *The Creative Writer's Style Guide* is a revolutionary resource. It provides the answers, advice, and rules you need to edit your manuscript with confidence. ISBN 1-884910-55-6, hardcover, 240 pages, #48054-K

**The Writer's Idea Book.** This is the guide writers reach for time after time to jump start their creativity and develop ideas. Four distinctive sections, each geared toward a different stage of writing, offer dozens of unique approaches to "freeing the muse." In all, you'll find more than 400 idea-generating prompts guaranteed to get your writing started on the right foot, or back on track! ISBN 1-58297-179-X, paperback, 272 pages, #10841-K

**Snoopy's Guide to the Writing Life.** This book presents more than 180 heartwarming and hilarious Snoopy "at the typewriter" comic strips by Charles M. Schulz, paired with 32 delightful essays from a who's who of famous writers, including Sue Grafton, Fannie Flagg, Elmore Leonard, and more. These pieces examine the joys and realities of the writing life, from finding ideas to creating characters. ISBN 1-58297-194-3, hardcover, 192 pages, #10856-K

**The Pocket Muse.** Here's the key to finding inspiration when and where you want it. With hundreds of thought-provoking prompts, exercises and illustrations, it immediately helps you to get started writing, overcome writer's block, develop a writing habit, think more creatively, master style, revision, and other elements of the craft. ISBN 1-58297-142-0, hardcover, 256 pages, #10806-K

*These and other fine Writer's Digest titles are available from your local bookstore, online supplier, or by calling 1-800-448-0915.*

# More of the best books for writers!

**Lessons from a Lifetime of Writing.** Best-selling author David Morrell distills more than 30 years of writing and publishing experience into this single masterwork of advice and instruction. A rare and intriguing mix of memoir and writer's workshop, *Lessons* pulls no punches. Morrell examines everything from motivation and focus to the building blocks of good fiction: plot, character, dialogue, description, and more. ISBN 1-58297-143-9, hardcover, 256 pages, #10808-K.

**Guerilla Marketing for Writers.** Packed with proven insights and advice, this book details 100 "classified secrets" that will help you sell your work before and after it's published. This wide range of weapons—practical low-cost and no-cost marketing techniques—will help you design a powerful strategy for strengthening your proposals, promoting your books, and maximizing your sales. ISBN 0-89879-983-X, paperback, 292 pages, #10667-K.

**How to Write and Illustrate Children's Books and Get Them Published.** Find everything you need to know about breaking into the lucrative children's market. You'll discover how to write a sure-fire seller, how to create fresh and captivating illustrations, how to get your manuscript into the right buyer's hand, and more! ISBN 1-58297-013-0, paperback, 144 pages, #10694-K.

**Writer's Guide to Places.** Imbue your settings with authentic detail—the kind of information that only an insider would know! Inside, you'll information on all 50 states, 10 Canadian provinces, and dozens of intriguing cities. From small town squares to city streets, you'll find great places to set a scene, the foods your characters eat, where they shop, and more. ISBN 1-58297-169-2, paperback, 416 pages, #10833-K.

*These and other fine Writer's Digest titles are available from your local bookstore, online supplier, or by calling 1-800-448-0915.*